Reading Apollinaire's *Alcools*

Reading Apollinaire's *Alcools*

Willard Bohn

UNIVERSITY OF DELAWARE PRESS
Newark

Published by University of Delaware Press
Copublished by The Rowman & Littlefield Publishing Group, Inc.
4501 Forbes Boulevard, Suite 200, Lanham, Maryland 20706
www.rowman.com

Unit A, Whitacre Mews, 26-34 Stannary Street, London SE11 4AB

British Library Cataloguing in Publication Information Available

Library of Congress Cataloging-in-Publication Data
Bohn, Willard, 1939- author.
Reading Apollinaire's Alcools / Willard Bohn.
Newark : University of Delaware Press, [2017] | Includes
    bibliographical references and index.
LCCN 2016039452 (print) | LCCN 2016042089 (ebook) | ISBN
    9781611496314 (cloth : alk. paper) | ISBN 9781611496321 (electronic)
LCSH: Apollinaire, Guillaume, 1880-1918 Alcools.
LCC PQ2601.P6 A7188 2016 (print) | LCC PQ2601.P6 (ebook) |
    DDC 841/.912—dc23
LC record available at https://lccn.loc.gov/2016039452

Printed in the United States of America

To Anita and Heather,
as always

Contents

List of Illustrations

~

Acknowledgments

First and foremost, I would like to thank Chris Young and the Interlibrary Loan staff at Illinois State University, without whose help in tracking down articles this book could never have been written. I am also greatly indebted to Anne Hyde Greet, whose translation of *Alcools* and copious notes have been my constant companion as I analyzed these seventeen poems. Published in 1965, it is still the best translation available and the only one that is fully annotated. I would also like to acknowledge my debt to Claude Debon's extremely useful bibliography of articles about poems in *Alcools*. It not only saved me a huge amount of time but also ensured that I did not miss anything. Thanks go as well to my friends and colleagues in France, who continue to support Apollinaire studies in many different ways, including the creation of a seminar, a conference, and a bi-annual journal. Finally, after forty years of teaching *Alcools* at Brandeis University, the University of California at Santa Cruz, and Illinois State University, I am grateful to my students for asking questions that spurred me to dig deeper and deeper into Apollinaire's poetry.

Preliminary versions of several sections have appeared in the following publications and are reprinted with their kind permission: "Apollinaire and the Broken Wine Glass," *Philosophy and Literature*, vol. 39, No. 2 (October 2015), 459–67, courtesy of The Johns Hopkins University Press; "Apollinaire, Poetry, and Fashion," *Romance Quarterly*, Vol. 62, No. 2 (2015), 106–12; "Apollinaire and the Gypsy Fortune Teller," *Modern Language Review*, Vol. 110, No. 3 (July 2015), 669–76, permission of the Modern

Humanities Research Association; and "Apollinaire and the Demise of Autumn," *Romanische Forschungen*, Vol. 126, No. 4 (2014), 511–18, Copyright Vittorio Klostermann GmbH, Frankfurt am Main, 2014. I am also grateful to the National Gallery of Art, Washington DC, for permission to reproduce *The Dance of Salomé*, by Benozzo Gozzoli, from their collections.

~

Introduction

The present project is unique in the history of Apollinaire studies. Given its meticulous nature and ambitious scope, it was necessary to limit the book to seventeen poems. Each section reviews all of the previous scholarship, analyzes the composition in detail, and combines previous insights with my own. Some of the poems, such as "Les Sapins" and "Rhénane d'automne," have received virtually no critical attention. Others, such as "Zone" and "Les Colchiques," have generated a large number of studies. By 1999, when Claude Debon published her bibliography of Apollinaire's collection *Alcools*, the first poem had become the subject of no fewer than thirty-one articles and the second poem the subject of twenty-six articles. Regrettably, it has not been possible to include "La Chanson du mal-aimé" in the present volume. Not only is it twice as long as any of the other poems, but it is also the subject of twice as many studies—including two entire books. In general, my studies are arranged in chronological order, beginning with the "Rhénanes" in 1901–1902 and concluding with "Zone" in 1912. At the same time, the poems in each chapter are grouped together according to a particular theme. Although each chapter is basically conceived as an independent unit, it is possible to follow the evolution of Apollinaire's aesthetics from his first mature creations through his subsequent experiments with fantastic, hermetic, visionary, and cubist poetry respectively. This also allows one to chart Apollinaire's personal evolution from his infatuation with Annie Playden through a period of deep depression, his love affair with Marie Laurencin, and the aftermath of that relationship.

In retrospect, the author of *Alcools* seems a much quieter figure than the poet who wrote *Calligrammes*. By 1918, Apollinaire had become a widely respected spokesman for modern art, the leader of the Parisian avant-garde, and a lieutenant in the French army. He had reinvented visual poetry, been wounded in the war, and had co-founded the Theater of the Absurd (together with Alfred Jarry). By contrast, the portrait that emerges of the young Apollinaire is curiously touching. Beginning his adult life with nothing but a love of poetry to sustain him, he was terribly insecure and immensely vulnerable. Had it not been for the year spent in Germany, where he blossomed into a full-blown poet, who knows what might have happened to him. Even so, Apollinaire was still living at home six years later and eking out a miserable living. And while everyone around him was publishing books of poetry, *Alcools* would not appear in print until six more years had passed. Spanning the period between Apollinaire's eighteenth and thirty-third birthdays, the volume bears witness to its difficult birth. Traces of its long gestation are not hard to discover. In retrospect, the fact that *Alcools* took so long to appear may have been a blessing in disguise. Apollinaire had plenty of time to develop his craft and to perfect his poetry. Indeed, some of the poems evolved over a period of several years. When the time came to publish the volume, finally, he had numerous poems from which to choose. Selecting only the very best examples, he assembled a truly remarkable collection.

The present volume was conceived above all as a cumulative venture. Building on previous scholarship, the book not only pays homage to earlier scholars but also presents a state-of-the-art survey of current Apollinaire criticism. It is my hope that future critics will find it easier to learn what has been written about a particular composition without having to conduct exhaustive research. For seventeen poems at least, it will acquaint them with the existing scholarship, outline the major arguments, and point them in the right direction. However, the volume is much more than a compilation of previous research, useful as that may be. I have subjected each poem to a rigorous, line-by-line analysis that engages in a succession of dialogues with other critics. Previous hypotheses have been closely scrutinized and accepted or rejected accordingly. Scholarly disputes have been re-examined and adjudicated according to the latest information. My ultimate goal has been to shed new light on each composition in question. Sometimes a fresh pair of eyes can see things others have missed. Sometimes a shift in critical perspective is all that is necessary to open up a new area of investigation.

First of all, I have tried to be completely objective. Let me add, after the chorus of laughter has died down, that I realize total objectivity is an illusion, if not a myth, but at least I have *tried* to be objective. I also realize that my analyses are inevitably colored by my own predilections. That is the unavoidable nature of literary criticism. What I mean by "objective" is that I have tried to remain completely neutral, carefully weighing competing interpretations and coming to a logical conclusion. It also means that I have thought long and hard about certain problems, in many cases disagreeing with previous interpretations and proposing new ones. Finally, it means that I do not have a hidden agenda or a special brand of criticism to promote. Like the French *explication de texte*, which has taught generations of students how to think and how to read, my approach is partially text-based. The critic's task is to divide the text into its constituent parts and show how they work together to produce a particular effect. Unlike the *explication*, my approach also considers the interaction between the author, the text, and the reader. The critic's task is also to explain how these factors contribute to our final understanding of the poem. Although the following analyses may appear monolithic to some readers, they are in no way intended to inhibit further discussion. On the contrary, I hope they will inspire readers to contribute ideas of their own.

My analyses basically follow the French model. Since discussion usually takes place in the present tense, a kind of leveling occurs in which temporal differences are partially obscured. My discussion strives above all to be synthetic. It combines previous theories, suggestions, and discoveries into a kind of critical collage in which, at least initially, each one is just as important as all the others. Although this approach makes it easier to compare and contrast certain ideas, it is inevitably ahistorical. As for widespread changes in critical approaches over the years, competing models, and so forth, there have essentially been none. For one thing, interest in the poet is a relatively recent phenomenon. Apollinaire studies are only about sixty years old. In 1967, when I began a doctorate under Michel Décaudin, his works were not even included in the French national curriculum. For another thing, most of Apollinaire's manuscripts were not freely available until very recently. Scholars are still struggling to absorb all the information in them. For yet another thing, although French clothing fashion changes every year, the French themselves do not share the American enthusiasm for the latest critical theory. Although they produce brilliant theorists, the latter are much better known in America than in their own country. Their most recent discoveries are basically structuralism and semiotics, which they use to good advantage. Ironically, the post-structuralist critics who appear in this volume are almost all Americans, mostly products of Yale University.

Apollinaire has been enormously influential over the years as his reputation has gradually risen to stratospheric heights. If anything, he seems to grow more influential day by day. All modern French poets and many well-known poets in other languages have been inspired by his works at one time or another. Most French people, even those with little formal education, can recite one or two of his poems from memory. In addition, many of his poems have been set to music. Yet, although Apollinaire authored two major books of poetry, most readers tend to prefer *Alcools*. Partly this is because they find *Calligrammes* too experimental, too self-consciously avant-garde, but mostly they feel that the first book speaks to them in ways the second book ignores. As *Alcools* abundantly demonstrates, Apollinaire is one of the finest lyric poets in French. "Le Pont Mirabeau," for example, became a classic the instant it appeared in print. "Les Colchiques" is a modern masterpiece. The only twentieth-century poet in the language who can match him is Paul Valéry, who wrote in a very different mode. Apollinaire's poetry is not only highly original, moreover, but intimate and intensely personal. As he once confided, every one of his poems commemorates an event in his life. More than anything, however, it is Apollinaire's lyrical voice, with its lilting music and variable rhythms, that readers respond to. Long after they have put down *Alcools*, that is what they remember.

~

Note on French Prosody

Since French poetry has a syllabic foundation rather than an accentual one, the length of a line is determined by its number of syllables rather than by its number of feet as in English. The most common lengths are octosyllables, decasyllables, and alexandrines, which contain twelve syllables. The silent "e" at the end of a line is not counted. Neither is the silent "e" at the end of the sixth syllable in alexandrines or after the fourth syllable in decasyllabic poetry. These two breaks are known as the caesura. The two segments are called *hémistiches*. Some of the more popular rhyme schemes employ *rimes croisées* (ABAB), *rimes embrassées* (ABBA), and *rimes suivies*—also called *rimes plates* (ABAB). However, composing a poem in French is more complicated than composing a poem in English. The rhymes may have one phonetic element (*rimes pauvres*), two phonetic elements (*rimes suffisantes*), or three *phonetic elements* (rimes riches). Rhymes that are too easy, like *bonheur* and *malheur*, are called *rimes banales* and are discouraged. As if that were not enough, rhymes are divided into masculine (ending with an accented vowel) and feminine (ending with an accented vowel plus a mute "e"). Traditionally, the two rhymes are supposed to alternate. Modern French poetry takes considerable liberties with these classic rules or, as in the case of *vers libres* (free verse), ignores them altogether. For better or for worse, this is a bare-bones description of French poetry. For additional information, readers should consult a more specialized volume such as Maurice Grammont's *Petit Traité de versification française*.

∼

CHAPTER ONE

The Wind on the Rhine

As Guillaume Apollinaire approached his twenty-first birthday, he encountered a rare opportunity. For several months he had been tutoring the daughter of a German aristocrat in Paris. Preparing to return home, the Viscountess Elinor de Milhau invited him to continue his French lessons in Germany. Following a leisurely automobile trip, they arrived in the Rhineland on August 29, 1901, where Apollinaire remained for the next year.[1] As Claude Debon remarks, this development was particularly fortuitous. The town of Honnef, where the Viscountess owned a villa, is situated "à l'endroit où le Rhin . . . est le plus pittoresque tout en restant navigable, où le passé légendaire et le présent actif . . . se côtoyaient" ("at the place where the Rhine . . . is the most picturesque, where the legendary past and the active present exist side by side").[2] In addition, Apollinaire soon fell in love with the English governess Annie Playden, who inspired some of his greatest poetry. This idyllic period was one of the richest in his entire career. For the next eleven months, Apollinaire wrote poem after poem in an amazing burst of creativity. In LeRoy C. Breunig's opinion, the wide range of subjects and styles suggests he was experimenting with new ways of writing poetry.[3] At the same time, Debon adds, he was also discovering the lyrical virtues of his own language. Although Apollinaire had been writing poems for years, he finally discovered how to exploit the French language to its fullest. In a sense, it was as if he had become a different poet. In the "Rhénanes," therefore, Apollinaire's mature style manifested itself for the very first time. The hesitations and lack of confidence of his earlier poems were replaced by a deftness of touch and a sureness of vision.

Apollinaire had trouble deciding what to call the volume of poetry he eventually published in 1913. At first it was to be entitled *Le Vent du Rhin* (*The Wind on the Rhine*), then *L'Année républicaine* (*The Republican Year*), and after that *Eau de Vie* (*The Water of Life* [Brandy]) before he finally settled on *Alcools* (*Alcohols*). These titles reflect some of the influences he was subject to during the intervening years. Didier Alexandre claims that Apollinaire chose *Le Vent du Rhin* initially because he sought to capture "le mystère ou l'étrangeté [du vent]" ("the mystery or the strangeness [of the wind]").[4] Unfortunately, although this describes some of the "Rhénanes," it fails to describe them all. In three poems, for example "Elégie," the wind is completely innocuous. In eleven others, including "Nuit rhénane," it is lacking altogether. Ernst Wolf speculates that the wind possessed a symbolic value for Apollinaire, that it represented something like the Rhineland's soul.[5] And yet, he continues, the banks of the Rhine are certainly very windy almost all year long. If anything, it is even windier around Neu-Glück, the Viscountess's country estate (Figure 1.1). Apollinaire mentions the frequent wind himself in "Le Dôme de Cologne." Eventually one begins to understand why he wanted to title the volume *Le Vent du Rhin*. Since the wind was always blowing, he associated it with the Rhineland (and vice versa). The relationship between the two entities was not metaphoric, as Wolf suggests, but rather metonymic. For Apollinaire, the wind was simply one of the region's distinctive characteristics.

The "Rhénanes" themselves, Wolf goes on to explain, contain references to two different kinds of wind: the true Rhine wind, which blows on the river and the river banks, and the wind that exists around Neu-Glück fifteen

Figure 1.1. *Neu-Glück*
Courtesy SiebenBergeGrizzly.

kilometers away. A careful reader can often tell which wind Apollinaire is evoking in his poetry. "Les Sapins" and "Les Femmes" are clearly associated with Neu-Glück, for example, which is surrounded by pine forests. Nevertheless, there are also pine trees in Honnef, where "Les Femmes" was written, so that it is impossible to generalize. In any event, Wolf observes, wind and pine trees always seem to be associated with each other in the "Rhénanes." Since they are found everywhere in the Rhineland, Apollinaire devoted a poem to each one of them: "Le Vent nocturne" and "Les Sapins." As we will see, the wind appears in one form or another in each of the following four poems.

"Le Vent nocturne"

Before being included in *Alcools*, Michel Décaudin notes, "Le Vent nocturne" appeared in both *Le Voile de Pourpre* in May 1909 and in an anthology edited by Florian-Parmentier in 1911.[6] On the first occasion, it was dated "Neu-Glück, 1901" and on the second "October 1901." Thus we know both the time and the place it was written. Composed of thirteen alexandrines forming a single block, the poem employs an unusual rhyme scheme that combines *rimes plates* with *rimes croisées*. While the first ten lines rhyme two-by-two, the last three deftly introduce an alternating rhyme. Although Apollinaire's poetry often deviates from the classical norm, "Le Vent nocturne" basically conforms to the traditional model. While it combines *rimes riches* with *rimes suffisantes*, the rhymes alternate between masculine and feminine. In addition, all the mute "e"s are meant to be counted and/or pronounced.

> Oh! les cimes des pins grincent en se heurtant
> Et l'on entend aussi se lamenter l'autan
> Et du fleuve prochain à grand'voix triomphales
> Les elfes rire au vent ou corner aux rafales
> Attys Attys Attys charmant et débraillé
> C'est ton nom qu'en la nuit les elfes ont raillé
> Parce qu'un de tes pins s'abat au vent gothique
> La forêt fuit au loin comme une armée antique
> Dont les lances ô pins s'agitent au tournant
> Les villages éteints méditent maintenant
> Comme les vierges les vieillards et les poètes
> Et ne s'éveilleront au pas de nul venant
> Ni quand sur leurs pigeons fondront les gypaètes.

> (Oh! the pine tops creak as they strike each other
> And you can also hear the south wind lamenting
> And from the nearby river the elves laugh at the

> Wind with great triumphal voices or shout at the windy gusts
> Attis Attis Attis charming and all unbuttoned
> It is your name the elves made fun of at night
> Because one of your pines fell in the gothic wind
> The forest flees far away like an ancient army
> Whose lances O pines jostle at the bend in the road
> The dark villages meditate presently
> Like virgins old men and poets
> And are not awakened by passers-by
> Nor when the vultures swoop down on their pigeons.)

According to Annie Playden, whom Breunig interviewed fifty years later, the text describes the view from Apollinaire's window at Neu-Glück.[7] One could see the forest on one side, she confided, and the little village of Bennerscheid on the other side. The fact that Annie was familiar with this view is interesting by itself. One wonders how often she visited the poet's room and under what conditions. Although Apollinaire claimed several times to have slept with her, most critics are skeptical. In any case, as Décaudin notes, "Le Vent nocturne" is a series of fleeting impressions rather than a realistic landscape.[8] Since it is night, the first four lines are dominated by sounds rather than by visual impressions. Judging from the first verse, the weather appears to be very windy. Although the tops of the pine trees are invisible, one can hear them creaking and scraping against each other. A second sound is produced by the wind, whose wailing contributes to the poem's eerie atmosphere. While "l'autan" rhymes nicely with "heurtant," its presence comes as something of a surprise. According to Le Petit Robert, the autan is associated not with Germany but with the south of France, where it can be quite forceful. Apollinaire uses the term here apparently to indicate that the wind is coming from the south. He takes additional geographical liberties with the river, moreover, which is supposedly nearby. In reality, the Rhine was some fifteen kilometers from Neu-Glück—too far away for him to hear the elves laughing and shouting. Here, as elsewhere in his poetry, Apollinaire indulges in a bit of poetic license.

Endowed with "grand'voix triomphales," the boisterous elves should not be confused with the Smurfs or the Seven Dwarves. Autochthonous beings who possess magic powers, elves are sometimes helpful, sometimes spiteful, and always unpredictable. One wonders what the elves in "Le Vent nocturne" have to be triumphant about and why they find the windy gusts so amusing. Have they conjured up the wind simply to entertain themselves? Are they wind elves? Interestingly, the fourth line was borrowed from another poem by Apollinaire, entitled "Mareye," which is set in the Ardennes forest in Belgium.[9] Ironically, although the elves in "Le Vent nocturne" are presumably German, they were taken originally from Belgian folklore.

"Rarely has a writer borrowed from himself so much as Apollinaire," Breunig declares.[10] The majority of the poems in *Alcools* and many in Apollinaire's other collection *Calligrammes*, he explains, contain lines, stanzas, or whole sections that have been transplanted from other poems. Paradoxically, Apollinaire embraced the collage aesthetic before there was a collage aesthetic to embrace. Years before Braque and Picasso began to experiment with *papiers peints* ("painted papers"), he literally cut and pasted his poems. Something about the collage process appealed to his eclectic sensibility and his penchant for abrupt transitions.

Suddenly, and without warning, the reader is transported from the realm of European folklore to that of Greek and Roman mythology. As Alexandre observes, Apollinaire employs myth as "une médiation qui transfigure le réel en matériau poétique" ("a mediation that transforms reality into poetic material").[11] The next three lines are addressed to Attys (or Atys), a fair young shepherd who was transformed into a pine tree by Zeus. That he is "débraillé," as Pilkington remarks, probably refers to the orgiastic rituals connected with his worship.[12] Although the elves belong to an entirely different world, for some reason they have been mocking Attys. At first glance, they appear to be amused that the wind has knocked down one of the pine trees. Or rather, since Attys has become a god, one of *his* pine trees. However, the story is more complicated than it seems. Upon learning that Attys was planning to marry another woman, the goddess Cybele, who was madly in love with him, drove him into such a frenzy that he castrated himself. This is why the elves are laughing at him—because the fallen tree mimics the act of his castration. There is even a suggestion that the tree represents Attys himself. During the yearly ceremonies held to commemorate his death, his body was represented by "a felled pine, wrapped in a shroud and adorned with wreaths."[13]

The next two lines recall a famous literary prophecy: "Macbeth shall never vanquished be until / Great Birnam wood to high Dunsinane hill / Shall come against him." In contrast to Shakespeare, who compares an army on the march to a forest, Apollinaire compares the forest around Neu-Glück to an army on the march. The wind rippling the tops of the trees makes it seem like they are moving. And since the trees are tall and straight, they resemble the lances that soldiers used to carry years ago. Up to this point, the scene in "Le Vent nocturne" mirrors the episode in *Macbeth*. Whereas Shakespeare's soldiers are approaching to do battle, however, Apollinaire's soldiers appear to be fleeing. The former are prepared to overthrow Macbeth, while the latter simply want to save their skins.

Despite the fact that the forest army is retreating, the villages seem to be in no danger. The lights are all extinguished, and everything is dark. The maidens, the old men, and the poets are not really "meditating," as

Apollinaire appears to suggest. Like the villages, they are merely asleep. No visitor's footsteps will wake them, not only because the villages are isolated but also because it is night. At the same time, there is a lightly veiled suggestion that all is not well. The fact that the villages are "éteints" (literally "extinguished") suggests they resemble cemeteries more than real villages. The possibility that the inhabitants may never wake up adds to the eerie atmosphere. Indeed, as the last line demonstrates, this situation prevails even in the light of day, when birds are active. The *gypaète* or bearded vulture is the largest Eurasian bird of prey. The fact that the Germans call it *lammer geier* ("lamb vulture") suggests that it is large enough to fly off with young sheep. Although the bird is primarily a scavenger, it sometimes attacks live animals—like the hapless pigeons in "Le Vent nocturne." Thus the poem concludes on a rather unexpected note. In contrast to the wind-whipped pines with which it opens, the villages are deathly still. Nothing moves but the hunters and the hunted, caught up in the dance of death.

"Les Sapins"

Since pine trees and fir trees are both coniferous evergreens, many people have trouble telling them apart. The easiest way to identify them is to examine their needles. If a branch has long needles in groups of two, three, or five, it is a pine tree. If it has large numbers of short, single needles, it is a fir tree. Despite these significant differences, Apollinaire uses the two terms interchangeably (as do many of his critics). Thus his comments regarding pine trees also apply to fir trees and vice versa. What differentiated Neu-Glück from the villa in Honnef, in any case, was not the conifers' genus but rather their large numbers. In effect, the country residence was situated in the middle of a forest.

Published in *Le Voile de Pourpre* in May 1909, along with several other Rhénanes, "Les Sapins" was originally dated "Neu-Glück, 1901."[14] Each of the six octosyllabic quintils (or quintains) has a six-syllable middle line and is rhymed AABAB. Apollinaire alternates masculine and feminine rhymes while combining *rimes suffisantes* with *rimes riches*. Interestingly, the vast majority of the poems in *Alcools* are written either in octosyllables or in alexandrines. Indeed, Apollinaire claimed on more than one occasion to have given new life to the eight-syllable verse. A similar claim could be made for the five-line stanza, which plays an important role in his poetry. As Maurice Piron notes, "Apollinaire a fait du quintil une de ses formes préférées" ("Apollinaire made the quintil one of his preferred forms").[15] While this form requires considerable skill, he wielded it effortlessly from the very beginning. In "Les Sapins," for instance, he moves easily from one stanza to the next. Treating the theme in a playful manner, Anne Hyde Greet explains,

Apollinaire exploits the Germanic tradition of attributing magic powers to fir trees.[16] Although only one of the stanzas mentions magicians, the trees possess a whole range of extraordinary powers.

> Les Sapins en bonnets pointus
> De longues robes revêtus
> Comme des astrologues
> Saluent leurs frères abattus
> Les bateaux qui sur le Rhin voguent
>
> Dans les sept arts endoctrinés
> Par les vieux sapins leurs aînés
> Qui sont de grands poètes
> Ils se savent prédestinés
> A briller plus que des planètes
>
> A briller doucement changés
> En étoiles et enneigés
> Aux Noëls bien heureuses
> Fêtes des sapins ensongés
> Aux longues branches langoureuses.
>
> (The fir trees in pointed bonnets
> And dressed in long robes
> Like astrologers
> Salute their fallen brothers
> The boats sailing on the Rhine
>
> Indoctrinated in the seven arts
> By the old fir trees their elders
> Who are great poets
> They know they are predestined
> To shine brighter than the planets
>
> To shine gently transformed
> Into stars and covered with snow
> At pleasant Christmases
> Feasts of fir trees lost in dream
> With long languorous branches.)

Perhaps because it seems so straightforward, "Les Sapins" has received virtually no critical attention. The few comments that have surfaced come from individuals who have been engaged in translating the poem. Everyone agrees, nonetheless, that it is unlike any of the other compositions in *Alcools*.

According to Garnet Rees, "Les Sapins" is unique because it represents a purely descriptive work.[17] In A. E. Pilkington's opinion, however, the poem is composed almost entirely of metaphors and similes.[18] How, one wonders, can two highly respected critics differ so widely in their evaluation of the same poem? Their assessments seem to be diametrically opposed. The answer in retrospect appears to be that they are both correct. "Les Sapins" is purely descriptive in the sense that very little happens. As one season gives way to the next, Apollinaire concentrates on the fir trees' visual qualities. Seeking to create an impression of *le merveilleux* ("the marvelous"), he replaces many of the transitive verbs with past participles. At the same time, in order to describe how the trees look, he resorts to metaphors and similes. The first stanza is an excellent example. The poem begins with a visual comparison based on the trees' physical appearance. Since the top of each fir tree resembles a pointed hat and its trailing branches a cloak, Apollinaire compares the tree to an astrologer. As Pilkington observes, "the trees are at once personified and endowed with magical powers."[19] The first quality stems from their appearance, the second from their new profession. From their location overlooking the river, the trees hail their fallen brothers as they sail by, whom carpenters have converted into wooden boats. In reality, as noted previously, Neu-Glück was fifteen kilometers from the Rhine.

The second stanza continues and expands the astrologer metaphor. Since the fir trees have been indoctrinated in the seven arts by their poet elders, they are not only educated but also very wise. In the Middle Ages, the seven liberal arts were divided into the Trivium ("the three roads") and the Quadrivium ("the four roads"). The former classification encompassed grammar, rhetoric, and logic, while the latter embraced arithmetic, geometry, astronomy, and music. And since the fir trees are very wise, they know they are destined to outshine the planets. While Apollinaire vacillated between "les planètes" ("the planets") and "des planètes" ("some planets"), he finally chose the latter. For some reason, hopefully explained in the next stanza, the trees will only outshine *some* of the planets. Unfortunately, the third stanza does not provide an adequate explanation. Somehow the trees will be subtly changed into stars covered with snow on blissful Christmas days. Since there will be celebrations involving fir trees "lost in dream," in all probability they will be transformed into Christmas trees. Rarely at a loss for words, Apollinaire invented this neologism *ensongé* to fill a linguistic vacancy, possibly by analogy with Old French *ensongié* ("anxious").[20]

> Les sapins beaux musiciens
> Chantent des noels anciens
> Au vent des soirs d'automne

Ou bien graves magiciens
Incantent le ciel quand il tonne

Des rangées de blanc chérubins
Remplacent l'hiver les sapins
Et balancent leurs ailes
L'été ce sont de grands rabbins
Ou bien de vieilles demoiselles

Sapins médecins divagants
Ils vont offrant leurs bons onguents
Quand la montagne accouche
De temps en temps sous l'ouragan
Un vieux sapin geint et se couche.

(The fir trees good musicians
Sing ancient carols
In the Autumn nights' wind
Or very grave magicians
Enchant the sky when it thunders

Rows of white cherubins
Replace the fir trees in winter
And balance their wings
In summer they are tall rabbis
Or else old spinsters

Fir trees wandering doctors
They proffer their excellent unguents
When the mountain gives birth
From time to time in a storm
An old fir tree moans and lies down.)

By this point, Pilkington demonstrates, the images have largely ceased to call attention to an object's physical features. The remainder of the poem consists of "a compressed succession of metaphors," some of which are completely gratuitous.[21] Apollinaire calls the trees musicians (i.e., singers) in the fourth stanza because the wind makes a rustling sound as it passes through their branches. Why they are singing Christmas carols in autumn, however, is hard to say. Similarly, when the trees are exposed to a violent storm, they creak and scrape against each other (cf. "Le Vent nocturne"). Although the sound reminds Apollinaire of magicians casting spells on the sky, one would be hard pressed to explain the connection. Once again one encounters a neologism: *incanter*, which means the same thing as *enchanter* ("to enchant").[22]

Since the fir trees are covered with snow in winter, it is easy to see why those in the fifth stanza resemble angels. However, it is much harder to find any resemblance between them and rabbis or old ladies. Perhaps the latter are dressed in triangular robes and thus possess the same shape as the trees. By contrast, the comparison with itinerant doctors is easier to justify. Since trees produce sap, they are able to provide their patients—perhaps even the pregnant mountain—with soothing unguents.

Unexpectedly, as Claude Morhange-Bégué and Pierre Lartigue point out, the poem ends abruptly with the image of death.[23] From time to time an old fir, succumbing to a strong wind, moans and falls to the ground—exactly like an old patient who succumbs to a heart attack or a stroke. Just as the fir trees are familiar with the medieval division of knowledge, it is tempting to conclude that "Les Sapins" itself represents another version of the seven arts. The Trivium would encompass astrology, poetry, and predestination, while the Quadrivium would embrace music, magic, religion, and medicine. The mastery of the former subjects would qualify one to study the latter subjects. For Pilkington, the poem represents "a cultivation of metaphor for its own sake."[24] In his opinion, it is an early example of Apollinaire feeling his way toward a new style and a new aesthetic.

"Rhénane d'automne"

The Viscountess Milhau and her entourage left Neu-Glück toward the end of October 1901 for her villa on the Rhine, where, since it was warmer, they all planned to spend the winter. Written one month after the previous text, "Rhénane d'automne" was originally dated "Honnef, novembre 1901."[25] Following its publication in Le Voile de Pourpre in May 1909, the poem was included in Alcools without a date but dedicated to Ange Toussaint-Luca. The latter was a former school friend from Nice whom Apollinaire encountered again in Paris years later. Although they were undoubtedly good friends, Apollinaire's tongue seems to have been firmly implanted in his cheek—since the poem takes place on All Souls' Day, the day before was All Saints' Day, known in French as "la Toussaint." Comprising fifty-two lines, "Rhénane d'automne" is surprisingly long for a Rhenish poem. Since the rhymes and the line lengths are irregular, the poem is technically written in free verse. And yet many of the verses are rhymed, and many are either octosyllabic or alexandrines. Thus, this represents another hybrid verse form, one that would serve Apollinaire well when he began to write "Zone" twelve years later. Combining order and adventure, tradition and invention, it provided him with a certain amount of structure but also the freedom to experiment. The first three stanzas of the poem are almost entirely descriptive:

Les enfants des morts vont jouer
Dans le cimetière
Martin Gertrude Hans et Henri
Nul coq n'a chanté aujourd'hui
Kikiriki

Les vieilles femmes
Tout en pleurant cheminent
Et les bons ânes braillent hi han et se mettent à brouter
les fleurs
Des couronnes mortuaires.

C'est le jour des morts et de toutes leurs âmes
Les enfants et les vieilles femmes
Allument des bougies et des cierges
Sur chaque tombe catholique
Les voiles des vieilles
Les nuages du ciel
Sont comme des barbes de biques.

L'air tremble de flammes et de prières.

(The children of the dead play
In the Cemetery
Martin Gertrude Hans and Henry
No cock has crowed today
Cock-a-doodle-do

The old women
Cry and walk
And the good donkeys
Bray he haw and begin to eat the flowers
On the mortuary crowns

It is the Day of the Dead and all their souls
The children and the old women
Light candles and tapers
On each Catholic grave
The old women's veils
The clouds in the sky
Are like nanny-goats' beards
The air trembles with flames and prayers.)

Since it is All Souls' day, whole families have come to the cemetery to
honor the dead, as is the custom in Germany, with offerings of flowers and

special grave lights. According to Claude Debon, Kurt Roessler has proposed the cemetery in Honnef as the place where the poem takes place.[26] However, many years earlier, Marc Poupon interviewed members of Elinor de Milhau's family, who explained that every year on All Saints' Day they all met at Krayer-hof (one of their five residences) and visited the cemetery in the nearby village of Eich, where their family tombs were.[27] Thus "Honnef, November 1901" refers to the place of composition, not to the cemetery in the poem. Since Annie and Apollinaire were part of the Viscountess's household, they were invited as well. As Poupon observes, the sight of families picnicking among the tombs (which Annie found shocking) and donkeys nibbling on flower crowns is better suited to a country cemetery than to one in the middle of town.

Judging from Apollinaire's description, the people in the poem welcome All Souls' Day as an opportunity to have a family outing. While the children play among the tombstones, the adults unpack the picnic hamper. Although no one denies that it is a religious occasion ("nul coq n'a chanté aujourd'hui"), the family atmosphere reduces the idea of mortality to manageable proportions. "The presence of death is everywhere in *Alcools*," Garnet Rees declares, "but as an inescapable fact of the human condition rather than as an obsession."[28] Since the scene is set in the Rhineland, Apollinaire employs a few tentative germanisms. "Kikiriki" is the sound a German rooster makes, and "de toutes leurs âmes" is the French equivalent of "aller Seelen" ("All Souls"). And be-cause children are present, he playfully compares the wispy clouds to nanny-goat beards. The last line incorporates a zeugma that reaffirms the religious nature of All Souls' Day and evokes the folk ceremony taking place outside the church. So many candles have been lit on the tombstones that the hot air makes everything appear to tremble. The next few stanzas introduce the reader to some of the cemetery's permanent inhabitants:

> Le cimetière est un beau jardin
> Plein de saules gris et de romarins
> Il vous vient souvent des amis qu'on enterre
> Ah que vous êtes bien dans le beau cimetière
> Vous mendiants morts saouls de bière
> Vous les aveugles comme le destin
> Et vous petits enfants morts en prière

> Ah! que vous êtes bien dans le beau cimetière
> Vous bourgmestres vous bateliers
> Et vous conseillers de régence
> Vous aussi tziganes sans papiers
> La vie vous pourrit dans la panse
> La croix vous pousse entre les pieds

Le vent du Rhin ulule avec tous les hiboux
Il éteint les cierges que toujours les enfants rallument
Et les feuilles mortes
Viennent couvrir les morts.

(The cemetery is a beautiful garden
Full of gray willows and rosemary
Buried friends come to mind repeatedly
Ah! how comfortable you are in the lovely cemetery
You beggars who died drunk with beer
You blindmen as blind as destiny
And you little children dead in prayer

Ah! how comfortable you are in the lovely cemetery
You mayors and boatmen
And you privy councilors
You too gypsies without papers
Life is rotting in your bellies
Crosses spring up between your feet

The Rhine wind ululates with all the owls
It extinguishes the candles children relight them
And dead leaves
Blanket the dead.)

The first two stanzas vie with each other to portray the cemetery in a positive light. Rather than a graveyard, it is a beautifully landscaped park adorned with weeping willows and fragrant patches of rosemary. Similarly, being buried in the cemetery is like staying in a comfortable hotel. Everybody knows everybody, and old friends arrive all the time. Some people, like the beggars, are probably better off than when they were alive. A whole series of apostrophes emphasizes the basic message: "Ah! que vous êtes bien dans le beau cimetière." According to Poupon, the graveyard in Eich contains both "tziganes sans papiers" and "conseillers de régence" ("gypsies with no papers" and "regency councilors"), two of whom were Elinor de Milhau's ancestors. Up to this point, the cemetery visit has been idyllic. Suddenly the wind kicks up and extinguishes all the candles, which the children hurry to relight. Judging from appearances, the wind that descends on the graveyard is a malevolent wind. Not only is it accompanied by a flock of hooting owls, but it also covers the graves with a blanket of dead leaves. Like the former, who are associated with darkness and death, the latter are an evil omen.[29] For a variety of reasons, Robert Champigny believes "Le vent du Rhin ulule avec tous les hiboux" is the most expressive verse in the poem.[30] Décaudin wonders if the eerie scene may have been inspired by Leconte de Lisle.[31] Pierre Brunel associates the wind with Hermes, who conducts the shades of the dead from the upper to the lower world.[32] Not only is it a mocking wind, he maintains, but the entire poem seems to be under the spell of Hermes. Following the appearance of the demonic wind, the tone becomes much more somber:

> Des enfants morts parlent parfois avec leur mère
> Et des mortes parfois voudraient bien revenir
>
> Oh! je ne veux pas que tu sortes
> L'automne est plein de mains coupées
> Non non ce sont des feuilles mortes
> Ce sont les mains des chères mortes
> Ce sont tes mains coupées.
>
> (Dead children sometimes talk to their mothers
> And dead women would like to return to life
>
> Oh! I don't want you to leave
> Autumn is filled with severed hands
> No no they are dead leaves
> They are the beloved hands of dead women
> They are your severed hands.)

The conversations in the first two lines probably refer to inscriptions on tombstones rather than to actual conversations. Whatever the explanation, they introduce a bizarre note that contributes to the eerie atmosphere. In addition, they anticipate similar conversations in "La Maison des Morts," which would be composed in Munich five months later.[33] Although the next stanza appears to continue the conversation, the first three lines are taken from another poem altogether entitled "La Clef."[34] While the severed hands inject new life into the familiar autumn leaves, as Pilkington declares, they also generate a considerable shock.[35] Since the tenor and the vehicle are reversed, the reader does not realize the hands represent a metaphor until the last moment. Despite the motif's association with French Symbolism, Décaudin believes its presence stems from Apollinaire's memory of oak leaves in the Ardennes.[36] As far as one can tell, the entire stanza consists of a dialogue between two people. Who these characters are, however, is impossible to say. Apparently frightened by the severed hands, the first person tries to prevent the second person from leaving. When the latter replies that they are only dead leaves, the former insists they are the hands of dead women. In fact, he or she continues, "They are your hands!" Apparently the demonic wind has managed to sow a great amount of confusion. Swirling around the speakers, symbols of mutilation alternate with active hallucinations in a kaleidoscopic *danse macabre*.

> Nous avons tant pleuré aujourd'hui
> Avec ces morts leurs enfants et les vieilles femmes
> Sous le ciel sans soleil
> Au cimetière plein de flammes
>
> Puis dans le vent nous nous en retournâmes
>
> A nos pieds roulaient des châtaignes
> Dont les bogues étaient
> Comme le coeur blessé de la madone
> Dont on doute si elle eut la peau
> Couleur des châtaignes d'automne.
>
> (We have cried so much today
> With these dead people their children and the old women
> Beneath the sunless sky
> In the cemetery full of flames
>
> Then we returned home in the sudden wind
>
> Chestnuts rolled around at our feet
> Whose husks resembled
> The blessed heart of the Madonna
> One doubts her skin was
> The color of autumn chestnuts.)

Speaking for the group as a whole, Apollinaire adopts the first-person plural. At the same time, he switches from the narrative present to the past tense. The visit has not been entirely joyous, he admits, for many tears have also been shed. Children have been mourning their dead parents, old women have been mourning their dead husbands. Leaving the flaming cemetery behind, the group walks back to the carriages as the wind blows fallen chestnuts in their direction. Their spiky husks remind Apollinaire of the Virgin Mary, whose skin, he suspects, was far from chestnut brown. More precisely, as we know from an earlier manuscript, the husks remind him of Notre Dame des Sept Douleurs, who is commonly depicted with seven swords piercing her heart (Figure 1.2).[37] The Sept Douleurs are the seven greatest sorrows she suffered during her lifetime. Evoked indirectly in "Rhénane d'automne," they would occupy a prominent place in "La Chanson du mal-aimé" in 1909. Champigny finds the final stanza particularly

Figure 1.2. *Notre Dame des Sept Douleurs.*
L'Ymagier, July 4, 1895.

impressive. Beginning and ending with the image of the chestnuts, it is essentially circular—like the chestnuts themselves. Nobody can compose a stanza like Apollinaire, he exclaims: "Sur ce point aucun poète français n'est son égal. Il dépasse Villon et Verlaine" ("No French poet can equal him on that point. He surpasses Villon and Verlaine").[38]

"Mai"

Originally dated "Leutesdorf, mai 1902," the next poem first appeared in the December 1905–February 1906 issue of *Vers et Prose*, edited by the poet Paul Fort, together with four other texts.[39] Leutesdorf was, and still is, a winemaking village on the right bank of the Rhine across from Namedy. On February 9, 1902, accompanied by the Viscountess de Milhau, her daughter, her mother, and Annie Playden, Apollinaire set off on a tour of Germany that would last until the middle of May.[40] He presumably visited Leutesdorf toward the end of the trip, where he also found time to compose "Mai." Unfortunately, May was also the month in which Annie definitively rejected Apollinaire, who had been courting her for eight months. Although he and Annie did not go their separate ways until August, Richard Stamelman explains, "it is in 'Mai' that he resignedly bids her farewell and, at the same time, says adieu to the Rhenish countryside."[41]

As Breunig remarks, the poem is composed of four separate blocks, "the connection among them remaining unexplained because it is one of mood rather than of logical sequence."[42] Pierre Curnier finds the classical form of Apollinaire's stanzas "presque impeccable" ("almost impeccable").[43] In general, they contain four alexandrines with a regular caesura at the hemistich. Unexpectedly, the third stanza possesses five alexandrines. Although Jacques Guilhembet complains that this unbalances the poem, none of the other critics share his concern.[44] All the stanzas utilize *rimes embrassées* for their rhyme scheme and a mixture of *rimes suffisantes* and *rimes riches*. Masculine and feminine rhymes alternate. While some of the rhymes are irregular, in Curnier's opinion they are scarcely noticeable. The most daring example occurs in the first stanza: "montagne" / "s'éloigne" followed by "ruines" / "vignes" in the final stanza. According to P.-R. Leclercq, these are simply examples of "la musique apollinarienne."[45]

> Le mai le joli mai en barque sur le Rhin
> Des dames regardaient du haut de la montagne
> Vous êtes si jolies mais la barque s'éloigne
> Qui donc a fait pleurer les saules riverains
>
> Or des vergers fleuris se figeaient en arrière
> Les pétales tombés des cerisiers en mai
> Sont les ongles de celle que j'ai tant aimée
> Les pétales flétris sont comme ses paupières.
>
> (May lovely May sailing on the Rhine
> Some ladies were watching from the mountaintop
> You are so lovely but the boat sails on
> Who caused the riverbank willow to weep
>
> Flowering orchards congealed behind us
> Lying on the ground the May cherry trees' petals
> Are the fingernails of the woman I loved so dearly
> The wilted petals resemble her eyelids.)

As Philippe Renaud remarks, "Mai" is "l'un des plus beaux poèmes rhénans" ("is one of the most beautiful Rhenish poems").[46] Among other things, this probably explains why it has received so much critical attention. While not a single article has been devoted to "Vent nocturne" or to "Les Sapins"—and only one article to "Rhénane d'automne"—eight different critics have published studies of this poem. To be sure, the flowery season and the romantic setting are very attractive, but the poem can also be quite challenging. Interestingly, as Curnier points out, Apollinaire did not write a lot of poetry about spring.[47] Autumn was actually his favorite season—his "saison mentale" ("mental season") as he says in "Signe." The shorter days, dimmer light, and occasional hard frost appealed to his melancholy sensibility. By contrast, the days are longer in May, the light is radiant, and everything is full of promise. In contrast to autumn's muted palette, colorful flowers are everywhere. In short, as the first line insists, May is very pretty. Surprisingly, this statement has engendered a considerable amount of debate. Since the names of the months are preceded by an article in German but not in French, Curnier and Stamelman believe that "le mai" is a deliberate germanism.[48] Apollinaire uses Germanic constructions elsewhere in the "Rhénanes" to heighten the local color. Nevertheless, it turns out that French months do occasionally take an article. In Leclercq's opinion, the first hemistich was borrowed from a well-known *comptine* (children's rhyme) beginning: "C'est le mai, joli mai / C'est le joli mois de mai."[49] A quick survey turns up other songs that contain similar verses.

Taking his clue from Pierre Orecchioni, Stamelman points out that the descent of the Rhine by boat is a classic motif—one that the German Romantics exploited to great effect.[50] Apollinaire tacitly acknowledges this tradition by putting the river in the center of the picture. But who is in the boat, one wonders, and where is he or she going? While the answer initially appears to be the ladies mentioned at the beginning of the second verse, this proves to be impossible. They are looking down on the river from the top of a bluff. Thus the first line completely defies grammatical logic. It is what is known to correctors of student themes as a "dangling modifier." There is a total disconnect between the first and the second verses. And in fact the third and fourth lines are as isolated as the first two. The entire stanza is governed by parataxis. Since the connective links are missing, it is essentially a collage.[51]

At long last, someone finally speaks—not to provide useful information but to express regret. Although he would like to pursue the ladies, this individual confides, unfortunately the boat is taking him away from them. Paralleling the musical quotation in the first line, "le mai le joli mai," the third verse begins with the refrain from a popular song: "Vous êtes si jolie" ("You are so lovely").[52] Apollinaire never identifies himself, never even says he is a passenger on the boat. As the clues accumulate, however, it eventually becomes clear that he must be the speaker. Once again, one wonders where he could be going. While in theory he could be taking a sightseeing trip, Stamelman is undoubtedly right that Apollinaire is leaving.[53] Since he has been unlucky in love, his decision to leave the Rhineland is understandable. This interpretation is confirmed by the fourth line, which poses the rhetorical question: "Qui donc a fait pleurer les saules riverains?" ("Who caused the riverbank willows to cry?"). As Curnier remarks, the answer is obviously Annie.[54] Drawing on a traditional topos, nature itself participates in the poet's sorrow.

Like the weeping willows, everything Apollinaire describes in the remainder of the poem reflects his emotional state. This is particularly true of the second stanza, which contains some highly unusual imagery. While he descends the Rhine, the poet watches the orchards disappear behind him until they seem to congeal. Whether this refers to an optical phenomenon or to a mental phenomenon is unclear. As objects recede from the viewer, for example, they eventually blur together. Alternatively, as Stamelman suggests, the scene could be preserved in Apollinaire's memory like a snapshot.[55] In either case, Decaudin discerns a certain irony: "'Mai' réussit ce paradoxe de faire du mois du renouveau et de floraison celui de l'éloignement et d'effacement" ("'May' manages paradoxically to transform the month associated with rebirth and flowering into one of leaving and obliteration").[56] Several critics attach a symbolic value not only to the Rhine but also to the boat. While Claude Morhange-Bégué concedes the river could symbolize either life or destiny, in her opinion it represents an image of time.[57] By contrast, Curnier believes the boat, rather than the river, symbolizes life as it carries Apollinaire away.[58] In actuality, their positions are not as far apart as they may seem. Whether an individual finds himself on the river or in the river, the mechanics are basically the same. In either case, he will be swept downstream. And because living takes place over days, weeks, and years, life and time are parallel yardsticks. Each can be used to measure the other.

Since *se figer* is commonly used to describe coagulated blood, it creates an eerie tone and introduces two uncanny images. Reflecting Apollinaire's infatuation with Annie, who is evoked here for the first and last time in the poem, he discovers traces of her everywhere. Not only do the cherry blossoms resemble her fingernails, he confides, but they also recall her delicately lined eyelids. According to Laurence Perfézou, the first two stanzas "s'articulent autour de la représentation de la mort" ("are organized around the representation of death").[59] Apollinaire's initial separation and suffering are followed by the death of the landscape, then by the death of his beloved's face.

> Sur le chemin du bord du fleuve lentement
> Un ours un singe un chien menés par des tziganes
> Suivaient une roulotte traînée par un âne
> Tandis que s'éloignait dans les vignes rhénanes
> Sur un fifre lointain un air de régiment

Le mai le joli mai a paré les ruines
De lierre de vigne vierge et de rosiers
Le vent du Rhin secoue sur le bord les osiers
Et les roseaux jaseurs et les fleurs nues des vignes.

(On the road along the river's edge
A bear a monkey a dog led by Gypsies
Slowly followed a donkey cart
While a regimental tune on a distant fife
Faded away in the Rhenish vineyards

May lovely May has adorned the ruins
With ivy with creepers and with roses
The Rhenish wind shakes the willows on the bank
The gossiping reeds and the vines' naked flowers.)

The third stanza, which is purely descriptive, offers a picturesque glimpse of some of the riverbank's inhabitants. As Apollinaire continues downstream, he passes a donkey pulling a gypsy caravan and followed by three animals. These are performing animals, rather than pets, with which the gypsies eke out their livelihood. The bear dances on its hind legs to the sound of a primitive drum, while the monkey and dog do more advanced tricks. Like Apollinaire, Stamelman points out, the gypsies are leaving one place en route to another.[60] Like him, they are essentially foreigners in the Rhineland. While Curnier is tempted to view the caravan as a symbol of life itself, nothing in the poem specifically justifies this interpretation.[61] Pursuing her mythological investigations, Madeleine Boisson deduces that the caravan and the three animals are terrestrial projections of the Big Dipper.[62] According to her, the dog is named Maira, otherwise known as Sirius the dog star. The stanza concludes with the sound of regimental music dying away, which, like all regimental music in Germany, is played on a fife. As Antoine Fongaro remarks, the last line parallels the first line, establishing a correspondence "entre le déplacement visuel (le cortège des tziganes) et le déplacement auditif (un air de régiment)" ("between the visual displacement [the file of Gypsies] and the auditory displacement [a regimental air]").[63] In Stamelman's words, "Everything in the stanza either disappears, flows away, or departs."[64] In this regard it resembles *Alcools* itself, so much of which vanishes or fades away in the distance.

The final stanza begins with the same musical phrase as the first stanza: "Le mai le joli mai." As far as one can ascertain, the words are uttered in pretty much the same spirit. Despite Apollinaire's miserable love life, May is just as beautiful as it was at the beginning of the poem. To Stamelman the stanza seems livelier than the rest of the poem.[65] No longer a dangling modifier, the musical phrase has become an active participant. May has completely transformed the appearance of the castle ruins along the Rhine by covering them with ivy, creeper, and rose bushes. In addition, the critics agree that the ruins are a symbol of Apollinaire's unfortunate love affair. With this in mind, he has chosen the plants carefully. The ivy symbolizes his fidelity, the creeper his persistence, and the roses his abiding love for Annie. At this point, a gust of wind buffets the willows on the riverbank, the chattering reeds, and the flowering vines. This is our fourth encounter with the Rhenish wind and by far the most pleasant. Instead of knocking down trees or covering everything with dead leaves, it merely livens things up a bit. Undoubtedly the fact that it is May, rather than November, has something to do with it.

The "roseaux jaseurs" recall the story of King Midas's barber, who, entrusted with an embarrassing secret, dug a hole in the ground, whispered the secret, and filled the hole up again. Unfortunately, a cluster of reeds grew up and gave the secret away with its chattering. According to Fongaro, "les fleurs nues des vignes" is a botanical reference.[66] It refers to flowers that lack a protective hood (perianth) formed by the calyx or the corolla. Together with the "vigne vierge," the expression evokes Apollinaire's passion for Annie and lends a slight erotic tinge to the proceedings. All things considered, Perfézou concludes that the stanza contains "l'espoir d'un renouveau" ("the hope of a renewal").[67] Guilhembet is even more explicit: "La vie du poète trouve un second souffle après le déclin de l'amour" ("The poet's life gets a second breath after the decline of love").[68] By contrast, Morhange-Bégué and Lartigue are more pessimistic. In their opinion, the last stanza evokes "la détérioration et . . . la vanité de toutes choses" ("the deterioration and . . . the vanity of all things").[69] What look like signs of a potential renewal to the first two critics strike them as signs of a general "dégradation."

During the precious year he spent in the Rhineland, Apollinaire suddenly matured as a poet. Although his love affair with Annie was frustrating, it provided the stimulus he needed to refine his craft. Thrust into different circumstances, Breunig explains, "he discovered a new language and new landscapes, customs, and legends which he made his own."[70] Faced with new demands, his poetry became more supple and more expressive. While he had been writing poems for years, "c'est en Allemagne," Décaudin remarks, "qu'Apollinaire [forgea] son univers poétique et les modalités de son expression" ("it is in Germany that Apollinaire [forged] his poetic universe and its expressive modalities").[71] Nearly half the poems in *Alcools*, several short stories, and a number of journalistic projects resulted directly from this experience.

While everyone agrees that the *année allemande* (German year) was a transformative experience, there is less agreement when it comes to describing how Apollinaire's poetry was transformed. Marie-Claire Bancquart believes that, compared to his previous poems, the "Rhénanes" are simpler and much more realistic.[72] Unlike his earlier poetry, Claude Debon adds, they fully exploit the musical resources of the French language.[73] Francis Steegmuller praises the poems for succinctly conveying "a strong physical picture."[74] According to Pilkington, they reveal unexpected links between things and transform them into highly expressive images.[75] While some of these assessments focus on stylistic criteria and others on the poetry's imagery, they are all basically correct. Since Apollinaire completely modified his poetry, every aspect underwent some kind of change. Some of the modifications were minor, and some were major. Together they enabled him to write poems that were simpler, more lyrical, more visual, and more perceptive.

Notes

1. The classic studies are Ernst Wolf's *Guillaume Apollinaire und das Rheinland* (1937; Frankfurt am Main: Peter Lang, 1988) and Pierre Orecchioni, *Le Thème du Rhin dans l'inspiration de Guillaume Apollinaire* (Paris: Lettres Modernes, 1956). For additional information, see Marc Poupon, "L'Année allemande d'Apollinaire," *Revue des Lettres Modernes*, Nos. 183–188 (1968), 9–45, and *Apollinaire: Revue d'Etudes Apollinariennes*, Nos. 5–7 (May 2009–May 2010).

2. Claude Debon, "L'Originalité des 'Rhénanes,'" *Histoire et critique littéraires en mouvement. Mélanges offert à Henryk Chudak*, ed. Wieslaw Kroker (Warsaw: University of Warsaw, 2009), 73–92.

3. LeRoy C. Breunig, *Guillaume Apollinaire* (New York: Columbia University Press, 1969), 15.

4. Didier Alexandre, *Guillaume Apollinaire. "Alcools"* (Paris: Presses Universitaires de France, 1994), 67.

5. Wolf, *Guillaume Apollinaire und das Rheinland*, 57–58.

6. Michel Décaudin, *Le Dossier d' "Alcools,"* rev. ed. (Geneva: Droz and Paris Minard, 1965), 155.

7. LeRoy C. Breunig, "Apollinaire et Annie Playden," *Mercure de France*, April 1, 1952, 645.

8. Décaudin, *Le Dossier d' "Alcools,"* 156.

9. Guillaume Apollinaire, *Oeuvres poétiques*, ed. Marcel Adéma and Michel Décaudin (Paris: Gallimard, 1965), 846.

10. Breunig, *Guillaume Apollinaire*, 20.

11. Alexandre, *Guillaume Apollinaire. "Alcools,"* 16.

12. A. E. Pilkington, *Apollinaire: "Alcools"* (Oxford: Blackwell, 1970), 135.

13. Sir William Smith, *Smaller Classical Dictionary* (New York: Dutton, 1958), 52.

14. Décaudin, *Le Dossier d' "Alcools,"* 191.

15. Maurice Piron, *Guillaume Apollinaire. "La Chanson du mal-aimé"* (Paris: Nizet, 1987), 18.

16. Anne Hyde Greet, *"Alcools." Guillaume Apollinaire* (Berkeley: University of California Press, 1965), 262.

17. Garnet Rees, ed., *Guillaume Apollinaire: "Alcools"* (London: Athlone, 1975), 166.

18. Pilkington, *Apollinaire: "Alcools,"* xxvii–xxviii.

19. Ibid., xxviii.

20. Claude Debon, *Apollinaire: Glossaire des oeuvres complètes* (Paris: La Sorbonne Nouvelle, 1988), 38.

21. Pilkington, *Apollinaire: "Alcools,"* xxviii.

22. Debon, *Apollinaire: Glossaire des oeuvres complètes*, 59.

23. Claude Morhange-Bégué and Pierre Lartigue, *"Alcools." Apollinaire* (Paris: Hatier, 1991), 25.

24. Pilkington, *Apollinaire: "Alcools,"* xxviii.

25. Décaudin, *Le Dossier d' "Alcools,"* 187–88.

26. Debon, "L'Originalité des 'Rhénanes,'" 73–92.

27. Poupon, "L'Année allemande d'Apollinaire," 23.

28. Rees, *Guillaume Apollinaire: "Alcools,"* 21.

29. J. C. Cooper, *An Illustrated Encyclopaedia of Traditional Symbols* (London: Thames and Hudson, 1978), 124.

30. Robert Champigny, "Analyse de 'Rhénane d'automne,'" *The French Review*, Vol. 33, No. 2 (December 1959), 127.

31. Décaudin, *Le Dossier d' "Alcools,"* 189.

32. Pierre Brunel, *Apollinaire entre deux mondes: Mythocritique II* (Paris: Presses Universitaires de France, 1997), 155.

33. Décaudin, *Le Dossier d' "Alcools,"* 120.

34. Apollinaire, *Oeuvres poétiques*, 553.

35. Pilkington, *Apollinaire: "Alcools,"* xxvii.

36. Décaudin, *Le Dossier d' "Alcools,"* 190.

37. Ibid., 190.

38. Champigny, "Analyse de 'Rhénane d'automne,'" 129.

39. Décaudin, *Le Dossier d' "Alcools,"* 179.

40. See Louis Brunet, "Le Voyage d'Apollinaire à travers l'Allemagne au printemps 1902," *Apollinaire: Revue d'Etudes Apollinariennes*, No. 5 (May 2009), 25–37, and No. 6 (November 2009), 25–37.

41. Richard Howard Stamelman, *The Drama of Self in Guillaume Apollinaire's "Alcools"* (Chapel Hill: North Carolina Studies in the Romance Languages and Literatures, 1976), 69.

42. Breunig, *Guillaume Apollinaire*, 16.

43. Pierre Curnier, *Pages commentées d'auteurs contemporains*, Vol. 2 (Paris: Larousse, 1965), 59.

44. Jacques Guilhembet, "'Rhénanes,'" *L'Ecole des Lettres*, No. 12 (June 1992), 67.

45. P.-R. Leclercq, "Etude de texte: Guillaume Apollinaire: '"Mai,'" *L'Ecole des Lettres*, April 1976, 10.

46. Philippe Renaud, *Lecture d'Apollinaire* (Lausanne: L'Age d'Homme, 1969), 105.

47. Curnier, *Pages commentées d'auteurs contemporains*, 56.

48. Ibid., 56, and Stamelman, *The Drama of Self*, 69–70.

49. Leclercq, "Etude de texte," 9.

50. Stamelman, *The Drama of Self*, 70.

51. For an analysis of the stanza's temporal and referential ambiguity, see Claude Morhange-Bégué, "'Mai': Essai d'application d'une méthode stylistique," *Langue Française*, No. 7 (September 1970), 29.

52. Stamelman, *The Drama of Self*, 70.

53. Curnier, *Pages commentées d'auteurs contemporains*, 59.

54. Stamelman, *The Drama of Self*, 72.

55. Michel Décaudin, "L'Année allemande," *Apollinaire: Revue d'Etudes Apollinariennes*, No. 6 (November 2009), 16.

56. Morhange-Bégué, "'Mai,'" 32.

57. Curnier, *Pages commentées d'auteurs contemporains*, 62.

58. Laurence Perfézou, *"Alcools." Apollinaire* (Paris: Bordas, 1988), 47.

59. Stamelman, *The Drama of Self*, 75.

60. Curnier, *Pages commentées d'auteurs contemporains*, 62.

61. Madeleine Boisson, *Apollinaire et les mythologies antiques* (Paris: Nizet, 1989), 177–79.

62. Antoine Fongaro, *Apollinaire poète: Exégèses et discussions 1957–1987* (Toulouse: Presses Universitaires du Mirail-Toulouse, 1988), 184.

63. Stamelman, *The Drama of Self*, 75.

64. Ibid., 76.

65. Fongaro, *Apollinaire poète*, 184.

66. Perfézou, *"Alcools." Apollinaire*, 47.

67. Guilhembet, "'Rhénanes,'" 75.

68. Morhange-Bégué and Lartigue, *"Alcools." Apollinaire*, 21. See Morhange-Bégué, "'Mai,'" 31 and 33–34.

69. Breunig, *Guillaume Apollinaire*, 15.

70. Michel Décaudin, "L'Ecrivain et son temps," in Jean Burgos et al., *Apollinaire en somme* (Paris: Champion, 1998), 125.

71. Marie-Claire Bancquart, *Fin de siècle gourmande: 1888–1900* (Paris: Presses Universitaires de France, 2001), quoted in Debon, "L'Originalité des 'Rhénanes.'"

72. Debon, "L'Originalité des 'Rhénanes.'"

73. Francis Steegmuller, *Apollinaire: Poet Among the Painters* (New York: Farrar, Straus: 1963), 77.

74. Pilkington, *Apollinaire: "Alcools,"* xxvi.

CHAPTER TWO

~

An Enchanted Land

Most of the poems in *Alcools* had been published previously before Apollinaire collected them in a single volume. Since they cover a fifteen-year period, from 1898 to 1913, this is not terribly surprising. Seeking to bolster his reputation as an *homme de lettres*, Apollinaire published forty-three of the poems in a variety of publications. These included prestigious literary reviews like *La Plume* and *La Revue Blanche*, but also a number of lesser journals such as *Les Argonautes* and *Le Voile de Pourpre*. Quite a few appeared in *Le Festin d'Esope* and *Les Soirées de Paris*, both of which Apollinaire edited himself. Only seven of the poems did not appear in print before *Alcools* was published. These include "Chantre," which was added to the proofs of the collection at the last moment, and "Automne malade," which seems to have been composed much earlier. Most of the *Alcools* manuscript was written on stationery from the Hotel Zu Den Vier Jahreszeiten in Munich, which the poet obtained in March 1902 during his tour of Germany, Vienna, and Prague.[1] Apollinaire himself resided in the Rhineland from August 29, 1901, to August 25, 1902—one of the richest periods in his career.[2] "Although he concealed the importance of this sojourn by grouping only nine poems in the 'Rhénanes' series in *Alcools*," LeRoy C. Breunig explains, "this single year produced many more works that were included in the collection."[3] Besides a number of longer poems, Breunig adds, it produced several one-page masterpieces such as "Les Colchiques," "La Tzigane," and "Automne malade."[4]

"Automne malade"

Unlike "Les Colchiques," which has received an unbelievable amount of attention (see Chapter 3), the others have generated relatively little critical interest. There have been only two or three serious studies of "Automne malade" since it was originally published. And yet, as Breunig maintains, it is one of the best-loved poems in *Alcools*. Critics cite it all the time without pausing to investigate it in more detail. Like "La Tzigane," "Automne malade" perpetuates the illusion that it can be apprehended quickly and effortlessly. Perhaps this explains why there is considerable disagreement about the poem's subject. According to Laurence Perfézou, for example, "le poète délivre un état d'âme, une émotion et un regard sur la vie" ("The poet delivers a mood, an emotion, and a view of life").[5] To be sure, this describes "Automne malade," but it describes a great many other poems as well—perhaps even most poems. Unfortunately, these characteristics are much too vague. Furthermore, even if one identifies the particular mood, the emotion, and the worldview in question, they do not constitute the poem's subject. Although Apollinaire consistently strives to create a melancholy mood, for example, it is the product, not the source, of the actions evoked in the poem. Anne Hyde Greet is more specific: "The poet links a mood to a season and turns a nineteenth-century theme, the death of the year, into a humorous, if nostalgic evocation of the Rhineland."[6] However, the poem's subject is not really the death of the year, nor is it concerned with the Rhineland. These are incidental motifs, chosen for their metaphorical value in the first instance and their metonymic value in the second. Like Greet, Timothy Mathews also detects a nostalgic dimension in "Automne malade."[7] Nevertheless, since Apollinaire had not left Germany when he composed the poem, it can hardly be nostalgic. According to Merriam Webster's Collegiate Dictionary, nostalgia is "a wistful or excessively sentimental yearning for return to or of some past period or irrecoverable condition." Curiously, Greet is the only critic who detects a humorous note to the poem, which strikes most readers as anything but amusing.

Roger Lefèvre approaches "Automne malade" from another, more promising angle. As he notes, poets usually portray autumn in one of two ways—either positively or negatively. They employ images associated either with richness and fecundity or else with poverty and sterility. The choice is essentially between ripe fruits and dead leaves, both of which are to be found in the present poem. "L'originalité d'Apollinaire," Lefèvre concludes, "est de sentir la faiblesse de la vie à l'intérieur même de la richesse épanouie" ("Apollinaire's originality consists in sensing life's frailty even at the heart of abundant riches").[8] Or, as Pierre Bourdieu puts it, "automne adoré *parce que malade*" ("autumn adored *because* it is sick").[9] The fact that the two themes are intertwined provides a more nuanced (and more rewarding) portrait of autumn. Scott Bates provides a more paradoxical assessment of the work's thematic complexity. For him "Automne malade" is a poem about "the melancholy, creative enjoyment of sterility."[10] Claude Morhange-Bégué and Pierre Lartigue remind us that fall is Apollinaire's favorite season, both for personal and for astrological reasons.[11] Born on August 26, 1880, the poet was a Virgo and thus "soumis au Chef du Signe de l'Automne" ("subject to the Chief of the Sign of Autumn") as he announces in "Signe."[12] In particular, he continues, fall is the season that most closely approximates his "saison mentale" ("mental season"). More than anything, the melancholy atmosphere that suffuses the work reflects Apollinaire's psychological condition. However, the source of his condition does not appear until the end of the poem, where even then it is evoked indirectly. As Morhange-Bégué and Lartigue declare, the subject of "Automne malade" is the ineluctable passage of time.[13] This finally explains why Apollinaire feels so melancholy. Writing to Jean-Yves Blanc during the war, he confided: "Rien ne détermine plus de mélancolie chez moi que cette fuite du temps. Elle est en désaccord si formel avec mon sentiment, mon identité, qu'elle est la source même de ma poésie" ("Nothing fills me with more melancholy than the flight of time. It disagrees so strongly with my feelings, my identity, that it is the very source of my poetry").[14]

As the reader quickly discovers, "Automne malade" is a highly idiosyncratic composition. Written in a kind of rhyming free verse and divided into four unequal stanzas, it is also a remarkable achievement. Although the verses vary in length, expanding to fifteen syllables near the beginning and shrinking to two syllables at the end, they generally rhyme. Except for lines 5–9, which are pure free verse, the poem consists of *rimes suffisantes* arranged according to traditional rhyme schemes. The initial stanza employs *rimes plates*, the next two stanzas *rimes croisées*, and the final stanza *rimes croisées* plus a tercet. Although the very first line is an octosyllable, the second line is nearly twice as long. Consisting of six and four syllables, respectively, the next two verses form a decasyllabic line with a displaced caesura. The poem continues in this manner, alternating different line lengths, until it concludes with a fragmented alexandrine. As Marie-Jeanne Durry comments, this arrangement "permet une constante variété, dans des strophes raccourcies ou allongées et avec des élargissements ou des resserrements de rythme. D'où une musique fluide et changeante" ("permits a constant variety in shorter or longer stanzas with rhythmical enlargements or shrinkings. Which produces a fluid and changing music").[15] Despite the poem's irregular appearance, A. E. Pilkington affirms, "the fluidity of [the] free verse is particularly effective."[16] Similarly, Mathews insists that "the flow of the language . . . is one of its distinctively 'lyrical' features":[17]

> Automne malade et adoré
> Tu mourras quand l'ouragan soufflera dans les roseraies
> Quand il aura neigé
> Dans les vergers.
>
> (Sick and adored Autumn
> You will die when the strong winds buffet the roses
> When it snows
> In the orchards.)

In his groundbreaking study *Semiotics of Poetry*, Michael Riffaterre argues that every poem results from "the transformation of . . . a minimal and literal sentence into a longer, complex, and nonliteral periphrasis."[18] If poems are generated by a single phrase or "matrix," as he calls it, then the origins of the present composition can be found in a statement such as "L'Automne est malade," which, slightly modified, becomes the title of this work. Repeated in the first verse, the title introduces the paradigm that will structure the entire work: *automne + malade*. Advancing line-by-line and stanza-by-stanza, Apollinaire develops both the initial image and the metaphor with which it is paired. Technically, therefore, the second term is actually an extended metaphor or *métaphore filée*. Although "adoré" is eventually echoed by "j'aime," its function is decorative rather than paradigmatic. Apollinaire may have merely wanted to create an octosyllabic line or, through homophony, to evoke the golden (*doré*) autumn leaves. Beginning with the title, fall is treated as if it were a patient confined to a hospital bed. The illness from which it is suffering appears to be old age, which, the second line reminds us, is invariably fatal. As Mathews notes, the authorial persona is elusive throughout much of the poem.[19] However, the authorial voice is evident from the very beginning. While the speaker is not identified, it can only be Apollinaire. Beginning with an apostrophe addressed to the moribund season, the poet proclaims that autumn will expire with the arrival of winter. Before long, howling winds will shake the summer rosebushes, and snow will cover the fertile orchards. Mathews protests that these images undercut the attempt at poetic lyricism because they are inappropriate: "Autumn—the season of orchard fruits in Europe—is implied by references to winter and snow."[20] Nevertheless, these references are to events that will take place in the future, not to contemporary affairs. Like a photographic negative, where black is replaced by white and vice versa, autumn is defined here by the *absence* of hurricanes and snow.

Beginning with another apostrophe, the following stanza is more forceful than the first:

> Pauvre automne
> Meurs en blancheur et en richesse
> De neige et de fruits mûrs
> Au fond du ciel
> Des éperviers planent
> Sur les nixes nicettes aux cheveux verts et naines
> Qui n'ont jamais aimé.
>
> (Poor Autumn
> Die buried in whiteness and riches
> In snow and ripe fruits
> In the depths of the sky
> Sparrow hawks glide
> Above nixies with green hair and dwarves
> Who have never loved.)

Apollinaire employs the imperative rather than the future and future perfect tenses. While he commiserates with the bedridden patient ("pauvre automne"), his sympathy extends only so far. No sooner has he uttered these words than he commands autumn to expire. Or rather, as Bourdieu insists, he delivers a philosophy lesson: "Accepte ton destin" ("Accepte your destiny").[21] Although the poem begins with a direct address, Mathews notes, "the promise of an open dialogue with autumn is not kept."[22] And yet, apostrophes are designed to allow the speaker to express his or her feelings. They do not normally promise much of anything. This time the poem contains a reference to objects associated specifically with autumn. The orchards evoked previously turn out to be laden with ripe fruit, some of which has fallen to the ground. As Mathews observes, the fruit "is so abundant that it need not be picked."[23] For this reason, apples and pears will still be hanging from the branches when winter arrives. In Apollinaire's eyes, the snow and the fruit are riches that embellish the Rhineland setting. Although they are normally incompatible, Bourdieu observes, they will be "reconciliées dans la beauté fatale d'une luxueuse décadence" ("reconciled in the fatal beauty of a luxurious decadence").[24] Despite their incompatibility, they will coexist for a brief moment when autumn encounters winter. For Ernst Wolf, the fruits, the orchards, the forest, and the wind are sure signs that the scene is set in the Rhineland.[25]

Up to this point, the poem has been a realistic, if metaphorical, portrait of the Rhenish countryside. The next few lines usher in a change of scenery and introduce us to a number of surprising characters. Some of these are wild animals, and some are mythical figures borrowed from Rhenish folklore. Clive Scott describes the shift as follows: "So the pastoral world of orchard and rose garden mixes with the uncultivated and untamed rural world of hawk and stag and forest, and world-weary knowledge mixes with ceremonies of innocence."[26] Borrowed from W. B. Yeats's "The Second Coming," the last phrase refers to the nixies with their long green hair. Scott is thinking of the word "nicette," which derives from the (archaic) masculine adjective *nicet*, meaning "nice," "simple," "harmless." Bates nicely translates the term as "naïve," but William Meredith goes completely astray with "nestling."[27] Cousins of the Cornish pixies, the German nixies are also found in "Nuit rhénane" and "Clotilde," where—as in the present poem—they contribute a supernatural note to the proceedings. According to Perfézou, the nixies are the souls of unhappy girls who have drowned themselves "par désespoir d'amour" ("out of lovelorn despair").[28]

Several critics have suggested that Apollinaire's choice of "nicettes" was dictated by the homophony between it and "nixes." Others insist that the term has a semantic function, which, in Scott's words, "[casts] the nixies as unfulfilled, [remaining] innocent not by choice but by bad fortune."[29] Viewed from this angle, they resemble the "naines qui n'ont jamais aimé." A brief foray into German folklore reveals that dwarves are commonly portrayed in one of two ways. Either they are helpful and hardworking, like Snow White's friends, or they are spiteful and malicious. Since those in "Automne malade" carry a negative marker, they undoubtedly match the second description. Like the dwarves in numerous medieval romances, they are intrinsically evil. And although the nixies seem to be completely innocent, their appearance turns out to be deceiving. In actuality, like Greek sirens and French on-dines, they attempt to seduce passers-by with their song.[30] Like the loveless dwarves, the nixies in "Automne malade" are associated with sterility and death. Half-woman and half-fish, they lure people into the water so they can drown them.[31] The difference between the cultivated part of the Rhineland and the uncultivated part is crystal clear. While orchards and rose bushes flourish elsewhere, the Rhine Valley is inhabited by malevolent spirits. Myth and magic, Apollinaire seems to say, are inherently dangerous enterprises.

Interestingly, the nixies and dwarves are framed by two groups of animals: hungry sparrow hawks and rutting stags. The introductory phrase "au fond du ciel" is ambiguous to say the least. Mathews points out that it can mean "on the horizon," "at the bottom of the sky," or "in the depths of the sky."[32] Bates renders the phrase as "at the top of the sky," which, since the hawks seem to be directly overhead, may be the most accurate translation.[33] The four translators are also split on how to translate *planer*. Donald Revell thinks the birds are gliding, Bates believes they are soaring, Greet imagines they are floating, and Meredith avoids the problem altogether. Nevertheless, according to all indications the birds are probably hovering overhead. The smallest of all the falcons, sparrow hawks are easy to identify because they frequently hover while looking for prey. Since they usually hunt alone, the presence of multiple sparrow hawks is puzzling. Perhaps Apollinaire is describing a mated pair who are looking for something to feed their young. Indeed, the fact that they are hovering over the nixies and the dwarves suggests they are preparing to pounce on them. Sparrow hawks may be small birds, but nixies are much smaller. Interestingly, Bates reports that falcons are associated with ondines in European folklore.[34] Numerous fairy tales exist, moreover, in which various "little people" are menaced by sparrow hawks. Ironically, while the nixies and dwarves are threatening to ambush the unwary human beings, the sparrow hawks are threatening to snatch the nixies and the dwarves. Faithful to his brand of "mythocritique," Pierre Brunel adopts what is essentially an allegorical perspective. For him, the episode represents "une menace aquiline suspendue sur mythes et légendes, prête à fondre sur ces résidus du 'monde ancien' pourtant ineffaçables et persistants" ("an aquiline menace hovering over myths and legends, ready to swoop down on those residues of the 'ancient world' that however are ineffable and persistent").[35]

> Aux lisières lointaines
> Les cerfs ont bramé.

> (In distant borderlands
> The stags have bellowed loudly.)

Consisting of only two verses, the third stanza scarcely qualifies as a stanza at all. Judging from the ABAB rhyme scheme, these lines were originally joined to the previous stanza, where they counterbalanced the nixies and the dwarves. For some reason, Apollinaire chopped off the last two lines and left them dangling in the middle of the page. Perhaps he wanted to call attention to them, or perhaps he wanted to create a pause after the preceding scene. Composed of two six-syllable lines, the stanza is essentially an alexandrine that has been cut in half. As the verses attest, fall is the mating season for European red deer. From

August to early winter, the dominant stags, who have magnificent branched antlers, form harems averaging about five does apiece. Not surprisingly, those that bellow the loudest attract the most females. Unfortunately, they also attract other stags, which try to steal the females away. During the fierce battle that ensues, both animals bellow continually. The sound is extremely loud and extends for quite some distance. Thus, even though the stags in "Automne malade" are far away, Apollinaire is still able to hear them. Their bellowing has such a mournful sound that Morhange-Bégué and Lartigue refer to it as "wailing."[36] Dying away on the wind, like the hunting horns in "Cors de chasse," the sound reminds us that the death of autumn is imminent. The final stanza continues this theme:

> Et que j'aime ô saison que j'aime tes rumeurs
> Les fruits tombant sans qu'on les cueille
> Le vent et la forêt qui pleurent
> Toutes leurs larmes en automne feuille à feuille
>> Les feuilles
>> Qu'on foule
>> Un train
>> Qui roule
>> La vie
>> S'écoule.

> (O season how I love your murmurs
> Fruits falling with no one to pick them
> The wind and the forest shedding
> All their tears in Autumn leaf by leaf
>> The trampled
>> Leaves
>> A moving
>> Train
>> Life
>> Flows by.)

Apollinaire finally makes a personal appearance in the last stanza, where he continues to explore the season's acoustic dimension. What he really likes about autumn, he confides, is the sounds that are heard at no other time of the year. These include the sounds of falling fruit, falling leaves, and the wind passing through the trees. Although the first four lines are clearly meant to serve as an encomium, they are seriously undercut by the imagery Apollinaire employs. Lying all over the ground, the rotten fruit merely evokes death and decay. Shedding copious tears, the wind and the trees resemble mourners at a funeral. From all appearances, they are mourning the death of autumn, which has finally succumbed to its metaphorical illness. The prediction at the beginning of the poem has finally come true.

Consisting of a single disjointed alexandrine, the final section was borrowed from "Un Soir d'été."[37] Anticipating Apollinaire's later experiments with visual poetry, three phrases are arranged vertically to mimic the falling leaves. As Bourdieu points out, Victor Hugo had previously employed this device in "Djinns":

> Tout fuit
> Tout passe,
> L'espace
> Efface
> Le bruit.
>
> (Everything flees
> Everything passes
> Space
> Effaces
> Sound.)[38]

At the verbal level, the leaves are juxtaposed with a speeding train and with the flow of life. Since all three are driven by powerful forces, the relationship between them is basically metaphorical. All three have moved away from their initial position and are en route toward another destination. Together they symbolize the transient aspect of life, which is all too brief, and the irresistible passage of time. Like Apollinaire's world in general, Bourdieu declares, "Automne malade" is characterized by "un amour du temps dans sa fugacité essentielle et de l'homme comme être de passage" ("a love of the basic evanescence of time and of man as a transient phenomenon").[39]

"Nuit rhénane"

Published initially in an anthology, where it was dated "Honnef 1902," "Nuit rhénane" has long delighted—and puzzled—readers of *Alcools*.[40] Composed of three quatrains plus a single last line, the poem basically adheres to the classical model. The verses are all alexandrines, they use alternating rhymes, and they are all *rimes riches* (or nearly). The first stanza describes a quiet evening on the banks of the Rhine:

> Mon verre est plein d'un vin trembleur comme une flamme
> Ecoutez la chanson lente d'un batelier
> Qui raconte avoir vu sous la lune sept femmes
> Tordre leurs cheveux verts et longs jusqu'à leurs pieds.

(My glass is full of wine trembling like a flame
Listen to the boatman's slow song
Telling of seven women in the moonlight
Wringing their green hair reaching down to their feet.)

According to Didier Alexandre, Apollinaire's poems open in one of three ways. They begin with a physical observation, a comment directed at someone else, or the first-person subject pronoun.[41] In this case, "Nuit rhénane" follows the first scenario. Apollinaire looks at his glass and notices that the wine is trembling. What this means is difficult to determine. It is amazing how little we know. Where exactly is Apollinaire, for example? Is he dining in a restaurant or sitting outside somewhere? How do we know he is sitting at all? Is he drinking white wine, which comes in a relatively slender glass, or red wine, which requires a glass with a rounder, wider bowl? Since the scene takes place in the Rhineland, where sixty percent of the grapes are white, the first scenario is more likely. However, why is the wine glass trembling? If it is resting on a table, there could have been a slight earth tremor. If Apollinaire is holding the glass, he could conceivably be nervous about something. Indeed, Jacques Guilhembet believes that he is suffering from existential anguish.[42] Or perhaps, as the line seems to imply, the wine itself is trembling but not the glass. Since this is a physical impossibility, "trembleur" must be a metaphor for something else. Roger Lefèvre suggests the wine is in a faceted glass that emits flashes from time to time.[43] This interpretation would explain why Apollinaire compares the wine to a flame. Philippe Renaud points out that the union of a liquid and a flame reflects the double nature of alcohol, which is simultaneously water and fire.[44] However, the verse is much more than the sum of its individual parts. It is charged with an unusual energy that sets the stage for the rest of the poem. As Lefèvre declares, "Ces mots suggèrent sourdement une ardeur enivrée et dévoratrice (*flamme*) et une inquiétude (*trembleur*)" ("These words evoke both an intoxicating and consuming ardor and an anxiety"). Evoking a scene in *Faust* where wine actually bursts into flame, Pierre Orecchioni claims the latter is a sign of the wine's diabolical origin and its magic power.[45] Although the glass of flaming wine in "Nuit rhénane" is wholly metaphorical, something magical is clearly about to happen.

The next three lines confirm this impression and introduce a slightly disquieting note. As we quickly learn, the scene transpires on the banks of the Rhine. Slowly sipping his wine, Apollinaire leans back in his chair and listens to a boatman's song slowly drifting across the water. Supposedly taken from Rhenish folklore, the song recounts how someone glimpsed seven

women wringing out their long green hair by the riverside. Apparently mis-
led by the number seven, critics persist in identifying these figures with the
legendary "sieben Jungfrauen von Oberwesel" ("seven maidens from Oberwesel") (near Honnef).[46] Mocking their suitors from a boat on the Rhine,
the maidens drowned when it suddenly capsized. However, in the song they
are obviously not drowning, and their long green hair immediately marks
them as nixies, who live in the river and prey on unwary travelers. Related to
Celtic pixies, the German nixies are also present in "Automne malade" and
"Clotilde." Laurence Perfézou reports that they are the souls of unhappy girls
who have drowned themselves from love.[47] Like Greek sirens and French
ondines, they woo passers-by with their bewitching songs.[48] As soon as their
victims approach, they pull them into the water and drown them.[49]Although
the boatman seems harmless enough, the mention of the nixies introduces
a supernatural element that the poet apparently finds threatening. While
the story would normally have fascinated Apollinaire, who loved Rhenish
folklore, for some reason he reacts violently:

> Debout chantez plus haut en dansant une ronde
> Que je n'entende plus le chant du batalier
> Et mettez près de moi toutes les filles blondes
> Au regard immobile aux nattes repliées.

> (Stand up sing louder while dancing a round
> So I no longer hear the boatman's song
> And bring me all the blond girls
> With their blank expressions and coiled braids.)

Since Apollinaire never explains why he is so frightened, critics have
come up with their own explanation. Judging from the poet's reaction, the
boatman's song must be associated with evil. Thus, Marc Poupon declares it
is "pernicieuse, mortelle," and Marie-Jeanne Durry asserts that it is a "com-
plainte maléfique" ("evil song").[50] Richard Stamelman believes that Apollinaire rejects the song because it is about mystery and the supernatural.[51]
Perfézou, Lefèvre, and Orecchioni are more specific: the song represents a
magic spell the boatman is attempting to cast over the crowd.[52] Hoping to
drown out his powerful voice, the poet jumps to his feet and encourages the
crowd to begin singing and dancing. Surrounding himself with a bevy of
blonde girls, who make a kind of magic circle, Apollinaire begins singing
and dancing himself. Jean-Claude Chevalier is struck by the way the "plus
d'excès" in the first line is transformed into a "plus négatif" in the second.

What looks initially like repetition, he notes, is actually "une opération de métamorphose portant sur les structures sémiques" ("a metamorphic opera-tion involving the semic structures").[53] Discussing the role of art in Apoll-inaire's early poetry, Margaret Davies reminds us that he loved *La Vierge à la fleur de haricot* (*Madonna with a Bean Flower*) (Figure 2.1), which he saw in Cologne in 1901.[54] Inevitably, one wonders if the blonde Madonna in the painting prefigured the impassive blondes in "Nuit rhénane." Despite Apol-linaire's best efforts, the boatman's spell eventually engulfs the entire region:

> Le Rhin le Rhin est ivre où les vignes se mirent
> Tout l'or des nuits tombe en tremblant s'y refléter
> La voix chante toujours à en râle-mourir
> Ces fées aux cheveux verts qui incantent l'été.

> (The Rhine the drunken Rhine mirrors the vines
> All the golden nights fall trembling and reflected
> The voice continues singing like a death rattle about
> These fairies with green hair who enchant the Summer.)

Although repetition plays an important role in Apollinaire's poetry, its function in "Nuit rhénane" is severely restricted.[55] While "le Rhin le Rhin"

Figure 2.1. Maître Guillaume, La Vierge à la Fleur de Haricot. Karl Schae-fer, Stephan Lochner, und die Kölner Malerschule (1923).
Dictionary of Words and Things (1895).

allows Apollinaire to fill out the first alexandrine, it accomplishes little else. At most, it resembles a kind of drunken stuttering as the river succumbs to general inebriation. Unfortunately, Apollinaire's efforts to protect himself and the rest of the company from the boatman's spell end in failure. There is only so much a human being can accomplish against supernatural forces. "La puissance du vin est trop grande," Orecchioni exclaims; "voici que le fleuve lui-meme semble saisi par l'ivresse" ("The wine's power is too great. The river itself seems to be seized with drunkenness").[56] From the river, the general intoxication expands to encompass the vineyards and finally the entire cosmos. As Renaud explains, "Le reflet tremblant dans le fleuve de l'or des nuits est la version cosmique du tremblement de l'alcool dans le verre" ("The golden nights' trembling reflection in the river is a cosmic version of the alcohol in the glass").[57]

This observation brings us back to the beginning of the poem, where it answers a previous question. The reason Apollinaire's wine, but not his wine glass, is trembling is because the boatman has put a spell on it. This recognition represents the first step as he continues to cast his supernatural net wider and wider. What it indicates, in retrospect, is that intoxication basically serves as a metaphor for enchantment. Because of the association between alcohol and the irrational, wine is the perfect vehicle for a magic spell. The reason the boatman likes to sing about nixies, one discovers, is that they too can cast spells. A neologism invented by the Symbolists, as mentioned in the previous chapter, *incanter* means approximately the same thing as *enchanter*.[58] That the boatman's voice sounds like a death rattle is also revealing. As his voice begins to assume diabolical proportions, it becomes clearer and clearer that he is associated with the underworld. Since *batelier* can also mean "ferryman," he seems in fact to be Charon, who ferries the souls of the dead across the Styx and the Acheron. Among other things, we finally know what the boatman looks like. According to one authority, Charon is typically represented as "an aged man, with a dirty beard and a mean dress."[59] Thus the boatman's physical appearance is nearly as menacing as his dreadful song. The final stanza consists of a single line: "Mon verre s'est brisé comme un éclat de rire" ("My glass has shattered like a burst of laughter").

This procedure, which Breunig calls "structural ellipsis," occurs throughout Apollinaire's poetry.[60] Setting the last line off from the rest of the text, he invites the reader to fill in the gap between the last two stanzas. It is the reader's responsibility, not the poet's, to supply the missing material. At the same time, Apollinaire also prepares to deliver a surprise. With no warning whatsoever, the wine glass suddenly shatters into a million pieces. As Jacques Guilhembet notes, "[La] chute du verre et [la] chute du poème sont

simultanées" ("[The] end of the glass and [the] end of the poem are simultaneous").[61] Like a burst (éclat) of laughter, the shards (éclats) fly everywhere.
According to Claude Morhange-Bégué and Pierre Lartigue, the single alexandrine "évoque la rapidité de l'éclat" ("evokes the sudden shatter").[62] As far
as one can tell, the whole episode is completely gratuitous. "Nuit rhénane"
ends as mysteriously as it began. Up until this point, the verbs all utilize the
present tense. Theoretically, the various events and the description of these
events take place simultaneously. However, Apollinaire suddenly introduces
the *passé composé* in the last verse. As if the broken glass were not surprising
enough, the reader experiences a dislocation both in space and in time. Since
the last line mirrors the first line, Chevalier claims that "Nuit rhénane" has
a circular structure.[63] Unfortunately, the lines are not similar enough to
complete the circle. They frame the text but do not surround it. According
to Guilhembet, the poem possesses a "structure brisée [a broken structure],
like the glass in the last line").[64] With only thirteen verses, it oscillates back
and forth between a sonnet and a hybrid form dictated by what Apollinaire
is trying to say.

In general, Garnet Rees declares, the poem's ambiguity arises from "the
juxtaposition of life and death, legend and reality, the supernatural and the
ordinary, which colors Apollinaire's vision."[65] As "Nuit rhénane" comes to
an end, one wonders how to interpret its conclusion. Who is responsible for
the broken wine glass, and what does it mean? Since the verse utilizes the
passive voice, the reader is left without a single clue. Like the first line of the
poem, the final line is suspended in midair. The explanations that have been
proposed for the broken glass vary from the purely practical to the symbolic
to the supernatural.[66] At the realistic level, one eventually realizes, the whole
incident could have been an accident. Apollinaire could have knocked the
glass over when he jumped to his feet to urge people to sing and dance. At
the symbolic level, Renaud believes that Apollinaire broke the wine glass on
purpose. In his opinion, the boatman (who is supposedly about to expire) was
vanquished by the vigorous singing and dancing. Since Apollinaire no longer
needs his glass, he bursts into laughter and breaks it as a "signe de contente-
ment" ("sign of happiness").[67] In a similar vein, but for different reasons, Kurt
Roessler calls the laughter "un rire quasi salutaire de libération" ("an almost
salutary laugh of liberation").[68]

At the supernatural level, by contrast, Lefèvre is convinced the poem has
a tragic ending. Although he does not go into detail, he sees no way that
Apollinaire and the others can escape the ferryman, who, sooner or later,
must carry them off. According to him, the final words evoke "la joie cruelle
de la puissance maléfique devant son triomphe" ("the cruel joy of the malefi-

cent presence after his triumph").[69] It is not Apollinaire who is laughing at the end, therefore, but mighty Charon. Unfortunately, this scenario is hopelessly pessimistic. Nevertheless, it is not the only supernatural interpretation available. Another scenario exists that provides a more satisfactory ending. As Stamelman notes, the intensity of the boatman's song increases from stanza to stanza.[70] Or rather, since the song is just a metaphor, the boatman's spell grows more and more powerful as the poem progresses. The fundamental analogy underlying "Nuit rhénane" is not with music or with magic, however, but with vulcanology. The poem resembles a slumbering volcano. Pressure builds up and up until it finally explodes—breaking the wine glass and the boatman's spell simultaneously. Orecchioni claims that Apollinaire awakens from a drunken sleep at this point, but nothing in the poem supports this interpretation.[71] Although Breunig speaks of "a sudden catharsis," the conclusion is basically orgasmic.[72] Rather than being instantaneous, it is the culmination of several previous events. Unexpectedly, since the spell has completely evaporated, the poem ends happily.

It remains to say a few words about an alternative reading of "Nuit rhénane" that offers interesting possibilities. Although no one has formally adopted this interpretation, traces surface often enough to reveal that it continues to interest people. According to Perfézou, for example, "Nuit rhénane" contains an important reflection about poetry. More specifically, it constitutes a "miroir humoristique de la brisure et de l'ivresse des vers" ("humorous mirror of the breaking and the intoxication of the verses").[73] What he and others are proposing is not an allegory, therefore, but rather a text-based interpretation. Discussing the first stanza, Morhange-Bégué and Lartigue remark that Apollinaire's poetic function is symbolized by the wine and the flame he is consuming.[74] While their remarks are based on observation, this is what the poet tells us himself when he is free to indulge in a little word play: "Mon *vers* est plein d'un vin trembleur comme une flamme" ("My *verse* is full of wine trembling like a flame"). As is well known, puns and other kinds of linguistic games play an active role in Apollinaire's poetry. The equation between poetry and alcohol is also widespread, which led him in 1913 to entitle his collection of verse *Alcools*.

Morhange-Bégué and Lartigue also call attention to the boatman, who turns out to be a remarkably gifted poet. Endowed with a powerful voice and a marvelous talent, he bathes the whole world in his poetry. As the third stanza demonstrates, his compositions are literally spellbinding. According to the same authors, the quatrain describes the "poétization de l'univers proche" ("the poeticization of the near universe"). The boatman's poetry is so powerful that everything comes alive. Nothing can resist it—neither the river nor the stars nor the grapevines. Continuing this scenario, the last line describes what happens when poetry attempts to invade reality. At this point, the critical interpretations diverge. "Apollinaire dramatizes the limits of poetry," Stamelman declares, "those frontiers beyond which the poet cannot go."[75] In his opinion, the broken glass represents the failure of poetry, which, forced to exceed its capability, basically self-destructs. According to Morhange-Bégué and Lartigue, by contrast, Apollinaire dramatizes his belief that poetic discourse has no limits. It exerts "un pouvoir magique sur les barrières de la réalité ('Mon verre'), qu'il [fait] exploser" ("a magic power on the barriers of reality, which it explodes"). In their opinion, the broken glass represents the triumph of poetry, which, faced with the limits of reality, develops new ways to transcend it.

"La Tzigane"

Published in La Phalange in 1907, together with "Les Colchiques" and "Lul de Faltenin," Apollinaire's poem "La Tzigane" has been the subject of only two articles over the years. Whereas the first two works have engendered numerous studies, the latter has been largely eclipsed by its flashier companions.[76] Originally accompanied by the notation "Honnef 1902," the poem appears to have been composed sometime between January 1 and February 9, when Apollinaire set out on a lengthy tour that lasted until the middle of May.[77] Like many of the "Rhénanes," Warren Ramsey declares, "La Tzigane" "renews late nineteenth-century themes in a way endlessly stimulating to twentieth-century readers and writers."[78] Unlike many of the "Rhénanes," however, it is conspicuously lacking in local color. Perhaps this explains why it was excluded from the group of "Rhénanes" in Alcools. The reader searches in vain for picturesque touches like those that characterize the rest of the group. Where are the castle ruins covered with ivy, one wonders, the slender blonde sorceress, the fairies with long green hair, the Hasidic Jews with their large fur hats, or Schinderhannes and his drunken band? For that matter, what has become of the gypsies, who play an important role in poems such as "Mai," "Les Cloches," and "Rhénane d'automne"? Although the gypsy fortune-teller is mentioned three times in the poem (including the title), we never actually meet her. In contrast to the composition itself, which, despite the presence of the imperfect and the passé simple, is narrated from a retrospective perspective, her actions are situated firmly in the past. Unlike the final stanza, which comments on the immediate problems of Apollinaire and Annie Playden, the first two stanzas recount events that occurred earlier. Serving as a convenient narrative device, the fortune-teller is little more than a memory. Composed of three octosyllabic quatrains, "La Tzigane" benefits from, among other things, the judicious use of *rimes embrassées*. As Anne Hyde Greet remarks, the rhyme scheme suggests "thoughts that circle and return upon themselves."[79] Like the two lovers themselves, the reader is dazzled by the circularity of the actions described in the poem. At first glance, it seems like a perfectly straightforward composition. Unlike, say, "Lul de Faltenin," which continues to puzzle scholars to this day, it appears to be completely transparent. Most critics would probably agree with Laurence Campa that "La Tzigane" is a melancholy lament "sur l'amour maudit et le poids du souvenir" ("on accursed love and the weight of memory").[80] In addition, a number of observers have noted the simplicity of the poem's basic scenario. According to Mechtild Cranston, "Les mots de la tzigane présagent un avenir funeste. Mais le voyageur ne les écoute pas. Il va vers la ville, dans l'espoir d'aimer en chemin" ("The Gypsy's words portend a gloomy future. But the traveler doesn't listen to them. He continues toward the city hoping to find love along the way").[81] Francis Steegmuller provides a succinct (and humorous) plot summary: "'Things between you won't go very far,' said that Rhineland gypsy. Nor did they."[82] Like Campa, he assumes that "La Tzigane" is yet another poem about lost love by Apollinaire the "mal-aimé." And in point of fact, this is the commonly held opinion. If the poem were really that simple, it would still be a significant accomplishment. However, "La Tzigane" is much more complex than it appears at first glance. For one thing, as will become apparent, it is not a melancholy complaint at all. For another thing, Annie was not as puritanical as some critics would like us to believe. She was not at all indifferent to Apollinaire's attentions initially. As Marie-Jeanne Durry observes, "Les trois petites strophes qu'on lit d'un trait sont . . . beaucoup plus énigmatiques qu'il ne paraît" ("The three brief stanzas that one reads in a single glance are . . . much more enigmatic than they seem").[83] The first stanza is an excellent example:

> La tzigane savait d'avance
> Nos deux vies barrées par les nuits
> Nous lui dîmes adieu et puis
> De ce puits sortit l'Espérance.

> (The gypsy knew in advance
> Our two lives barred by the nights
> We said goodbye and then
> Hope emerged from this well.)

Discussing the poem's assertiveness and its syntactical overdetermination, Barbara Johnson focuses on what the fortune-teller knew. Although "La

Tzigane" begins and ends with the verb *savoir* ("to know"), she complains, the extent of the gypsy's knowledge is not readily discernible.[84] The "syntax of affirmation" fools readers, like the two lovers, into believing they have actually been told something. In reality, she insists, the poem is riddled with ambiguity from beginning to end. Despite Johnson's obvious frustration, it is surprising that this situation constitutes a problem. Whether one prefers terms such as "indeterminacy," "undecidability," or "aporia," ambiguity is a fundamental condition of poetry. Rather than a hindrance, as William Empson and many others have demonstrated repeatedly, it is a valuable resource that poets—especially modern poets—have exploited to the fullest.[85] This is especially true of Apollinaire's work, Roger Shattuck adds, whose primary quality is in fact its ambiguity.[86] The problem with the second verse, Johnson continues, is that it can be translated four different ways: as "Our lives criss-crossed by nights of love"; "Our lives crossed out by darkness"; "Our lives fettered by intimations of mortality"; or "Our lives ruined by our love." Nevertheless, although these readings may be theoretically possible, they are not all legitimate. To qualify as a valid interpretation, each version must dovetail perfectly with all of the other elements in the text. Each version needs to contribute to the poem's total gestalt. Although it needs to be slightly modified, the second version is the only one that fits. According to clues embedded in the text, the verse means something like: "Our lives together thwarted by forces associated with the night."

Five translators and virtually all of the critics basically agree with this interpretation. Greet speaks of "Night's shadow on our lives," Margaret Davies opts for "our night-crossed lives," William Meredith chooses "Our nights would cancel out our days," Donald Revell prefers "Our two lives thwarted by the nights," and Roger Shattuck offers "Our secret night-imprisoned lives."[87] What Apollinaire actually meant by the verse, however, remains to be seen. Where the critics inevitably differ is in regard to the details. Like Durry, for example, Pol-P. Gossiaux suggests that "nos deux vies" refers to the lifelines ("lignes de vie") on the lovers' palms, which, the gypsy discovered, were canceled out by other lines.[88] Although the exact sense of "barrées" is not immediately evident, the expression clearly has negative connotations. By contrast, "nuits" is more difficult to pin down. Why are the nights an obstacle to the lovers' happiness? Is it because they occupy separate bedrooms, Durry wonders, or because Annie continues to rebuff Apollinaire's advances?[89] Perhaps we should be looking for a metaphorical interpretation instead of a biographical one. However, the most convincing explanation exploits metonymy rather than metaphor. Night is when the stars come out, which for centuries were believed to control our individual destinies. As the poet himself proclaims in "Sanglots," published ten years later, "Notre amour est réglé par les calmes étoiles" ("Our love is controlled by the calm stars").[90] Like Romeo and Juliet, therefore, Apollinaire is depicting himself and Annie as star-crossed lovers. Through no fault of their own they are destined to be unhappy. Although Gossiaux invokes their "désespoir" (despair) at one point, the word that best describes their predicament is "désastre" (disaster; <latin: dis + astrum).[91] According to *Le Petit Robert*, the term originally meant "né sous une mauvaise étoile" ("born under a bad star").

Despite Johnson's protestation to the contrary, what the gypsy knew is in fact perfectly clear. Since she possessed the ability to see the future, she obviously knew everything that would happen. Deceived by her own difficulties, Johnson uses the "syntax of affirmation" herself to convince us that the fortune-teller's knowledge is irretrievable. In the last analysis, however, what the gypsy knew is far less important than what she said. What she told Apollinaire and Annie when they came to see her (if in fact they really did) is more elusive. Without betraying the fortune-tellers' confidentiality, the third and fourth lines hint at her prediction. One of Apollinaire's many contributions to modern poetry was to rehabilitate the lowly pun, illustrated here by the juxtaposition of "puis" ("then") and "puits" ("well"). One of the first poets to recognize the creative possibilities of paronomasia, he experimented with this rhetorical innovation as long as he lived. Less well known is Apollinaire's fondness for echolalia, which Michel Décaudin defines as "la relance d'un son" ("the repetition of a sound").[92] In addition to puns, this includes such rhetorical devices as consonance, assonance, and simple repetition. Besides allowing the poet to achieve certain aesthetic effects, echolalia furnished him with an important compositional tool. A particular sound (or word) would generate a second sound (or word), suggesting new possibilities for the poet to explore. As Jean-Claude Chevalier remarks, "Le calembour est rarement séparable de la métaphore" ("Puns are rarely separable from metaphors").[93] This observation is confirmed by "La Tzigane," where "puits" makes absolutely no sense if taken literally. Durry and Johnson both observe that a well is traditionally considered to be a source of truth.[94] Gossiaux offers an astrological explanation according to which "nuits" designates the space occupied by the lovers' star and "puits" its position in the sky.[95] In contrast to Davies and Shattuck, who choose to translate "puits" literally, Greet changes the noun into a verb: "Then hope welled from hiding." For some inexplicable reason, in Revell's translation, the well becomes "holes in the ground." Recognizing that "puits" is a metaphor for the situation described in line 2, Meredith translates it as "dark pit," which seems closer to the mark. Like the

Slough of Despond in *The Pilgrim's Progress*, Apollinaire's well is associated with despair and depression.

Although "La Tzigane" is generally considered to be a melancholy poem, Gossiaux remarks, "c'est l'espoir, non la tristesse, qui naît de la rencontre avec la tzigane" ("it is hope, not sadness, that emerges from the meeting with the gypsy").[96] Apollinaire waits until the end of the stanza to spring his surprise on the reader. Unexpectedly, the well turns out to be a source of Hope in addition to despair. That "Espérance" begins with a capital letter conveys the joy that accompanies this discovery. But how on earth, one wonders, can these two contradictory emotions coexist simultaneously? The answer seems to be that rather than being simultaneous they are sequential. Beginning with depression and ending with elation, they represent the two poles of the lovers' emotional spectrum. Hope is not always associated with the well but is something that emerges on this particular occasion. The question that occurs at this point is why now? What is the source of the lovers' renewed optimism? Since there are no other candidates, one inevitably concludes, it has to be the gypsy. Or rather, as Gossiaux intimates, it has to be what the gypsy told them. Steven Winspur believes that she deliberately deceived Apollinaire and Annie, promising them "a rosy future" while knowing their love was doomed.[97] Judging from the second stanza, however, the fortune they received was neither entirely good nor entirely bad. Their love would have its ups and downs, the fortune-teller confided, but it was worth pursuing all the same. This provisional conclusion is confirmed by the remainder of the poem.

> L'amour lourd comme un ours privé
> Dansa debout quand nous voulûmes
> Et l'oiseau bleu perdit ses plumes
> Et les mendiants leurs *Ave*.

> (Awkward as a tame bear
> Love danced upright when we wanted
> And the bluebird lost its feathers
> And the beggars their prayers).

The second stanza evokes the lovers' successful and unsuccessful attempts to follow the fortune-teller's advice. As Annie told Breunig years later, Apollinaire often spent time with the gypsies who passed through Honnef, following the course of the Rhine.[98] Although traces of this experience occur in other poems, "Mai" contains what is perhaps the most memorable scene: "Sur le chemin du bord du fleuve lentement / Un ours un singe un chien menés par des tziganes / suivaient une roulette traînée par un âne" ("On the road bordering the river / A bear a monkey a dog led by gypsies / slowly followed a donkey cart").[99] As Ramsey remarks, the animals' symbolism is deeper than it appears at first glance. Like the bear in "La Tzigane," they contribute "another analogy to the carnival theme as an analogy for the human predicament."[100] The animals in "Mai" were all trained animals whose performance provided the band with a meager livelihood. While the monkey and the dog could do several different tricks, the bear had only one. Accompanied by a small drum, he would dance awkwardly on his hind legs as the gypsies led him around on a leash. While "privé" means "tame," Durry adds, it can also be translated as "deprived" or "frustrated." Judging from the stanza's first two lines, the lovers' initial attempts at making love—however one chooses to understand that expression—were equally clumsy. For Pilkington, the trained bear metaphor suggests "the ignoble reduction of love to a sort of circus," thus condemning their efforts to failure.[101] Although the poet told James Onimus, and later Madeleine Pagès, that he managed to sleep with Annie, Apollinaire specialists tend to be skeptical.[102] Which is not to say that Apollinaire didn't try. Durry and Steegmuller both suspect that they engaged in bouts of heavy petting.[103] Besides the lovers' chagrin at being so clumsy together, the image of the dancing bear conveys their inevitable disappointment. Encouraged by the gypsy to give love a chance, they bungled what should have been an easy assignment. Coming from two very different countries, Annie and Apollinaire were seriously mismatched. Whereas sex was something to be suppressed in England, it was something to be enjoyed in France. Buoyed by their initial optimism, the lovers found their confidence slipping away before long. Before they knew it, the pendulum had swung in the other direction, from hope to despair.

This development is confirmed by the two remaining verses, which contain additional images of disappointment. While scholars have sought to relate the bluebird to Mme d'Aulnoy's fairy tale of the same name, there is no need to travel back to the seventeenth century. As Pilkington points out, the bluebird is found throughout Apollinaire's works, where it is associated with happy occasions.[104] For that matter, it has the same joyful reputation in popular culture. Jeanine Kohn-Etiemble thinks that a reference in Rimbaud's "Bottom" may have served as an intertext. In any case, she declares, "l'on retrouve la hantise apollinarienne des phallus ailés" ("once again Apollinaire is haunted by flying phalluses").[105] Whether the bluebird of happiness has lost its feathers because it is molting, as Meredith thinks, or because it has plucked them out itself, as Durry proposes, ultimately makes little difference.[106] In either case,

Kohn-Etiemble observes, the bird has been stripped of its erotic attributes. The symbolism is perfectly clear. According to Winspur, the bluebird loses its association with faithful love.[107] The deterioration in its condition parallels the deterioration in the lovers' relationship. Whether one attributes this situation to love being degraded, as Pilkington maintains, or simply to a lack of success, it is certainly not a happy predicament.

These remarks describe line 8 as well, which contains yet another image of disappointment and loss. As Annie and Apollinaire approach a Catholic church, the beggars clustered around its front entrance, who have been praying to the Virgin Mary, fall silent. At least this is how the verse is usually interpreted. The original wording, which insists that the beggars "lost" their prayers, is frankly puzzling. Since prayers are not normally something that can be misplaced, one wonders how to interpret this information. How were the actual prayers lost, and where have they gone? Durry sidesteps these questions by assuming the lovers are so wrapped up in each other that they simply don't hear the prayers.[108] Sooner or later, nevertheless, suspicion arises that the beggars have permanently given up praying. In this sense, their prayers have been lost forever. Abandoned by humanity and ignored by the Virgin Mary, the beggars have finally lost all hope. This situation marks the lowest point of the poem, which is momentarily dominated by despair. In the third stanza, however, the pendulum begins to swing in the opposite direction.

> On sait très bien que l'on se damne
> Mais l'espoir d'aimer en chemin
> Nous fait penser main dans la main
> A ce qu'a prédit la tzigane.

> (We know very well that we are damned
> But the hope of finding love meanwhile
> Makes us think hand in hand
> Of what the gypsy predicted.)

Composed in the present tense, the final stanza brings the reader up to date. The thoughts that it relates occur at the same time as the writing of the poem, or nearly so. Despite the ruin that threatens to overwhelm the lovers, despite the conflicting emotions that permeate the poem, they are determined to persevere. At one level, the concept of "damnation" refers to their topsy-turvy relationship, which, as the gypsy told them, will always be a problem. The bipolar mood swings between hope and hopelessness will continue indefinitely. At another level, Davies believes the term refers to the "heavy, guilt-ridden sexuality" that permeates the poem.[109] She thinks Apollinaire feels as guilty as Annie about their carnal adventures. This is certainly not the image of the poet that has come down to us. However, Durry also thinks the lovers are consumed by guilty feelings. Carried away by the intensity of their illicit passion, she explains, "ils acceptent pour [elle] le péché, la damnation" ("they accept sin and damnation.")[110] The problem with this (literal) interpretation, however, is that it requires the lovers to actually believe in sin and damnation. Although Annie may still have belonged to the Church of England, Apollinaire had rejected Catholicism years before.

Despite the risk involved, in any case, they feel it is amply compensated by the strength of their passion. What keeps the lovers going, one learns in the next line, is the hope of loving "en chemin" (nicely translated by Greet and Shattuck as "along the way"). This thought reminds them in turn of the gypsy's prophecy—and for a very good reason. What the fortune-teller originally advised them to do was precisely that: to love each other through thick and thin. Bringing the poem full circle, Hope returns once again and with it the resolve to stick together. That the lovers are holding hands as the poem concludes conveys both their commitment to each other and their determination to resist the baleful influence of the stars.

Notes

1. Michel Décaudin, *Le Dossier d' "Alcools,"* rev. ed. (Paris: Minard, 1965), 215–16. The manuscript is reproduced in the *Revue des Lettres Modernes*, Nos. 276–279 (1971), 16 and 17. The Viscountess, her mother, and Annie stayed at the Hotel den Vier Zahrezeiten, while Apollinaire found cheaper quarters elsewhere. Louis Brunet, "Le Voyage d'Apollinaire à travers l'Allemagne au printemps 1902," *Apollinaire: Revue d'Etudes Apollinariennes*, No. 6 (November 2009), 25.

2. The classic study is Ernst Wolf's *Guillaume Apollinaire und das Rheinland* (1937; Frankfurt am Main: Peter Lang, 1988). For additional information, see Marc Poupon, "L'Année allemande d'Apollinaire," *Revue des Lettres Modernes*, Nos. 183–88 (1968), 9–45, and *Apollinaire: Revue d'Etudes Apollinariennes*, Nos. 5–7 (May 2009–May 2010).

3. LeRoy C. Breunig, *Guillaume Apollinaire* (New York: Columbia University Press,1969), 15.

4. Ibid., 18.

5. Laurence Perfézou, *"Alcools"—Apollinaire* (Paris: Bordas, 1988), 67.

6. Anne Hyde Greet, tr. *"Alcools." Guillaume Apollinaire* (Berkeley: University of California Press, 1965), 280.

7. Timothy Mathews, *Reading Apollinaire: Theories of Poetic Language* (Manchester: Manchester University Press, 1987), 87. Elsewhere he calls "Automne malade" an "anti-nostalgic poem of absence and being" (10).

8. Roger Lefèvre, *"Alcools": choix de poèmes* (Paris: Nouvaux Classiques Larousse, 1965), 85.

9. Pierre Bourdieu, "Apollinaire, 'Automne malade,'" *Cahiers d'Histoire des Littératures Romanes / Romanistiche Zeitschrift für Literaturgeschichte*, Vol. 19, Nos. 3–4, 330. Jérôme David relates this article to Bourdieu's sociological studies in "On an Enigmatic Text by Pierre Bourdieu," *Paragraph. A Journal of Modern Critical Theory*, Vol. 35, No. 1 (2012), 115–30.

10. Scott Bates, *Guillaume Apollinaire*, rev. ed. (Boston: Twayne, 1989), 36.

11. Claude Morhange-Bégué and Pierre Lartigue, *"Alcools" / Apollinaire* (Paris: Hatier, 1991), 41.

12. Guillaume Apollinaire, *Oeuvres poétiques*, ed. Marcel Adéma and Michel Décaudin (Paris: Gallimard, 1965), 125.

13. Morhange-Bégué and Lartigue, *"Alcools." Apollinaire*, 27.

14. Letter from Guillaume Apollinaire to Jean-Yves Blanc, August 4, 1916. Repr. in Apollinaire, *Oeuvres complètes*, ed. Michel Décaudin (Paris: Balland-Lecat, 1965–66), Vol. IV, 686.

15. Marie-Jeanne Durry, *Guillaume Apollinaire: "Alcools,"* Vol. III (Paris: SEDES, 1964), 96.

16. A. E. Pilkington, ed., *Apollinaire: Alcools* (Oxford: Blackwell, 1970), 157.

17. Mathews, *Reading Apollinaire*, 8.

18. Michael Riffaterre, *Semiotics of Poetry* (Bloomington: Indiana University Press, 1978), 19.

19. Mathews, *Reading Apollinaire*, 7.

20. Ibid., 8–9.

21. Bourdieu, "Apollinaire, 'Automne malade,'" 331.

22. Mathews, *Reading Apollinaire*, 203.

23. Ibid., 47.

24. Bourdieu, "Apollinaire, 'Automne malade,'" 331.

25. Wolf, *Guillaume Apollinaire und das Rheinland*, 81–82.

26. Clive Scott, *Vers Libre: The Emergence of Free Verse in France 1886–1914* (Oxford: Clarendon Press, 1990), 290.

27. Bates, *Guillaume Apollinaire*, 37, and William Meredith, tr., *Alcools: Poems1898–1913* (Garden City, NY: Doubleday, 1965), 211.

28. Perfézou, *"Alcools"—Apollinaire*, 71.

29. Scott, *Vers Libre*, 290.

30. Pierre Brunel, *Apollinaire entre deux mondes: Mythocritique II* (Paris: Presses Universitaires de France, 1997), 115–16.

31. *New World Encyclopedia*, "Nix," www.newworldencyclopedia.org/entry/Nix.

32. Mathews, *Reading Apollinaire*, 11.

33. Bates, *Guillaume Apollinaire*, 37.

34. Ibid., 37.

35. Brunel, *Apollinaire entre deux mondes*, 110.

36. Morhange-Bégué and Lartigue, *"Alcools." Apollinaire*, 27.

37. Apollinaire, *Oeuvres poétiques*, 529.

38. Bourdieu, "Apollinaire, 'Automne malade,'" 333.

39. Ibid.

40. Décaudin, *Le Dossier d'"Alcools*," 178.

41. Didier Alexandre, *Guillaume Apollinaire "Alcools"* (Paris: Presses Universitaires de France, 1994), 82–85.

42. Jacques Guilhembet, "'Rhénanes': Etude comparée de 'Nuit rhénane,' 'Mai,' 'La Loreley,' 'Les Femmes,'" *L'Ecole des Lettres*, No. 12 (1992), 74.

43. Roger Lefèvre, *"Alcools": choix de poèmes*, (Paris: Nouveaux Classiques Larousse, 1965), 74.

44. Philippe Renaud, *Lecture d'Apollinaire* (Lausanne: L'Age d'Homme, 1969), 134–35.

45. Pierre Orecchioni, *Le Thème du Rhin dans l'inspiration de Guillaume Apollinaire* (Paris: Lettres Modernes, 1956), 102.

46. See Michel Décaudin, "Compléments à un dossier," *Revue des Lettres Modernes*, Nos. 69–70 (Spring 1962), 61; Marc Poupon, "Sources allemandes d'Apollinaire," *Revue des Lettres Modernes*, Nos. 530–536 (1978), 43; and note 2.

47. Perfézou, *"Alcools"—Apollinaire*, 71.

48. Pierre Brunel, *Apollinaire entre deux mondes: Mythocritique II* (Paris: Presses Universitaires de France, 1997), 115–16.

49. *New World Encyclopedia*, "Nix" www.newworldencyclopedia.org/entry/Nix.

50. Poupon, "Sources allemandes d'Apollinaire," 43, and Marie-Jeanne Durry, *Guillaume Apollinaire: "Alcools*," vol. 3 (Paris: SEDES, 1964), 78.

51. Richard Howard Stamelman, *The Drama of Self in Guillaume Apollinaire's "Alcools"* (Chapel Hill: University of North Carolina Department of Romance Languages and Literatures, 1976), 57.

52. Perfézou, *"Alcools"—Apollinaire*, 45; and Roger Lefèvre, ed. *"Alcools": choix de poèmes*, 75; Orecchioni, *Le Thème du Rhin*, 102.

53. Jean-Claude Chevalier, *"Alcools": analyse des formes poétiques* (Paris: Minard, 1970), 161.

54. Margaret Davies, "Apollinaire, la peinture et l'image," *Que Vlo-Ve?: Bulletin de l'Association Internationale des Amis de Guillaume Apollinaire*, Nos. 21–22 (July–October 1979), 2. Apollinaire wrote a poem about the famous painting, which he gave to Annie Playden at the time. See Guillaume Apollinaire, *Oeuvres poétiques*, ed. Marcel Adéma and Michel Décaudin (Paris: Gallimard, 1965), 534.

55. See, for example, Chevalier, *"Alcools": analyse des formes poétiques*, 243–51.

56. Orecchioni, *Le Thème du Rhin*, 102.

57. Philippe Renaud, "L'Effraie et le rossignol ou les énigmes du tremblement," *Revue des Lettres Modernes*, Nos. 249–253 (1970), 49.

58. Claude Debon, *Apollinaire: Glossaire des oeuvres complètes* (Paris: Sorbonne Nouvelle, 1988), 59.

59. Sir William Smith, *Smaller Classical Dictionary*, rev. ed. (New York: Dutton, 1958), 80.

60. Breunig, *Guillaume Apollinaire*, 16.

61. Guilhembet, "'Rhénanes,'" 67.

62. Garnet Rees, ed. *Guillaume Apollinaire: "Alcools"* (London: Athlone, 1975), 162.

63. Chevalier, *"Alcools": analyse des forme spoétiques*, 159.

64. Guilhembet, "'Rhénanes,'" 67.

65. Morhange-Bégué and Lartigue, *"Alcools." Apollinaire*, 20–21.

66. Pursuing another line of inquiry, Stamelman concludes that the burst of laughter is cynical, hysterical, and self-mocking. See *The Drama of Self*, 59–61.

67. Renaud, *Lecture d'Apollinaire*, 136.

68. Kurt Roessler, "Le Rire d'Apollinaire dans 'Nuit rhénane," *Apollinaire et les rires 1900*, ed. Claude Debon (Paris: Calliopées, 2011), 155.

69. Lefèvre, *"Alcools": choix de poèmes*, 75.

70. Stamelman, *The Drama of Self*, 57–58.

71. Orecchioni, *Le Thème du Rhin*, 102.

72. Breunig, *Guillaume Apollinaire*, 16.

73. Perfézou, *"Alcools"—Apollinaire*, 44.

74. Morhange-Bégué and Lartigue, *"Alcools." Apollinaire*, 20.

75. Stamelman, *The Drama of Self*, 216.

76. See Claude Debon, "Ouvrages et articles sur les poèmes d'*Alcools*," *"Alcools" en corps: Lectures et situation du recueil d'Apollinaire*, ed. Jean-Yves Debreuille (Grenoble: Université Stendhal 3, 1999), 197–224.

77. Brunet, "Le Voyage d'Apollinaire à travers l'Allemagne au printemps 1902 (suite et fin)," 36. Theoretically the poem could also have been composed several years later.

78. Warren Ramsey, "Foreword" to Guillaume Apollinaire, *Alcools*, tr. Anne Hyde Greet (Berkeley: University of California Press, 1965), xiii.

79. Greet, tr. *"Alcools." Guillaume Apollinaire*, 245.

80. Laurence Campa, *Guillaume Apollinaire* (Paris: Gallimard, 2013), 227.

81. Mechtild Cranston, "Voyage en Rhénanie," *Du Monde européen à l'univers des mythes: Actes du Colloque de Stavelot* (Paris: Minard, 1968), 35.

82. Francis Steegmuller, ed., *Alcools: Poems 1898–1913*, tr. William Meredith (Garden City, NY: Doubleday Anchor, 1965), 244.

83. Marie-Jeanne Durry, "Sur 'La Tzigane,'" *Revue des Lettres Modernes*, Nos. 85–89 (Fall 1963), 81. This article was extracted from her book *Guillaume Apollinaire: "Alcools,"* Vol. III (Paris: SEDES, 1964), 15–30.

84. Barbara Johnson, *The Critical Difference: Essays in the Contemporary Rhetoric of Reading* (Baltimore: Johns Hopkins University Press, 1985), 73–75. Future references to her discussion of "La Tzigane" are to these pages.

85. William Empson, *Seven Types of Ambiguity* (London: Chatto and Windus, 1930).

86. Roger Shattuck, *The Banquet Years: The Origins of the Avant-Garde in France, 1895 to World War I* (Garden City, NY: Doubleday, 1961), 314.

87. Greet, tr. *"Alcools." Guillaume Apollinaire*, 119; Margaret Davies, *Apollinaire* (New York: St. Martins, 1964), 78 n17; Meredith, tr. *Alcools: Poems 1898–1913*, 131; Donald Revell, tr. *Poems by Guillaume Apollinaire. "Alcools"* (Middletown, CT:

Wesleyan University Press, 1995), 97; Roger Shattuck, tr. *Selected Writings of Guillaume Apollinaire* (New York: New Directions, 1971), 63.

88. Pol-P. Gossiaux, "Clef de la 'Tzigane' de Guillaume Apollinaire," *Les Lettres Romanes*, Vol. XXXIII, No. 3 (August 1979), 306.

89. Durry, "Sur 'La Tzigane,'" 81.

90. Apollinaire, *Oeuvres poétiques*, 365.

91. Gossiaux, "Clef de la 'Tzigane,'" 303.

92. Michel Décaudin, *"Alcools" de Guillaume Apollinaire* (Paris: Gallimard, 1993), 59.

93. Jean-Claude Chevalier, "Apollinaire et le calembour," *Europe*, Vol. XLIV, Nos. 451–452 (November–December 1966), 60.

94. Durry, "Sur 'La Tzigane,'" 81, and Johnson, *The Critical Difference*, 74–75.

95. Gossiaux, "Clef de la 'Tzigane,'" 304–6.

96. Ibid., 303.

97. Steven Winspur, "The Uncertainties of Apollinaire's Language," *French Literature Series*, No. 18 (1991), 128.

98. L. C. Breunig, "Apollinaire et Annie Playden," *Mercure de France*, April 1, 1952, 648.

99. Apollinaire, *Oeuvres poétiques*, 112.

100. Ramsey, "Foreword," ix.

101. Pilkington, ed. *Apollinaire: Alcools*, 137.

102. Guillaume Apollinaire, *Oeuvres complètes*, ed. Michel Décaudin, 4 vols (Paris:Balland-Lecat, 1965–1966), 715. Guillaume Apollinaire, *Tendreecomme le souvenir* (Paris: Gallimard, 1952), 70. Durry has seen a letter addressed to Louise de Coligny-Chatillon in which Apollinaire makes the same claim.

103. Durry, "Sur 'La Tzigane,'" 88, and Steegmuller, ed. *Alcools*, 244.

104. Pilkington, ed. *Apollinaire: Alcools*, 137.

105. Jeanine Kohn-Etiemble, "De 'Bottom' à 'La Tzigane' par les chemins de traverse," *En hommage à Michel Décaudin*, ed. Pierre Brunel et al. (Paris: Minard, 1988), 11.

106. Meredith, tr. *Alcools*, 131; Durry, "Sur 'La Tzigane," 80.

107. Winspur, "The Uncertainties of Apollinaire's Language," 127.

108. Durry, "Sur 'La Tzigane,'" 81–82.

109. Davies, *Apollinaire*, 78.

110. Durry, "Sur 'La Tzigane,'" 82.

CHAPTER THREE

~

Two *Femmes Fatales*

This chapter examines two examples of a theme that was widespread at the end of the nineteenth century and the beginning of the twentieth: lethal, usually seductive, women who lure men to their death. That this was a popular theme of the French Symbolists is commonly known, Gustave Moreau being the first that comes to mind, followed by Stéphane Mallarmé. The best twentieth-century example is a film rather than a literary work: Josef von Sternberg's *Der Blaue Engel* (*The Blue Angel*). Since Apollinaire began his poetic career as an aspiring Symbolist, it is not surprising to find him experimenting with the theme. Although the deadly female in "Les Colchiques" is basically a metaphor, the biblical protagonist in "Salomé" is supposedly a historical figure. Neither woman consciously lured her male partner to his death—metaphorical or otherwise—but, deliberately or not, their actions were responsible for the unpleasant fate that awaited their partners. Since Apollinaire was unsuccessful in love, at least at the beginning of his career, the theme likely appealed to him on a personal level, as well.

"Les Colchiques"

Like most of the poems in *Alcools*, "Les Colchiques" was published previously before Apollinaire decided to issue a volume of poetry. In fact, the poem was published twice—in the neo-Symbolist journal *La Phalange*, on November 15, 1907, and in an anthology edited by Florian-Parmentier in 1911.[1] Originally dated "Neu-Glück 1902," this was corrected in the anthology to "Neu-Glück

Septembre 1901," which is generally accepted as its date of composition. At the time he wrote "Les Colchiques," Apollinaire had only recently arrived at Neu-Glück but had managed to fall in love with Annie Playden. While Annie would ultimately reject her attentive suitor, at the time "Les Colchiques" was written she welcomed his attention. Although the poem portrays her as a *femme fatale*, to Apollinaire the future seemed, if not rosy, at least fairly promising.

According to various dictionaries, the *colchique* supposedly comes from Colchis, an ancient district on the eastern shore of the Black Sea. Known in English as "meadow saffron" or "autumn crocus," it is extremely poisonous. As such it is associated with Medea, also from Colchis, who poisoned both of her children to punish Jason for abandoning her. Since the flowers are widespread in Europe, they have come to represent various things over the years. According to *La Grande Encyclopédie Larousse*, for example, autumn crocuses signify "beaux jours passés" ("my best days are gone"), which doesn't seem to describe either Annie or Apollinaire. Depending on the region, Georges Legros declares, the crocuses can also symbolize bitter thoughts, the end of love, unexpressed desire, or unsatisfied passion.[2] While the last term certainly describes Apollinaire, the flowers in "Les Colchiques" resemble Annie, who was demure and somewhat puritanical. The poem takes place against a background of unsatisfied passion, symbolized by the field of crocuses. In addition, the flowers have acquired a series of nicknames over the years. According to *Le Petit Robert*, these include *tue-chien* ("dog killer") and *veillottes*. According to Legros, they are also called *femmes nues* ("naked women")—probably because they have no leaves for much of the year (Figure 3.1).[3] Although the last name is provocative, it tells us more about the autumn crocuses than about the poem itself.

Since so much has been written about "Les Colchiques," some of the critical approaches have inevitably been of questionable value. The list of these is headed by methodologies that purport to discover secret messages, either by selecting or by rearranging certain letters in the text. Thus, Michel Deguy believes the three "é"s in the first half of the first line are intended to evoke Medea (Médée).[4] And Legros claims the second hemistich contains an anagram of "Jason," who married Medea and had two children with her.[5] Similarly, Françoise Dininman identifies a series of paragrams in the poem that include not only Annie's name but those of nearly all the women in Apollinaire's novel *L'Enchanteur pourissant*.[6] This is proof once again that critics tend to find exactly what they are looking for. Philippe Renaud casts an equally audacious eye on the same hemistich that supposedly contains an anagram of "Jason": "mais joli en automne." Substituting "mai" for "mais" and reversing

Figure 3.1. Autumn Crocus
Dictionary of Words and Things (1895).

the adjective and noun, he concludes the juxtaposition of May and autumn represents "la surimpression de deux âges de la femme" ("the superimposition of two women's ages").[7] What this has to do with Annie or Apollinaire, who were both young, is anybody's guess. In Michel Décaudin's opinion, this type of approach is no more valid than "les blagues de l'almanachVermot" ("the jokes in the Vermot Almanac").[8]

Divided into three stanzas of unequal length, "Les Colchiques" is composed almost entirely of alexandrines. With two exceptions, Jean-Pierre Bobillot declares, the verses can all be reduced or expanded to twelve syllables and to a 6 + 6 metrical pattern.[9] As elsewhere in Apollinaire's poetry, it is not always easy to tell if a line has twelve syllables. Whether or not to count a mute "e," for example, depends primarily on the way the poet read the verse himself. In contrast to classical French poetry, where a mute "e" must be pronounced, the decision is left up to the reader, whose reading reflects his or her expectations.[10] For this reason, Deguy calls the flexible verses "phantom alexandrines."[11] In his opinion, "c'est le *e muet* qui empoisonne le poème" ("the mute e poisons the poem").[12] By contrast, Bobillot explains, "Apollinaire recourt aux potentialités stylistiques jusqu'alors inexploitées, de . . . l'élasticité métrico-prosodique ("Apollinaire draws on stylistic resources that were unexploited until then . . . involving metrico-prosodic elasticity").[13] Depending on various factors, for instance, the sixth line of "Les Colchiques" may contain twelve, thirteen, or fourteen syllables. Because the composition possesses fifteen lines instead of fourteen, Deguy refers to it as a "sonnet travesti" ("a disguised sonnet"), which is actually quite accurate.[14] In point of fact, the poem was first conceived as a sonnet.[15] When Apollinaire was correcting the final proofs, he cut the second line in half in order to provide greater rhythmic variety. This explains why the (new) second and third lines have only six syllables each and why the former does not participate in the rhyme scheme. Otherwise, the verses rhyme two-by-two and alternate between masculine and feminine endings. The first stanza progresses in three distinct stages. It begins with a description of a meadow, introduces the crocuses, and then focuses on Annie's eyes:

> Le pré est vénéneux mais joli en automne
> Les vaches y paissant
> Lentement s'empoisonnent
> Le colchique couleur de cerne et de lilas
> Y fleurit tes yeux sont comme cette fleur-là
> Violâtres comme leur cerne et comme cet automne
> Et ma vie pour tes yeux lentement s'empoisonne.

> (The meadow is poisonous but lovely in Autumn
> The cows grazing there
> Are slowly poisoning themselves
> The color of eye rings and lilacs the crocuses
> flourish there your eyes resemble that flower
> Violet like their eye rings and like this Autumn
> And my life is slowly poisoning itself for your eyes.)

As Renaud notes, "Les Colchiques" is considerably more complex than it appears at first sight.[16] Much of its apparent simplicity derives from the large amount of repetition that confronts the reader. Words echo back and forth not only within individual stanzas but also from one end of the poem to the other. Of the twenty-one nouns examined by Domenica Iaria and Jean-Yves Tillmans, for example, eight occur twice and one occurs three times.[17] In addition to repetitive verbs like s'empoisonner and battre, "Les Colchiques" contains no fewer than five similes, three of which occur in the first stanza. The poem also contains two examples of an informal simile: "couleur de." Like formal comparisons and the occasional metaphor, they enable the functioning of poetic discourse. Roland Le Mollé points out that the first verse contains a syntactic illogicality.[18] Since "mais" ("but") expresses a hesitation, the general term should be expressed first, then its limitation. The sentence should proceed from the positive to the negative: "Le pré est joli mais vénéneux en automne" ("The meadow is lovely but poisonous en Autumn"). As it stands, however, "joli" is treated as an inconvenience. If the sentence were prose, Le Mollé explains, this would present a problem. But since poetry strives to disrupt mental habits, it is perfectly acceptable. Semantic inversion increases the poem's poetic value. While this may very well be true, it is worth pointing out that Apollinaire had no choice. If he had switched "vénéneux" and "joli," the caesura would have fallen between the fifth and the sixth syllables, and the verse would have been horribly disjointed.

Unlike the rest of the stanza, the first three lines are purely descriptive. Comprising two declarative sentences, they are also completely straight-forward. It is autumn, cows are grazing in the meadow, and the meadow is poisonous. No metaphors or other rhetorical devices interrupt the narrative flow. All that suddenly changes with the fourth verse, which introduces at least six comparisons in the space of only four lines. According to Le Mollé, "Le colchique couleur de cerne et de lilas" is another example of semantic inversion.[19] Flowers should be compared to other flowers first, he declares, and thus "cerne" and "lilas" should trade places. In any event, the fourth verse unleashes a veritable tidal wave of comparison. We learn: 1) that the crocuses resemble the rings around Annie's eyes; 2) that the crocuses resemble lilac bushes; 3) that the crocuses resemble Annie's eyes; 4) that Annie's eyes resemble the rings around her eyes (tautology); 5) that her eyes resemble autumn; and 6) that her eyes resemble crocuses (repetition). While the first five comparisons are based on the flower's color, the sixth comparison exploits one of its properties. The crocuses resemble Annie (and vice versa) because they both are poisonous. Unlike the first five comparisons, which are based on metonymy, the sixth is metaphorical. As this example demonstrates, all of the comparisons are reversible. "Ainsi," Jean-Michel Adam observes, "le comparant est-il aussi bien comparé et le comparé comparant" ("the comparer is also the compared and the compared the comparer").[20] Whereas the first three lines are devoted to linear narrative, Shuhsi Kao points out, the next four lines are characterized by circularity, reversibility, and repetition.[21]

Since the crocuses resemble the rings around Annie's eyes and lilac bushes (line 4), the rings around her eyes resemble lilac bushes (and vice versa). For similar reasons, they also resemble autumn (and vice versa) in line 6. So far we have been talking about horizontal comparisons, but a number of vertical comparisons are possible as well. Thus Annie's eyes resemble lilac bushes, and autumn resembles her eyes. In the last analysis, everything basically resembles everything else. The scene is bathed in a lovely violet light. "Y fleurit" (line 5) was originally a run-on line followed by a period. When Apollinaire deleted all the punctuation in *Alcools*, he introduced a certain amount of ambiguity. While some readers are frustrated by mutually exclusive readings, others find them stimulating. Delighted to encounter the construction "Y fleurit tes yeux," Louis Daubier exclaims: "La fleur renvoie aux yeux et les yeux à la fleur" ("The flower leads to the eyes and the eyes to the flower").[22] As Le Mollé has demonstrated, "yeux" (eyes) occupies a privileged place in lines 4, 5, and 6.[23] It is preceded by four references to eyes and flowers and followed by four more references to eyes and flowers. The first group mirrors the second: flower—eyes—flower—flower—EYES—flower—flower—eyes—flower. What makes Annie so attractive (and so dangerous) is clearly her eyes, which were either blue or gray and apparently very provocative.[24] Anne Hyde Greet reminds us that the poisonous eyes conceit goes back at least to the troubadours.[25]

Renaud takes issue with Apollinaire's decision to include cows in "Les Colchiques" because they do not normally appear in love poetry. And since the cows are grazing on the crocuses, he complains, metaphorically they are grazing on Annie's eyes![26] The first observation is correct. Sheep, not cows, are the animals most commonly found in love poetry, beginning with *Daphnis and Chloe*. However, that does not mean that the cows constitute a liability. Their presence in "Les Colchiques" simply emphasizes Apollinaire's originality. Renaud's second objection is actually incorrect. Annie's eyes are linked to the crocuses not by metaphor but by simile. They are *like* the crocuses since they share the same color, but they are not identical to them. She is in no danger of being injured after all. Jean-Claude Coquet points out that the reflexive verb *s'empoisonner* is misleading. The cows are not poisoning themselves, they are being poisoned by the crocuses.[27] The same observation applies to Apollinaire, who is being poisoned by Annie's eyes. Most of the critics believe the poem embodies the following four-term homology: crocuses / vaches = eyes / Apollinaire. Daubier substitutes "ma vie" ("my life") for "Apollinaire" but cannot believe the poet is comparing his life to that of the cows.[28] Since the poem is centered around the crocuses, he argues, the reader forgets that this vulgar equation exists. Renaud is equally incredulous.[29] Since a cow is a maternal image, he asks, how can Apollinaire possibly compare himself to one? Is it because he thinks he is as stupid as a cow for letting Annie poison him? Following a lengthy psychoanalytic interpretation, he deduces that the poet has experienced "une vertigineuse régression psychique" ("a dizzying psychic regression").

The first stanza concludes exactly as it began—with the very same rhymes and the very same (end) words. As Le Mollé remarks, these produce "une impression de mouvement circulaire, à quoi s'ajoute la sensation de valse lente" ("an impression of circular movement, to which is added the feeling of a slow waltz").[30] Indeed, the first stanza seems positively elegant compared to the following one. Unlike the former, which flows relatively smoothly, the latter proceeds by fits and by starts. Whereas the first stanza seeks to create an état d'âme ("mood"), the second is filled with frenetic activity. In contrast to its predecessor, which draws heavily on être ("to be") and comme ("like"), the second stanza employs four action verbs: "viennent," "jouant," "cueillent," and "battent." Interestingly, it follows the same progression as the first stanza. Beginning with a description of the meadow, it focuses on the crocuses before moving on to Annie's eyes:

> Les enfants de l'école viennent avec fracas
> Vêtus de hoquetons et jouant de l'harmonica
> Ils cueillent les colchiques qui sont comme des mères
> Filles de leurs filles et sont couleur de tes paupières
> Qui battent comme les fleurs battent au vent dément.

> (Schoolchildren arrive noisily
> Dressed in *hoquetons* and playing harmonicas
> They pick the crocuses which resemble mothers
> Daughters of their daughters and the color of your eyelashes
> Which flutter like the flowers fluttering in the demented wind.)

All of a sudden, a bunch of schoolchildren burst upon the scene and begin picking the crocuses. Although Le Mollé calls this scene an "irruption immotivée" ("an unmotivated eruption"), Robert Faurisson suggests they are coming home from school.[31] Since it is autumn, the schools are back in session. From the fact that the children are dressed in *hoquetons*—rough cloth coats—we know that they come from peasant families. Although Daubier doubts the poetic efficacy of these garments, Claude Lévi-Strauss praises the word's awkward sound and its choppy rhythm.[32] Whereas the cows graze according to an anapestic rhythm, he declares, the "hoquetons" and "harmonicas" evoke the children's destructive behavior.[33] Other scholars have sought to discover additional information. Trying to extract the maximum benefit from "hoquetons," Deguy has constructed an imaginary scenario involving hiccups and rags.[34] Like previous secret messages, however, these basically lead nowhere. In 1974, interestingly, Legros wondered if the noisy schoolchildren might mirror an ancient rite associated with picking flowers.[35]

Although the word *hoqueton* is attested as early as the twelfth century, it had fallen out of use by Apollinaire's time. In 1998, after much ink had been spilled trying to locate the source of this reference, Etienne-Alain Hubert published a fascinating piece of scholarship. Pursuing a fragmentary citation by Apollinaire, he discovered a book with a description of an ancient Greek ceremony, which the poet had copied. Celebrated annually by the Spartans and dedicated to the memory of Hyacinth, the festival was interrupted at a pre-arranged point by a raucous band of "enfanz equippez avec de petits hoquetons [qui] alloient jouäns de la cistre et chantans quant et quant au son des fluttes et hautbois" ("infants wearing *hoquetons* playing zithers and singing along to the music of flutes and oboes").[36] The noisy schoolchildren in "Les Colchiques" are wearing "hoquetons," it turns out, because they are descended from the Spartans. Like their ancient ancestors, they introduce a welcome intermission. Instead of zithers, flutes, and oboes, however, they are playing harmonicas. Or rather, since they are only children, they are probably making a terrible racket. Renaud gives the scene a psychoanalytical twist. Since the crocuses resemble breasts, he declares, the children who are picking flowers are tearing at the maternal body.[37] Whereas the meadow represents the mother in his opinion, Dininman identifies it with "le corps de la femme aimée" ("the body of the beloved woman")—presumably Annie.[38] The fact that the children are picking autumn crocuses, and getting the poisonous juice all over their hands, is unsettling to say the least. Although Iaria and Tillmans believe their innocence will protect them, there is certainly no guarantee.[39] "Les Colchiques" is not a fairy story. Inevitably, the fact that the flowers are "comme des mères" ("like mothers") reminds one of Medea, who poisoned both her children.

The expression "mères / Filles de leurs filles" ("mothers / Daughters of their daughters") has bedeviled readers ever since the poem was published. A surprising number of scholars have been disturbed by the apparent transformation of the masculine *colchiques* into female figures. Pages and pages have been written attempting to account for this puzzling anomaly. In reality, Apollinaire simply says the flowers are *like* mothers and daughters. They resemble the latter in one respect, but otherwise they retain their masculine characteristics. Since the crocuses are closely identified with Annie, it would never have done to refer to them as fathers and sons. Apollinaire essentially had no choice. Nevertheless, the question remains: how can a mother possibly be the daughter of her own daughter? Or conversely, how can a daughter be the mother of her own mother? Lest we forget how shocking this formulation really is, Legros calls it "[une] monstruosité à peine concevable" ("a barely conceivably monstrosity").[40] The easiest way to grasp this illogical concept is to distance oneself from it as far as possible. Thus Lévi-Strauss declares that the instability of the mother/daughter relationship in the poem parallels that between the signifier and the signified.[41] Both relationships are infinitely reversible. The problem is, of course, that mother/daughter relationships are not reversible in real life. For this reason, Kao prefers to view the illogical phrase as a subversive gesture.[42] By reversing the irreversible, Apollinaire demonstrates his poetry's refusal to recognize any authority but itself.

All this is basically irrelevant to scholars who don't care for abstract generalizations. Convinced that the puzzling phrase must have another explanation, numerous critics have come up with theories of their own.

The prize for the most ingenious explanation goes to Robert Faurisson. The middle-aged mothers are acting so coquettishly and wearing so much makeup, he declares, "qu'on les prendrait pour . . . les filles de leurs filles" ("that one would take them for . . . the daughters of their daughters").[43] Other critics have argued that Apollinaire was inspired by Leviticus, Dante's *Divine Comedy*, the Catholic liturgy, the myth of Persephone and Demeter, and so forth. Unfortunately, simply locating a potential source is not enough. While these texts satisfy some of the technical requirements of being a source, they do not help us to understand the original expression. At the time he wrote "Les Colchiques," in any case, Apollinaire was immersed in German poetry and German folklore. He would not have been reading Dante or anyone else from outside that tradition. Over the years, a consensus has gradually emerged in favor of a botanical explanation. The autumn crocus is noteworthy for two characteristics: it is poisonous, and its flowers appear six months before its leaves do. The second feature is reflected in a number of intriguing nicknames such as "filius ante patrem," cited by Lévi-Strauss, and "Sohn vor dem Vater," cited by Bengt Hasselrot.[44] Apollinaire did not need to translate or feminize these examples, however, because a perfectly good French name already existed: "la fille avant la mère" ("the daughter before the mother"). Indeed, as several authorities remark, this expression applies to a few other flowers too.[45] Against all expectations, the mother/daughter relationship turns out to be reversible after all—at least in the eyes of the beholder.

The second stanza concludes with the image of Annie's eyelashes (literally "eyelids") fluttering like flowers in a strong wind. Since the repetition of "battent" mimics the mutual fluttering, the verse is auto-illustrative. It describes what it does, and it does what it describes. Although the "vent dément" ("demented wind") comes as something of a surprise, it provides a forceful conclusion. Why Annie's eyelashes should be fluttering so furiously is hard to say. Since the scene has been absolutely idyllic up to this point, a violent wind is extremely unlikely to be the cause. Most scholars assume that Apollinaire is speaking metaphorically. Margaret Davies concludes, for example, that the wind represents destiny, which governs flowers and human beings alike.[46] In Dininman's opinion, by contrast, it functions as the Freudian father.[47] Iaria and Tillmans associate the wind with Apollinaire himself, whose "ardeur maladroite" ("awkward ardor") continually caused problems.[48] However, another possibility exists that is much more likely. Since Annie became involved with Apollinaire during their year in Germany, the wind almost certainly reflects their mutual passion—which is "crazy" because it is so intense. Among other things, this explains why

Annie's eyelashes are fluttering so rapidly. She feels like a flower caught up in a hurricane. The final stanza contains three verses:

> Le gardien du troupeau chante tout doucement
> Tandis que lentes et meuglant les vaches abandonnent
> Pour toujours ce grand pré mal fleuri par l'automne.

> (The cowherd sings softly
> While mooing and slowly moving the cows abandon
> Forever this large meadow poisoned by Autumn's flowers.)

Unexpectedly, the poem ends on a subdued note. A cowherd quietly singing to himself replaces the noisy harmonica players, who have presumably gone home. Somehow, the fact that he is singing a gentle song is reassuring. Despite his decidedly minor role, the cowherd continues to interest a number of critics, who would like to know more about him. Why has he let the cows eat poisonous flowers in the first place, for example, and where is he taking them when he leaves? Interestingly, as Le Mollé points out, his complete lack of concern parallels that of the children and the cows themselves.[49] No one seems to know or care that the crocuses are dangerous. Is it lack of concern, one wonders, or just plain ignorance? Dininman is convinced that the cowherd is the most important character in "Les Colchiques." Since he represents Apollinaire's creative ego, she explains, the song he is singing is the poem itself.[50] The last two lines have generated an amazing amount of debate. Since the cows have been eating poisonous plants, what exactly is going to happen to them?

At least three individuals deny that the flowers constitute a danger. Faurisson and Adam Stepnowski both insist that cows don't eat autumn crocuses, while D. C. Potts claims that crocuses are not poisonous to cattle.[51] In any case, he adds, the cowherd leads the cows away before anything can happen. Unfortunately, all three of them are seriously mistaken. According to an agricultural authority, "many horses, cattle, and pigs have been killed by meadow saffron. . . . Sheep and goats are believed to be very slightly affected."[52] In a last ditch effort to save the cows, Faurisson claims that they are only leaving for the winter, Coquet that they are merely going to another meadow, and Renaud that they are tired of being poisoned.[53] Despite their valiant efforts, it is abundantly clear that the cows are doomed. Otherwise the four-term homology would not work: crocuses / vaches = eyes / Apollinaire. The cows' destiny is meant to serve as a warning to Apollinaire, who is in danger of succumbing to a different poison. Thus, Décaudin concludes, "les vaches vont à la mort en s'éloignant dans le pré, comme l'année va aussi à sa fin" ("the cows go off to their death in the meadow, as the year is also is moving toward its end").[54] Their fate is sealed by the force of the run-on line: "abandonnent / Pour toujours." If any doubt remains, the progressively shorter stanzas illustrate the cows' disappearance visually.

In Dininman's opinion, "Les Colchiques" retraces Apollinaire's unconscious conflicts step by step and stage by stage.[55] The first stanza dramatizes the poet's oral mode, she declares, the second illustrates his "maîtrise sadique-anale" ("sadistic-anal mastery"), and the third resolves the conflict between the two by renouncing and sublimating his unconscious desires. By contrast, Davies detects a spiral structure centered around the comparison: flowers = eyes.[56] Each time the spiral revolves, it adds a new theme such as love, sickness, or poison. Opening out to embrace the eternal feminine ("filles de leurs filles"), it contracts briefly before opening again to embrace the wind. Noting that the poem begins and concludes with the same end words and rhymes, other critics have been struck by its circular structure. The last verse also mirrors the first verse, and the penultimate verse reflects the second verse. Unexpectedly, readers suddenly find themselves back at the beginning of "Les Colchiques," ready to start all over. In a sense, the poem never seems to end. Le Mollé attributes this impression to the important role played by repetition.[57] Interestingly, Décaudin argues that the dominant structure is linear rather than circular. The key concepts in his opinion are those associated with "l'éloignement, le départ, la fuite, l'effacement" ("going away, leaving, flight, and obliteration").[58] Since these words describe Apollinaire's Rhenish poetry in general, structural concerns are forced to compete with thematic concerns for the reader's attention. What happens to the cows is as important as what happens to the poet.

"Salomé"

Published in *Vers et Prose* in 1905, "Salomé" has attracted considerable attention over the years. Since it revolves around a legendary *femme fatale*, this is not particularly surprising. Celebrated by the Symbolists in particular, Salomé was an extremely popular character at the dawn of the twentieth century. As Décaudin remarks, she was "une figure privilégiée, chargée des rêves et des phantasmes de l'époque" ("a privileged figure, loaded with dreams and the fantasies of the period").[59] In France alone, according to Maurice Kraft, 2,789 poets celebrated the dancer during the fifty years preceding World War I.[60] By the time Apollinaire decided to write about her, she had acquired mythic proportions. Nevertheless, while the cult of Salomé was widespread, the literary theme was gradually coming to an end. Few aesthetic options remained that had not already been explored. For someone like Apollinaire, who prized originality above all else, this presented a serious problem. Instead of simply writing a pastiche, he chose to create a revolutionary new poem, one that would make the literary world sit up and take notice. Toward this end, he devised four principal strategies.

Apollinaire decided first to create a radical new *mise-en-scène*. Defying spatial and temporal conventions, he transposed the biblical tale to a different country and a different historical period. Readers expecting to revisit ancient Palestine are astonished to encounter a medieval French court. Herod and his wife have been transformed into the king and queen of France, and Salomé has become a French princess. Commentators have generally assumed that the drama takes place in France and the Holy Land simultaneously. Thus, Durry calls the poem "une bigarrure d'époques juxtaposées" ("a hodgepodge of juxtaposed periods") and Robert Couffignal calls it "une rêverie envoûtante, où se mêlent les époques: temps évangéliques, moyen âge, temps modernes" ("a magical fantasy that combines several different periods: evangelical times, the Middle Ages, and modern times").[61] Most critics find the chronological mixture disturbing or confusing (or both). While Durry accuses Apollinaire of creating a carnival atmosphere, others complain that the poem is filled with anachronisms.

Nevertheless, close examination fails to substantiate these and similar complaints. In actuality, "Salomé" is situated neither in multiple countries nor during different historical periods. The medieval French setting displaces, effaces, and replaces the biblical setting altogether. While the transition from one to the other is startling, with a little effort it is possible to discover a logical explanation. As Jacqueline Bellas mentions, Apollinaire may have been inspired by a medieval painting or drawing.[62] Indeed, since he possessed a keen interest in art, this is quite likely. An exquisite painting like that by Benozzo Gozzoli (Figure 3.2) could have provided the necessary inspiration. The center depicts Salomé dancing for Herod and his guests, all of whom are dressed in fifteenth-century finery. On the left, John the Baptist prepares to be beheaded by a soldier wearing medieval armor. At the rear, Salomé presents the severed head to her mother.

Couffignal offers a different explanation entirely. He suggests that Apollinaire's poem is concerned with a French princess who has lost her mind and believes she is Salomé.[63] However, there is really no need to justify the geographical and chronological changes in "Salomé." Like modern directors who situate *Hamlet* in Brazil or *Heart of Darkness* in Vietnam, Apollinaire may simply have decided that medieval France would make a good location. In order

Figure 3.2.   Benozzo Gozzoli, *The Dance of Salomé*.
National Gallery of Art, Washington DC, Samuel H. Kress Collection.

to make the transition more convincing, he added a number of contemporary details. Herodias is dressed like a French countess, while her eldest son is called the Dauphin. The king has a jester to entertain him and soldiers with halberds to protect him. Even the trees are arranged in a French pattern.

Apollinaire decided next to center the poem around a single, symbolic date. The day he selected was June 24, which, as Rafael Cansinos-Asséns notes, traditionally marks the summer solstice.[64] However, the events recounted in "Salomé" do not take place on Midsummer's Day but rather the evening before—on Midsummer's Night. The composition is precisely situated both in time and in space. While the full significance of this date will become evident as the discussion progresses, several aspects are readily apparent. In France, for example, Midsummer's Night is called *la nuit de la Saint-Jean* because it is the eve of John the Baptist's birthday. In addition, as Shakespeare's *A Midsummer's Night's Dream* attests, it was associated in the popular imagination with the height of madness—foolishness as well as insanity. Marveling at Malvoglio's strange behavior in *Twelfth Night*, Olivia protests: "Why, this is very midsummer madness" (Act III, Scene 4). Although it is not immediately apparent, this theme is introduced at the very beginning of "Salomé."

Whereas Apollinaire's first two strategies set the stage for the story, the last two focused on the story itself. They determined not only how the narrative would be presented but also how it would be structured. Rejecting the dialogue form adopted by Mallarmé in *Hérodiade*, which interrupts the alexandrines' stately flow, Apollinaire decided to compose a dramatic

monologue. By reducing the descriptive elements to a minimum, he allowed the hapless protagonist to reveal her innermost thoughts and feelings.
Though troubling, the resulting portrait of Salomé's psychological distress is
intimate and unforgettable. Surprisingly, the portrait that gradually emerges
does not conform to her traditional depiction. Generally having been portrayed as cruel and unfeeling, Apollinaire's Salomé seems strangely vulnerable. In contrast to Mallarmé's princess contemplating her reptilian nudity,
she seems immensely human.

Apollinaire's final stroke of genius was to focus on the aftermath of Salomé's actions rather than on the actions themselves. Eschewing the anecdotal
approach favored by many writers, the poem commences where the traditional story leaves off. It begins not with John the Baptist's denunciation of
Herodias's incestuous marriage, nor with her plans for revenge, nor even with
Salomé's famous dance, but after the prophet has been beheaded. Apollinaire
had treated Salomé once before, in a short story published in 1902 (collected
in L'Hérésiarque et Cie). Entitled "La Danseuse," it contains the following
description: "Salomé, enjolivée, attifée, diaprée, fardée, dansa devant le roi
et, excitant un vouloir doublement incestueux, obtint la tête du Saint refusée
à sa mère" ("Embellished, decked out, beautified, made up, Salome danced
before the king and, exciting a doubly incestuous desire, obtained the saint's
head refused to her mother").[65] This account, which reflects the fin-de-siècle
myth, depicts her not only as a willing participant but also as a scheming
accomplice. By contrast, Salomé was transformed into a completely different
figure three years later. Instead of a voluptuous temptress, Apollinaire cast
her as a naive adolescent.

Consisting of five quatrains loosely rhymed ABAB, "Salomé" is composed
largely of alexandrines. Apollinaire varied the formula by introducing a deca-
syllable in the fourth stanza, rhyming the final stanza ABBA, and appending
three half lines at the end. The reader's first glimpse of Salomé is profoundly
astonishing. Although she had asked Herod to bring her the head of John the
Baptist, she is overcome by grief when she finally receives it.

> Pour que sourie encore une fois Jean-Baptiste
> Sire je danserais mieux que les séraphins
> Ma mère dites-moi pourquoi vous êtes triste
> En robe de comtesse à côté du Dauphin
>
> (If John the Baptist could smile again
> Sire I would dance better than the seraphim
> Tell me mother why you are so sad
> Dressed like a countess beside the Dauphin.)

The first stanza orients the reader with respect to the story and evokes Salomé's extraordinary talent. Elsewhere, Apollinaire calls her "la danseuse au pied prompt" ("the dancer with quick feet").[66] As this felicitous phrase implies, Salomé is totally consumed by dance. Dancing is not only her favorite pastime but also her *raison d'être*. And yet, while the first two lines acknowledge her remarkable gift, they are also deeply ironic. Although her marvelous dancing brought about John the Baptist's death, it is powerless to restore him to life. Even the heavenly seraphim—who according to talmudic lore are dancing masters—could not accomplish such a feat.[67] While the third line is uttered by Salomé, as is the entire work, in reality it is concerned with her mother. Here and elsewhere, Salomé serves as an unconscious mirror, reflecting the actions of those around her. We never view the other characters directly. Only through her, for example, do we learn that Herodias has a sad expression on her face.

Like that of Salomé's sudden grief, this discovery comes as a considerable surprise. Since her mortal enemy John the Baptist is dead, one would expect Herodias to be jubilant. As the story unfolds, however, the reader gradually perceives that her daughter has lost her mind. This is the source of Herodias' sadness. But what could have happened to drive Salomé insane? As it turns out, there are two answers to this question. The first one is relatively simple: she is suffering from midsummer madness. Her illness stems from Midsummer's Night itself, which exerts a mysterious influence over her. The second explanation is more complicated.

> Mon coeur battait battait très fort à sa parole
> Quand je dansais dans le fenouil en écoutant
> Et je brodais des lys sur une banderole
> Destinée à flotter au bout de son baton
>
> Et pour qui voulez-vous qu'à présent je la brode
> Son baton refleurit sur les bords du Jourdain
> Et tous les lys quand vos soldats ô roi Hérode
> L'emmenèrent se sont flétris dans mon jardin
>
> (My heart beat how very fast it beat
> Dancing in the fennel as I listened to him
> And I embroidered lilies on a banner
> Meant to fly from the tip of his staff
>
> For whom should I embroider it now
> His staff blooms on the Jordan's banks
> And all the lilies withered in my garden
> King Herod when your soldiers led him away.)

The conclusion that inevitably emerges from these two stanzas is that Salomé was in love with John the Baptist. The construction "battait battait" mimics her quickening heartbeat, for instance, and betrays her excitement at hearing his voice. And the banner she is embroidering recalls a similar device in courtly romances. Whenever a knight enters a jousting tournament, his lady presents him with a scarf or a handkerchief to affix to his lance as a sign of her favor. Serving as a badge of his authority, John's staff even resembles a lance. Depicted in countless paintings and drawings, it is long and straight with a short crosspiece near the top. Since the fleur-de-lys pattern was reserved for French royalty, the fact that Salomé chose to embroider it on the banner is also significant. Like the king of France, who governs the secular domain, John is the supreme authority in the spiritual realm. As the flower of Easter, moreover, the lily symbolizes rebirth and spiritual renewal. Viewed in this perspective, it alludes to the fact that John is the great Precursor whose role prefigures that of Jesus. His staff not only resembles Aaron's rod in the Bible but also is imbued with the same symbolism as the lily. Blooming on the banks of the Jordan River (where he used to baptize his disciples), it symbolizes the coming of Christ.

Since Salomé possesses lilies of her own, however, the situation is considerably more complicated. Insofar as she is concerned, the flowers are associated with purity and virginity. In many paintings of the Annunciation, the angel carries a stalk of lilies for the same reason. The theme of purity would seem to indicate that the love between her and John the Baptist was strictly platonic. An argument could even be made that she was in love with his religious message, rather than with the man himself, and thus that she was a potential convert. This interpretation is subverted by other symbols that imply that she was passionately in love with John. In particular, several critics have called attention to the sexual symbolism that permeates the two stanzas. Bates points out that the staff is a common symbol for the phallus and that fennel traditionally represents pubic hair.[68]Refuting Marc Poupon's contention that the lilies are associated with violent death, Antoine Fongaro emphasizes their phallic nature and the fact that they are planted in the yonic garden.[69] He concludes from this that Salomé and John the Baptist were lovers. Whichever interpretation one chooses, the spiritual or the carnal, the withered flowers (borrowed from "La Dame") clearly parallel John the Baptist's death. Both groups of lilies, the heraldic and the biblical, are eclipsed at the same moment.

Ultimately, the withered flowers reflect far more than the death of John the Baptist. Since they are related to Salomé metonymically, their unfortunate fate mirrors her own. Serving as objective correlatives, they translate her deteriorating mental condition into concrete terms. Retracing the preceding chain of events, it is clear that Salomé's madness stems above all from the death of the man she loved. The recognition that she was to blame has caused her to lose her mind. And yet the question remains: how could Salomé have done such a thing? How could she have betrayed the man she loved? Since she asked for John's head in person, it is hard to believe she didn't know what she was doing.[70] Couffignal attributes her actions to her "demonic personality," but this describes the mythical Salomé better than it does the sorrowful adolescent in the poem.[71] The best explanation is doubtless the traditional one: that she was manipulated by her evil mother. How Herodias managed to achieve this goal is left to the reader's imagination.

Ironically, despite her murderous history, Salomé is a surprisingly sympathetic character. This is due partly to her mother's manipulation, partly to her obvious remorse, and partly to the fact that she has lost her mind. Like John the Baptist, she is a victim of Herodias' thirst for revenge. Until this point, however, there has been no obvious indication that Salomé is insane. Only in the last two stanzas does the reader perceive that she is demented. The earlier experience has so unhinged her that she has become a child again. Her mental age is perhaps five or six. Unlike the first three stanzas, which are situated in the royal palace, the final two appear to take place on the palace grounds. All of a sudden, Salomé invites everyone to come outside and dance.

> Venez tous avec moi là-bas sous les quinconces
> Ne pleure pas ô joli fou du roi
> Prends cette tête au lieu de ta marotte et danse
> N'y touchez pas son front ma mère est déjà froid
>
> (Come with me under the quincunxes everyone
> Please don't cry charming jester
> Take this head for your scepter and dance
> Don't touch mother his forehead is already cold.)

Consisting of four objects at the corners of a square and a fifth in the middle, a quincunx is a common floral pattern in public gardens. However, the first line refers not to flowers but to plane trees, which have been planted in alternate rows. Salomé's sudden gaiety contrasts vividly with the weeping jester who, like Herodias, is distressed by her madness. Presenting him with John the Baptist's head, which she has been cradling in her arms, she advises him to lay down his scepter and join in the future dancing. Since the scepter is adorned with bells and topped by a hooded fool's head, her suggestion possesses a certain bizarre logic. Finally, Salomé commands the king and his attendants, including a Spanish princess, to form a procession.

Sire marchez devant trabants marchez derrière
Nous creuserons un trou et l'y enterrerons
Nous planterons des fleurs et danserons en rond
Jusqu'à l'heure où j'aurai perdu ma jarretière
    Le roi sa tabatière
    L'infante son rosaire
    Le curé son bréviaire

(Sire march before halberdiers march behind
We will dig a hole and bury it
We will plant flowers and dance in a ring
Until I have lost my garter
    The king his snuff-ox
    The Infanta her rosary
    The priest his breviary.)

Suddenly, as Durry remarks, "tout se met à tourner au galop" ("everything begins to whirl around").[72] The accelerating rhythm at the end is complemented by the quadruple rhyme scheme, both of which contribute to the general gaiety. The poem concludes on an unexpected note with the royal party joining hands and dancing around John the Baptist's grave until they are exhausted. Although we can visualize their actions easily enough, the conclusion is entirely imaginary. The reader is swept up by the accelerating rhythm like the characters themselves. Not surprisingly, since she has reverted to her former childhood, Salomé is attracted to childish games. "The final three lines dissolve away into a dance of pure unreality," Pilkington comments, "with an incantation like that of a children's rhyme."[73] Similarly, Anna Boschetti declares that the poem concludes "au rythme de comptine" ("to the rhythm of a children's rhyme").[74] In addition, the final scene recalls a traumatic experience that befalls every child at one time or another—the death of a beloved pet. Like a group of children who have organized a mock funeral, the king and his followers march to the appointed spot and bury the object they are carrying with all the pomp and ceremony they can muster.

Bellas provides an even closer link to the experience of childhood. Evoking her youth in the Ardennes, where Apollinaire spent the summer of 1899, she recalls a similar song that she and her friends used to act out.[75] Accompanying a dead heroine who refused to marry the "p'tit roi d'Angleterre" ("the little king of England"), they would dig a hole, pretend to bury her, plant flowers, and dance around her grave. Finally, as Serge and Hélène Auffret note, Salomé herself resembles a character in a popular comptine. Like her, the miller's daughter loves to dance but ends up losing her garter.[76]

C'est la fille de la meunière
Qui dansait avec les gars;
Elle a perdu sa jarretière,
Sa jarretière ne tenait pas.
Gibouli, giboula,
On dit qu' elle est malade;
Gibouli, giboula,
On dit qu'elle en mourra.[77]

(It's the miller's daughter
Who liked to dance with the boys;
She lost her garter
Her garter wouldn't stay up.
Gibouli, giboula,
They say that she is sick;
Gibouli, giboula,
They say that she will die.)

Although "Salomé" ends "in the whirl of a nonsense rhyme," as Garnet Rees puts it, the conclusion itself is far from nonsensical.[78] C. M. Bowra offers an allegorical interpretation, for instance, in which the frenzied dancing constitutes a myth of artistic creation.[79] In addition, the conclusion was clearly inspired by an ancient folkloric rite handed down through the centuries. It is modeled not on a maypole dance, as I suggested in an earlier study, but on another picturesque custom known as *le feu de la Saint-Jean.*[80] "Coutume populaire qui subsiste encore dans nombre de villages et de faubourgs," *La Grande Encyclopédie* reported in 1902, "la veille ou le jour même de la fête de saint Jean-Baptiste (23 ou 24 juin), on allume des feux autour desquels on danse, par-dessus lesquels on saute" ("A popular rite that still exists in a number of villages and suburbs: the evening before John the Baptist's feast day, or the day itself [June 23rd or 24th], people light bonfires and dance around or leap over them"). After a decline in popularity, the custom is currently experiencing a massive revival in France.

An extensive discussion of this pan-European phenomenon can be found in Sir James George Frazer's book *The Golden Bough*, which describes several French celebrations. "In Provence," he declared in 1922, "the midsummer fires are still popular. Children go from door to door begging for fuel, and they are seldom sent empty away. Formerly the priest, the mayor, and the aldermen used to walk in procession to the bonfire, and even deigned to light it; after which the assembly marched thrice round the burning pile."[81] According to *La Grande Encyclopedie*, a similar ceremony used to take place in Paris, at the Place de Grève, until it was abolished in 1768. Apollinaire was obviously familiar with the midsummer celebration—which he probably witnessed in Provence during his youth—from which he borrowed two key elements. The conclusion to "Salomé" incorporates not only the circular dance around the fire but also the formal procession that preceded it.

Surprisingly, several critics find "Salomé" to be amusing, presumably because of its curious ending.[82] By contrast, LeRoy Breunig emphasizes the anxiety that the composition elicits in the reader, which I think is closer to the mark.[83] The impression of gay abandon that accompanies the conclusion is patently artificial—too much gloom hangs over the poem for it to be convincing. Although Salomé's gaiety is doubtless sincere, her companions are simply humoring her. They know the princess is mad and that their behavior is totally inappropriate. For these and other reasons, "Salomé" is not an amusing poem—nor was it ever intended to be. On the contrary, as I have tried to show, Apollinaire created a psychological study that is deeply disturbing. Although it begins and concludes with the theme of dancing, Salomé's childish game at the end bears little resemblance to the performance that beguiled Herod. Ironically, despite her royal blood, she fares little better than John the Baptist did. By the end of the poem, she is reduced to a pathetic figure, a poignant shadow of her former self.

Notes

1. Michel Décaudin, Le Dossier d' "Alcools," rev. ed. (Paris: Minard, 1965), 107.

2. Georges Legros, "'Sens' et 'Source.' A propos des vers 10-11 des 'Colchiques,'" Cahiers d'analysetextuelle, No. 16 (1974), 119 n20.

3. Ibid., 114.

4. Michel Deguy, "Encore une lecture des 'Colchiques' ou un poème de l'apophonie," Poétique, No. 20 (1974), 453.

5. Legros, "'Sens' et Source,'" 123.

6. Françoise Dininman, "Toujours à propos des 'Colchiques,'" Etudes autour d'"Alcools," ed. Anne de Fabry and Marie-France Hilgar (Birmingham: Summa, 1985), 30-31.

7. Philippe Renaud, "Herbiers et rituels ("Une Relecture de 'Colchiques,')" in Apollinaire, ed. Pierre-Olivier Walzer (Fribourg: Editions Universitaires Fribourg, 1983), 60-61.

8. During the discussion following Adam Stepnowski's presentation: "'Les Colchiques' et le renouvellement du lyrisme," later published in Les Cahiers de Varsovie, No. 11 (1984), 243.

9. Jean-Pierre Bobillot, "L'élasticité métrico-prosodique chez Apollinaire: une lecture formelle des 'Colchiques,'" Poétique, No. 84 (November 1990), 421.

10. Bobillot analyzes the competition between the metric approach and the prosodic approach in exhaustive detail. See also Roland Le Mollé, "'Les Colchiques' de Guillaume Apollinaire (architecture du poème et nature de la poésie)," *Annali della Scuola Normale Superiore di Pisa, Lettere, Storia e Filosofia*, Series 2, Vol. 37, fasc. 1–2 (1968), 178.

11. Michel Deguy, "Encore une lecture," 453.

12. Ibid., 457.

13. Bobillot, "L'élasticité métrico-prosodique chez Apollinaire," 414.

14. Deguy, "Encore une lecture," 452.

15. Décaudin, *"Le Dossier d'*'Alcools,'" 107.

16. Renaud, "Herbiers et rituels," 61.

17. Domenica Iaria and Jean-Yves Tillmans, "Apollinaire et ses filles-fleurs," *Nuovi Annali della Facoltà di Magistero dell'Università di Messina*, No. 1 (1983), 310.

18. Le Mollé, "'Les Colchiques' de Guillaume Apollinaire," 175.

19. Ibid., 181.

20. Jean-Michel Adam, *Pour lire le poème* (Paris: Duculot, 1985), 62.

21. Shuhsi Kao, "'Les Colchiques' d'Apollinaire et la modernité," *Essays in French Literature*, No. 17 (November 1980), 65.

22. Louis Daubier, "'Les Colchiques' et les philtres d'Apollinaire," *Le Thyrse*, Vol. 70, No. 4 (July–August 1968), 20 n1.

23. Le Mollé, "'Les Colchiques' de Guillaume Apollinaire," 181–83. The actual demonstration is much more extensive.

24. Margaret Davies, *Apollinaire* (New York: St. Martin's, 1964), 76.

25. Anne Hyde Greet, tr. *"Alcools." Guillaume Apollinaire* (Berkeley: University of California Press, 1965), 223.

26. Renaud, "Herbiers et rituels," 61.

27. Jean-Claude Coquet, "Sémantique du discours poétique. 'Les Colchiques' de Guillaume Apollinaire," *Littérature*, No. 6 (May 1972), 70.

28. Daubier, "Les Colchiques et les philtres d'Apollinaire," 20.

29. Renaud, "Herbiers et rituels," 61.

30. Le Mollé, "'Les Colchiques' de Guillaume Apollinaire," 183.

31. Ibid., 186, and Robert Faurisson, "Notes sur *Alcools*," *L'Information Littéraire*, No. 1 (January–February 1967), 39.

32. Daubier, "Les Colchiques et les philtres d'Apollinaire," 20.

33. Claude Lévi-Strauss, *Le Regard* éloigné (Paris: Plon, 1983), 296.

34. Deguy, "Encore une lecture des 'Colchiques,'" 456.

35. Legros, "'Sens' et 'Source,'" 118.

36. Etienne-Alain Hubert, "Autres Scolies sur *Alcools* d'Apollinaire," *Revue d'Histoire Littéraire de la France*, January–February 1998, 115.

37. Renaud, "Herbiers et rituels," 62–63.

38. Dininman, "Toujours à propos des 'Colchiques,'" 28–29.

39. Iaria and Tillmans, "Apollinaire et ses filles-fleurs," 312.

40. Legros, "'Sens' et 'Source,'" 120.

41. Lévi-Strauss, *Le Regard* éloigné, 297.

42. Kao, "'Les Colchiques' d'Apollinaire," 67–68.

43. Robert Faurisson, "Notes sur *Alcools*," *L'Information Littéraire*, No. 1 (January–February, 1967), 39.

44. Lévi-Strauss, *Le Regard* éloigné, 294, and Bengt Hasselrot, "Les Vertus devraient être soeurs, ainsi que les vices sont frères. Accord genre-sexe dans les figures généalogiques," *Revue Romane*, Special No. 1 (1967), 35–44.

45. See Legros, "'Sens' et 'Source,'" 117; Marc Poupon, "Sources allemandes d'Apollinaire," *Revue des Lettres Modernes*, Nos. 530–536 (1978), 27; and Renaud, "Herbiers et rituels," 65.

46. Margaret Davies, "Apollinaire, la peinture et l'image," *QueVlo-Ve?*, Nos. 21–22 (July–October 1979), 3 (paginated separately).

47. Dininman, "Toujours à propos des 'Colchiques,'" 35.

48. Iaria and Tillmans, "Apollinaire et ses filles-fleurs," 312.

49. Le Mollé, "'Les Colchiques' de Guillaume Apollinaire," 192.

50. Dininman, "Toujours à propos des 'Colchiques,'" 36. Following Lévi-Strauss, she concludes on page 37 that the cowherd represents Jesus, the *mère fille de sa fille* represents the Virgin Mary, and the wind represents the Holy Spirit.

51. Faurisson, "Notes sur *Alcools*," 39; Stepnowski, "'Les Colchiques' et le renouvellement du lyrisme," 244; D. C. Potts, "The Interpretation of Apollinaire's 'Les Colchiques," *French Studies*, Vol. 27, No. 4 (October 1972), 430.

52. Harold C. Long, *Plants Poisonous to Live Stock*, 2nd ed, (Cambridge: Cambridge Agricultural Monographs, 1924), 80.

53. Faurisson, "Notes sur *Alcools*," 39; Coquet, "Sémantique du discours poétique," 71; Renaud, "Herbiers et rituels," 64.

54. Decaudin, *Apollinaire* (Paris: Livre de Poche, 2002), 92.

55. Dininman, "Toujours à propos des 'Colchiques,'" 26.

56. Davies, "Apollinaire, la peinture et l'image," 3 (paginated separately).

57. Le Mollé, "'Les Colchiques' de Guillaume Apollinaire," 190.

58. Stepnowski, "'Les Colchiques' et le renouvellement du lyrisme," 243.

59. Michel Décaudin, "Un Mythe 'fin de siècle': Salomé," *Comparative Literature Studies*, Vol. 4, Nos. 1–2 (1967), 110.

60. Cited in ibid., 109.

61. Durry, *Guillaume Apollinaire: "Alcools"* (Paris: SEDES, 1964), Vol. 3, 146, and Robert Couffignal, *L'Inspiration biblique dans l'oeuvre de Guillaume Apollinaire* (Paris: Minard, 1966), 35.

62. Jacqueline Bellas, "L'Equivoque de Salomé dans la littérature et l'art 'fin de siècle'" in *Poésie et peinture du symbolisme au surréalisme en France et en Pologne*, ed. ElzbietaGrabska (Warsaw: University of Warsaw, 1973), 46.

63. Couffignal, *L'Inspiration biblique*, 35.

64. Rafael Cansinos-Asséns, *Salomé en la literatura (Flaubert, Wilde, Mallarmé, Eugenio de Castro, Apollinaire)* (Madrid: América, 1919), 241–43.

65. Guillaume Apollinaire, *Oeuvres en prose*, Vol. 1, ed. Michel Décaudin (Paris: Gallimard, 1977), 125.

66. Guillaume Apollinaire, *Oeuvres poétiques*, ed. Marcel Adéma and Michel Décaudin (Paris: Gallimard, 1965), 1030.

67. Scott Bates, "Notes sur 'Simon Mage' et Isaac Laquedem," *Revue des Lettres Modernes*, Nos. 123–26 (1965), 68.

68. Scott Bates, *Dictionnaire des mots libres d'Apollinaire* (Sewannee, TN: privately printed, 1991), 247 and 160 respectively.

69. Poupon, "Sources allemandes d'Apollinaire," *Revue des Lettres Modernes*, Nos. 530–36 (1978), 14–18, and Antoine Fongaro, "Des 'lys,'" *Que Vlo-Ve? Bulletin International des Etudes sur Guillaume Apollinaire*, 4th series, No. 14 (April–June 2001), 42–45.

70. Décaudin, *Le Dossier d' "Alcools,"* 140.

71. Couffignal, *L'Inspiration biblique*, 35.

72. Durry, *Guillaume Apollinaire: "Alcools,"* 3:146.

73. A. E. Pilkington, ed., *Apollinaire, "Alcools"* (Oxford: Blackwells, 1970), 130.

74. Anna Boschetti, *La Poésie partout: Apollinaire, homme-époque (1898-1918)* (Paris: Seuil, 2001), 74.

75. Bellas, "L'Equivoque de Salomé," 47.

76. Serge and Hélène Auffret, *Le Commentaire composé* (Paris: Hâchette, 1968), 163.

77. Jean Baucomont et al, eds., *Les Comptines de la langue française* (Paris: Seghers, 1961), 310.

78. Garnet Rees, ed., *Guillaume Apollinaire: "Alcools"* (London: Athlone, 1975), 147.

79. C. M. Bowra, *The Creative Experiment* (London: Macmillan, 1949), 74.

80. Willard Bohn, *Apollinaire and the International Avant-Garde* (Albany: State University of New York Press, 1997), 190.

81. Sir James George Frazer, *The Golden Bough: A Study in Magic and Religion*, abridged ed. (New York: Macmillan, 1963), 730.

82. See, for example, Pilkington, ed., *Apollinaire, "Alcools,"* 129.

83. L. C. Breunig, "Les Phares d'Apollinaire," *Cahiers du Musée d'Art Moderne*, Vol. 81, No. 6 (1981), 66.

CHAPTER FOUR

~

Fashion Trends and Trendy Fashions

The following poems describe some of Apollinaire's experiences with the world of fashion. One of them is a fictional account that takes place in a fashionable tailor's shop in London, and the other relates an encounter with a fashion model in Paris that turns out to have really happened, although not quite as Apollinaire describes it. Although "L'Emigrant de Landor Road" is pure fantasy, a product of his unhappy love affair with Annie Playden, "1909" describes an actual experience. Possessing impeccable taste, the tailor on Savile Row in the first poem caters to royalty. Dressed in the latest Parisian style, the model of the second poem acts as if she were royalty. While the tailor possesses a disturbing resemblance to Sweeney Todd, the model seems to have stepped right out of a toothpaste commercial.

"L'Emigrant de Landor Road"

As charming and accomplished as the "Rhénanes" are, Margaret Davies declares, they pale in importance beside "La Chanson du Mal-Aimé" and "L'Emigrant de Landor Road." Completed some two years after the "Rhénanes" were, these poems are "the final, aesthetically triumphant outcome of all the desire and tears and frustration and rage of that year in Germany."[1] Apollinaire needed both the time and the space to recover from his experience in the Rhineland. Only when he stepped back could he begin to process what had happened between him and Annie. Unlike "La Chanson du mal-aimé," which treats this subject on an epic scale, "L'Emigrant de Landor

Road" adopts a more condensed approach. Despite its much shorter length, the composition is highly experimental. As Philippe Renaud remarks, it is "un mélange unique de fantaisie, d'humour, de cocasserie et de tristesse soudaine mais passagère" ("a unique mixture of fantasy, humor, bizarre events, and sadness").[2] For the first time, Apollinaire dares to break all the rules. From now on, he will continue to ignore the restrictions imposed by realism and logic. Writing in 1964, Marie-Jeanne Durry argued that the placement of "L'Emigrant de Landor Road" in the exact center of *Alcools* reflects the central role of the original experience in his life.[3] Unfortunately, Pierre Laforgue has recently pointed out that the poem does not occupy the exact center.[4] It is twenty-eighth out of fifty poems. What has become increasingly evident is that Apollinaire was striving to develop a bold new poetics. As Le-Roy Breunig notes, the poem's patchwork structure prefigures the 1907–1908 period, when "structural ellipses and free association . . . will be most fully developed and incorporated in a new aesthetic."[5]

Published in the December 1905 issue of *Vers et Prose*, "L'Emigrant de Landor Road" was accompanied by "Mai," "Les Cloches," and "Salomé."[6] André Billy, to whom the composition is dedicated, was a critic and friend who later wrote several books about Apollinaire. As a sign of his eagerness to experiment, Apollinaire takes unprecedented liberties with the poem's prosody. While the composition consists almost entirely of quatrains, for example, one stanza is a quintil. In addition, Apollinaire experiments with different line lengths in five of the thirteen stanzas. Whereas the majority are composed of alexandrines, the third stanza contains an octosyllable, and the sixth consists entirely of six-syllable lines (alexandrines cut in half). Concluding with a tiny three-syllable verse, the eighth stanza is probably the most daring. However, the eleventh stanza contains two octosyllables and an extra seven-syllable line, and the twelfth alternates alexandrines and octosyllables. As Durry explains, "Les brusques changements de mètres accompagnent la brusquerie des contrastes" ("The sudden changes of meter accompany the brusqueness of the contrasts").[7] In a similar manner, Apollinaire varies the rhyme scheme from one stanza to another. While he alternates masculine and feminine rhymes throughout, quatrains composed of *rimes plates* are juxtaposed with others employing *rimes croisés* or *rimes embrassées*. The rhymes themselves exhibit a similar freedom. Some are banal ("avidement" / "serments"), one is rich ("Amérique" / "lyriques"), and others are approximative. Thus, "Indes" supposedly rhymes with "singes" and "vitrine" with "victimes."

"L'Emigrant de Landor Road" practically radiates with creativity from beginning to end. What strikes the reader more than anything is its originality.

Although Gilberte Jacaret calls the poem a "double pastiche" of Rimbaud's "Le Bateau ivre" and Baudelaire's "Le Voyage," the resemblance is superficial at best.[8] Since Apollinaire did not like to repeat himself, moreover, he never tried to duplicate this experiment—which in any case was engendered by a specific set of circumstances. One of the things that distinguished him from his contemporaries was that each of his compositions represented a particular stage in his poetic development. Discussing "L'Emigrant de Landor Road" and three other poems, André Breton called Apollinaire "le champion du *poème-événement*" ("the champion of the poem-event"). In Breton's opinion, he was "l'apôtre de cette conception qui exige de tout nouveau poème qu'il soit une refonte totale des moyens de son auteur . . . hors des chemins déjà tracés, au mépris des gains réalisés antérieurment" ("the apostle of the belief that every new poem must be a total recasting of the author's talents . . . far from previous accomplishments, with nothing but disdain for earlier achievements").[9]

> Le chapeau à la main il entra du pied droit
> Chez un tailleur très chic et fournisseur du roi
> Ce commerçant venait de couper quelques têtes
> De mannequins vêtus comme il faut qu'on se vête
>
> La foule en tous les sens remuait en mêlant
> Des ombres sans amour qui se traînait par terre
> Et des mains vers le ciel plein de lacs de lumière
> S'envolaient quelquefois comme des oiseaux blancs.
>
> (Hat in hand and right foot first he entered
> A stylish tailor's shop patronized by royalty
> This merchant had just decapitated several mannequins
> Dressed in the very latest fashion
>
> The crowd stirred restlessly in every direction
> Dragging loveless shadows on the ground as
> Hands lifted toward the sky full of lakes of light
> Occasionally took flight like white birds.)

Paradoxically, although "L'Emigrant de Landor Road" was meant to be read by the literate public, it is essentially a private poem. For this reason, it strikes the uninitiated reader as mysterious rather than poignant. To fully appreciate the work, one needs to know about Apollinaire's courtship of Annie Playden, which is never mentioned, and that Annie lived at 75 Landor Road in London (Clapham). The three-story Victorian row house she grew up in is still standing, although it has been divided into two flats. The ground floor is stone, the top two stories are brick, and the door and windows are nicely framed in limestone. Although Apollinaire left the Rhineland feeling he had lost Annie forever, he visited her twice in London, where he renewed his courtship—in November 1903 and May 1904. It was during the second visit that Annie told him she was emigrating to America. Shocked and dismayed, Apollinaire decided to write a poem in which he would take Annie's place. In part, this decision allowed him to appropriate her voyage for himself, and in part it allowed him to partially assuage his pain. Ironically, while the entire poem describes his attempt to emigrate, there is no obvious trace of Apollinaire anywhere. As far as the naïve reader can tell, the composition is about somebody else—the disembodied "il" (he) in the first line—who is never identified.

According to Renaud, Apollinaire's imaginary voyage symbolizes his determination to break with the past and to make a new future for himself.[10] After all, that is why people have always immigrated to America. Preparing to assume a new identity, he hurries to a tailor shop to buy a new suit for the voyage. Although the reader may not know where Landor Road is, the second line situates the scene in England. Laforgue wonders why Apollinaire removes his hat before entering the shop instead of waiting until he has entered.[11] Perhaps, since the British are famous for their politeness, he simply errs on the side of caution. Or perhaps, since he was also writing "L'Emigrant de Landor Road," he simply needed six syllables. As for why Apollinaire enters the shop right foot first, Renaud explains that he scorns the superstition that this will bring bad luck. In reality, the explanation is exactly the reverse. The left foot is the unlucky foot. Like his Roman forebears, who always began a journey or entered a building right foot first, Apollinaire wants to "get off on the right foot." In addition to being very fashionable, the tailor possesses a prestigious royal warrant. His advertisements are able to include the phrase "by appointment to his majesty the King." Together with this honor, the fact that his tailoring is absolutely correct ("comme il faut") suggests that he is located on Savile Row. Despite the tailor's elegant pretensions, Apollinaire seems to say in the third line, he is basically just a merchant like all the others.

The first stanza concludes, in Claudine Gothot-Mersch's words, with "une petite scène de humour noir" ("a little example of black humor").[12] Made of stuffed black cloth, Durry explains, British mannequins usually had arms, sometimes legs and feet with ankle boots, but were always headless.[13] Encountering them for the first time in London, Apollinaire jokes that the tailor must have lopped off their heads. At one stroke (actually several), the tailor is transformed into a fiendish butcher. While I. Merlin detects a possible reference here to Cromwell's men, who enjoyed decapitating royalists, one wonders if Apollinaire was familiar with Sweeney Todd.[14] The fictitious hero of a well-known Victorian melodrama, Todd was a barber who wielded a straight razor with uncommon ferocity. At any event, as Laforgue observes, the decapitation theme is widespread in *Alcools*.[15] In addition, "L'Emigrant de Landor Road" is filled with images of suffering, mutilation, and death, reflecting Apollinaire's anguish at Annie's departure. Curiously, the street outside the tailor's shop is filled with people who appear to be waving good-bye. Breunig theorizes that the poem was inspired by two different events: Apollinaire's departure at Waterloo Station, where Annie wished him goodbye when he returned to France, and her departure for America a few days later.[16] The first scene is evoked in the second stanza, where amputated hands seem to be flying in every direction like birds. As Merlin comments, "La foule n'est pas plus humaine que les mannequins ("the crowd is no more human than the mannequins").[17] All we see are their anonymous hands and their loveless shadows crawling on the ground. A sense of desolation pervades the restless scene:

> Mon bateau partira demain pour l'Amérique
>   Et je ne reviendrai jamais
> Avec l'argent gagné dans les prairies lyriques
> Guider mon ombre aveugle en ces rues que j'aimais
>
> Car revenir c'est bon pour un soldat des Indes
> Les boursiers ont vendu tous mes crachats d'or fin
> Mais habillé de neuf je veux dormir enfin
> Sous des arbres pleins d'oiseaux muets et de singes.
>
> (My boat leaves tomorrow for America
>   And I will never return
> With money earned on the lyrical prairies
> To guide my blind shadow down streets that I loved
>
> For returning is fine for a colonial soldier in India
> The pawnbrokers have sold all my medals of fine gold
> But dressed in new clothes I want to sleep at last
> Beneath trees full of mute birds and monkeys.)

At this point the action shifts from the immediate past to the present. Whereas the first two stanzas employ the impersonal third person, the next two are written in the first person. However, one wonders exactly who is speaking. Is it the narrator who suddenly intervenes or the author himself or the man we encountered in the first stanza? For a moment, the situation is ambiguous. Sooner or later, one realizes the speaker must be the first individual. Apollinaire originally enclosed the two stanzas in quotation marks to help the reader make this connection. Ultimately, of course, the narrator, the author, and the well-dressed man are one and the same. As the monologue continues, the speaker insists emphatically, by inserting a single octosyllable, that he will never return. He has no intention of promenading his mutilated shadow down English streets. The prospect of earning money on America's "lyrical prairies" is somewhat puzzling. Anne Hyde Greet wonders if Apollinaire imagines the prairies covered with singing cowboys.[18] Renaud is convinced the prairies contain the promise of a new kind of poetry.[19] Several critics think the speaker is going to America to seek his fortune. As proof, they point out that he was forced to sell his gold medals (see the next stanza). However, several other critics are not convinced. Despite assertions to the contrary, the speaker does not seem to be destitute. Instead of buying a suit off the rack, for example, he insists on patronizing an expensive tailor. In addition, he is able to buy a transatlantic ticket on an ocean liner. The second and third lines are open to at least three interpretations. The speaker will not return with money he has earned either because he doesn't want to or because he doesn't plan on earning any money. In which case, he is free to return or not as he chooses.

The first line of the next stanza, "Car revenir c'est bon pour un soldat des Indes," refers to a poem by Rudyard Kipling. Entitled "Mandalay," a French version appeared in Apollinaire's journal Le Festin d'Esope in February 1904. Essentially a lament, the poem is spoken by a former colonial British soldier who regrets not staying in Burma, where life was much easier than it is in London. Apollinaire's verse is problematic for at least two reasons. First, although car (for) implies that what follows will justify his decision never to return, the example he cites is of an ex-soldier who is happy to have returned ("revenir c'est bon"). Second, in point of fact, Kipling's ex-soldier was not happy at all. Apollinaire drops the subject altogether in the following verse and complains of having to sell his medals (which Scott Bates thinks may refer to his unappreciated poems).[20] This suggests that the first verse is meant to be taken ironically and that the "soldat des Indes" is Apollinaire himself, whose situation resembles that of the ex-soldier in "Mandalay." The proof that the first verse is ironic is furnished by the third verse, which basically contradicts what he said earlier. The key word here is the conjunction mais (but). "Returning home may be well and good for ex-soldiers," Apollinaire appears to say, "but

I want to buy a nice suit and go to America." This statement supports Roger Lefèvre's claim that the emigrant doesn't intend to seek his fortune in America: "Il ne désire que l'anéantissement (*dormir, muets*), loin du monde qui fut le sien" ("He only desires annihilation ['sleep,' 'mute'], far from the world that was his").[21] While the silent birds do not pose a problem, the monkeys come as a bit of a surprise. Perhaps Apollinaire had been reading *Paul et Virginie* by Bernardin de Saint-Pierre, who also imagined a tropical America. Or perhaps the monkeys were suggested by the thought of Kipling's Burma:

> Les mannequins pour lui s'étant déshabillés
> Battirent leurs habits puis les lui essayèrent
> Le vêtement d'un lord mort sans avoir payé
> Au rabais l'habilla comme un millionnaire

> > Au-dehors les années
> > Regardaient la vitrine
> > Les mannequins victimes
> > Et passaient enchaînées

> Intercalées dans l'an c'étaient les journées veuves
> Les vendredis sanglants et lents d'enterrements
> De blancs et de tout noirs vaincus des cieux qui pleuvent
> Quand la femme du diable a battu son amant.

> (The mannequins having undressed for him
> Brushed off their clothes then tried them on him
> The suit of a lord who died before he could pay
> marked down made him look like a millionaire

> > Outside the years
> > Observed the shop windows
> > The mannequin victims
> > And passed by chained together

> Inserted into the year were widowed days
> Slow bloody Fridays with burials
> White days and black days conquered by rainy skies
> When the Devil's wife beats her lover.)

The remainder of "L'Emigrant de Landor Road" is written in the impersonal third person. The first of the next three stanzas returns to the tailor's shop, where Apollinaire has been waiting to buy a suit. Unexpectedly, the headless mannequins remove the clothes they are wearing and try them on him. For some reason, Durry and Merlin think these actions are really performed by the shop attendants.[22] However, as several critics note, Apollinaire simply resumes the humorous fantasy he introduced at the beginning of the poem. In particular, he associates poetic renewal with the renewal of poetic forms, Laurence Perfézou explains: "La surprise, la fantaisie dont il est épris s'expriment à travers le parti-pris d'audace de ses compositions" ("The surprise and the fantasy he adores are expressed by the compositions' audacious orientation").[23] Fortunately, a suit ordered by a wealthy customer but never claimed fits Apollinaire perfectly. Since he is planning to leave the next day, he doesn't have time to wait anyway. In addition, like any sensible person in his place, he is delighted to receive a discount. Contrary to what some critics have alleged, nothing about the experience is humiliating.

This time, when Apollinaire turns to inspect the crowd outside the shop window, he discovers it gazing back at him. In the interim, the crowd's composition has changed dramatically. Instead of anonymous shadows and hands, he encounters allegorical figures representing the passing years. Apparently fascinated by the decapitated mannequins, they pass by the window one after another, chained together like a group of prisoners. As Claude Morhange-Bégué and Pierre Lartigue note, the swiftness of the years' passage is underlined by the brevity of the verses.[24] The third quatrain, which is worthy of Baudelaire, was borrowed from an earlier poem entitled "Adieux."[25] Like the previous stanza, it is concerned with the passage of time—measured in days this time rather than years. Unlike in the previous stanza, however, time seems to pass extremely slowly. Indeed, Gothot-Mersch thinks the slow, plodding rhythm resembles that of the funeral processions evoked in the second line.[26] In addition, the stanza is filled with gloomy imagery. "Les journées veuves" evokes a procession of widows all dressed in black. At the metaphoric level, it describes a succession of dark, overcast days. Although some scholars think "vendredis sanglants" designates Holy Friday, the fact that the expression is plural would seem to rule out this interpretation. The general impression of defeat is reinforced by the image of rain-drenched mourners gathered around a gravesite. The last line is modeled on a colorful expression employed when the sun and rain appear simultaneously: "Le diable bat sa femme et marie sa fille" ("The Devil beats his wife and marries off his daughter"). Although "la femme du diable" could conceivably refer to Lilith, it is hard to imagine what role she could play here.

> Puis dans un port' d'automne aux feuilles indécises
> Quand les mains de la foule y feuillolaient aussi

Sur le pont du vaisseau il posa sa valise
      Et s'assit

Les vents de l'Océan en soufflant leurs menaces
Laissaient dans ses cheveux de longs baisers mouillés
Des émigrants tendaient vers le port leurs mains lasses
Et d'autres en pleurants'étaient agenouillés.

(Then in an Autumn port with hesitant leaves
When the crowd's hands fluttered like leaves too
He set his suitcase on the ship's deck
      And sat down

Breathing their threats the Ocean winds
Left long moist kisses in his hair
Some emigrants held their weary hands out toward the port
And others knelt and cried.)

At this point, Apollinaire fast-forwards to the next day, which, as he announced earlier, is when his ship is scheduled to leave. The fact that it is autumn guarantees the scene will be steeped in melancholy. In contrast to the poet, who is determined to depart, the leaves on the trees are "indécises." They can't decide whether to stick to the branches or to fall to the ground. Once again, Apollinaire makes use of one of his favorite images. Whereas the leaves in "Rhenane d'automne" resemble hands (see Chapter 1), the hands in "L'Emigrant de Landor Road" resemble leaves. Accordingly, the crowd waving goodbye to their friends and relatives—the third crowd we have encountered—reminds him of leaves fluttering to the ground. In contrast to everyone else, Apollinaire has no one to see him off. Making his way through the delirious multitude, he boards the ship, finds a place to sit, and puts his suitcase down beside him.

The last two lines convey his indifference to the spectacle around him. Gothot-Mersch concludes that, since Apollinaire has only one suitcase, he is traveling in steerage.[27] However, other bags could be waiting for him in his stateroom, where he could plan to retire after the ship gets under way. At the moment, he is simply watching the preparations for departure. While many of the emigrants are overcome by emotion as the ship departs, Apollinaire is simply glad to be leaving.

Il regarda longtemps les rives qui moururent
Seuls des bateaux d'enfant tremblaient à l'horizon

Un tout petit bouquet flottant à l'aventure
Couvrit l'Océan d'une immense floraison

Il aurait voulu ce bouquet comme la gloire
Jouer dans d'autres mers parmitous les dauphins
    Et l'on tissait dans sa mémoire
    Une tapisserie sans fin
    Qui figurait son histoire.

(He looked a long time at the dying shores
Only a few toy boats trembled on the horizon
A tiny bouquet floating at random
Covered the Ocean with an immense flowering

He would have liked to hold that bouquet like glory
Playing in other seas among all the dolphins
    And an endless tapestry
    Was woven in his memory
    That pictured his story.)

As the ship draws farther and farther away from land, Apollinaire stares at the receding shore. While he is happy to be leaving England, the intensity of his gaze suggests that he has a few regrets. Unlike the subject of "Mandalay," who yearns to return to a tropical paradise, he has no idea what to expect in America. Whereas the former has a girlfriend waiting for him, he has no one at all. If only things had worked out between him and Annie!

By this time, his ship has come so far that the boats back in the port look like children's toys. Several critics have pointed out the resemblance between the first two lines and the conclusion of Rimbaud's "Le Bateau ivre."[28] Looking over the railing, Apollinaire spies a tiny bouquet floating in the water. While Robert Faurisson thinks he dropped it in the water himself *in memoriam*, it is impossible to say where it has come from.[29] Unexpectedly, the bouquet expands to cover the entire ocean. Faurisson suggests that the petals are widely dispersed by the waves. It is also possible that Apollinaire is hallucinating. The first two lines in the second stanza are far from clear. The speaker seems to associate the bouquet with glory and fantasizes about frolicking with dolphins "dans d'autres mers." To be sure, Faurisson interjects, Apollinaire would have preferred a wedding bouquet and a honeymoon somewhere nice with Annie. Whatever the explanation for the image, all sorts of memories come flooding back. Noting that they form "une tapisserie sans fin," Laforgue detects a reference to Penelope in the *Odyssey*.[30]

Mais pour noyer changées en poux
Ces tisseuses têtues qui sans cesse interrogent
    Il se maria comme un doge
Aux cris d'une sirène moderne sans époux

Gonfle-toi vers la nuit Ô mer Les yeux des squales
Jusqu'à l'aube ont guetté de loin avidement
Des cadavres de jours rongés par les étoiles
Parmi le bruit des flots et les derniers serments.

    (But in order to drown these stubborn weavers
Changed into lice that ceaselessly interrogated him
      He got married like a Doge
To the cries of a modern siren with no spouse

Swell up toward the night O Sea until dawn
The sharks' eyes have watched avidly from afar
The days' corpses gnawed by the stars
Among the sound of the waves and last promises.)

As Morhange-Bégué and Lartigue state, the way in which Apollinaire treats memories is virtually unprecedented. Amazingly, "le souvenir n'est jamais associé au bonheur, à la joie de vivre: c'est un thème de mort" ("memories are never associated with happiness, with the joy of living: the theme is associated with death").[31] The image of the memorial tapestry continues into the next stanza, where a host of weavers torture Apollinaire with painful memories of the past. If the situation weren't so serious, the pun would be amusing. The weavers are "têtues" not only because they are relentless but also because they are situated inside the poet's head. In fact they are so irritating, so hard to get rid of, that he compares them to head lice. Seeking to rid himself of these parasitic memories, he adopts a drastic solution. He dives head first into the water in order to drown them. Instead of marrying Annie, ironically, he chooses to marry the sea—like the Doge of Venice every year on Ascension Day. Whereas the Venetian leader's action is purely symbolic, Apollinaire's action is presumably fatal. Alerted by one of his officers that a passenger has jumped overboard, the captain repeatedly sounds the ship's siren. Because sirens also figure in the Odyssey, like the "tapisserie sans fin," Laforgue argues that "L'Emigrant de Landor Road" is modeled on Homer's text.[32] At the same time, he is forced to confess that there are major problems with this interpretation.

The final stanza was taken from a poem entitled "Le Printemps," which Apollinaire cannibalized on several other occasions.[33] As several writers have pointed out, it is also reminiscent of the sixth stanza of "Le Bateau ivre."[34] Except for the two quatrains containing a monologue, "L'Emigrant de Landor Road" is written entirely in the past tense. Beginning with a puzzling apostrophe addressed to the sea, the last stanza brings the story up to the present. After a terrible night, during which lovers whisper tender words to each other as the stars gnaw on remnants of the day, it is finally morning. Unfortunately, now that it is daylight, hungry sharks are prepared to eat whatever is left—including Apollinaire's waterlogged corpse. Not surprisingly, there is some disagreement about how the conclusion should be interpreted. As Laforgue notes, the reference to the "cadavres des jours" completes the thematic circle of mutilation. According to him, the poem concludes with "le tableau macabre d'un démembrement cosmique" ("the macabre picture of a cosmic dismembering").[35] However, Gothot-Mersch is considerably more optimistic. According to her, the poem ends with the birth of a new day "lavé de tout souvenir de ce petit drame humain" ("cleansed of any memory of this little human drama").[36] Like these two interpretations, "L'Emigrant de Landor Road" alternates between melancholy and optimism, which, as Renaud points out, are the two principal sources of Apollinaire's poetry.[37]

Ultimately, how one interprets the poem depends on how one understands Apollinaire's suicidal gesture. Whether the reader is buoyed by hope or gives in to despair hinges on this single climactic act. Since most critics are convinced that his character drowned to death, they view "L'Emigrant de Landor Road" as a tragedy. For them it is the story of an honorable man, who, rejected by the woman he loves and haunted by painful memories, decides to kill himself. At the same time, a small but vocal minority insists that the character in the poem does not die at all. For Michel Décaudin, the suicide serves as a kind of symbolic shorthand. The emigrant drowns his terrible thoughts and memories but not himself.[38] In a similar vein, Marc Poupon views the suicide as a blessing in disguise. Relieved of his terrible burden, the emigrant is free to become a new man.[39] Critics interested in mythography are also convinced that he does not drown, but for a wholly different reason. Since he is a solar hero, they explain, his fate is intimately bound up with that of the sun. Instead of dying, he rises and falls with the solar disc, drowning himself in the sea every evening but reappearing without fail in the morning.[40] As long as the sun continues to shine, therefore, the emigrant will continue to live.

"1909"

The history of Apollinaire's opinions regarding the world of fashion has yet to be written. Whoever undertakes this fascinating task will need to include

"Chapeau-Tombeau" and "1909," both of which satirize contemporary fashions. The first poem was inspired by stuffed birds that had begun to appear on women's hats in the early twentieth century.[41] It ridiculed both the original designers and the women who wore these strange creations. The second poem was inspired by a similar experience and is equally scathing. Unlike most of the poems in *Alcools*, "1909" was not published beforehand. The only known manuscript is a punctuated version consisting of two sheets numbered 88 and 89.[42] Following the third stanza, another stanza has been crossed out: "Pareils au col candide / De l'amant divin et ailé / De cette Léda solitaire / Que deux étoiles appellent une mère" ("Like the candid neck / of the divine and winged lover / Of that solitary Leda / Whom two stars call mother"). As Décaudin points out, the final version contains several lines borrowed from a draft of "Vendémiaire," which he believes dates from Fall 1909.[43] In all probability, therefore, "1909" was composed at about the same time. Although Décaudin suggests the poem was inspired by Baudelaire's "Recueillement," the resemblance is distant at best.[44] In actuality, Verlaine's "Une Grande Dame" is a much more likely candidate. The similarity between it and "1909" is simply striking. A satirical poem like "Monsieur Prudhomme," it describes an extremely beautiful woman whose arrogance leaves the viewer only two choices:

> Belle "à damner les saints," à troubler sous l'aumusse
> Un vieux juge! Elle marche impérialement,
> Elle parle—et ses dents font un miroitement—
> Italian, avec un léger accent russe.
>
> Ses yeux froids où l'émail sertit le bleu de Prusse
> Ont l'éclat insolent et dur du diamant.
> Pour la splendeur du sein, pour le rayonnement
> De la peau, nulle reine ou courtisane, fût-ce
>
> Cléopâtre la lynce ou la chatte Ninon,
> N'égale sa beauté patricienne, non!
> Vois, ô bon Buridan: "c'est une grande dame!"
>
> Il faut—pas de milieu!—l'adorer à genoux,
> Plat, n'ayant d'astre aux cieux que ses lourdes cheveux roux,
>
> Ou bien lui cravacher la face, à cette femme!
>
> (Beautiful enough "to damn the saints," to trouble
> An old judge beneath his robes! She walks imperially,

> She speaks—and her teeth sparkle wildly—
> Italian, with a slight Russian accent.
>
> Her cold eyes whose enamel clasps the Prussian blue
> Have the hard, insolent brightness of a diamond
> As for her splendorous breast, the effulgence
> Of her skin, no queen or courtesan, even
>
> Cleopatra the lynx or the cat Ninon,
> equals her patrician beauty, no!
> Observe, my good Buridan: "she is a great lady!"
>
> One must—nothing less—adore her on one's knees,
> Since there is no other star in the sky than her luxurious red hair,
> Or else take a horsewhip to the woman's face!)

As mentioned earlier, Apollinaire was essentially a collage poet. Long before Cubism was invented, he developed a patchwork method of constructing his works that suited his restless intelligence. When he encountered the Cubists, this method simply accelerated. Borrowing phrases, verses, indeed whole stanzas from his large repository of personal documents, Apollinaire managed to integrate them into seamless compositions. He never seemed to throw anything away. Bits and pieces of other poems, rough drafts of earlier projects, notes scribbled down in haste—everything was grist for his poetic mill. As will gradually become apparent, "1909" was constructed in a similar manner. Written almost entirely in free verse, the poem is divided into seven unequal stanzas, one of which is a single line. Unexpectedly, some of the lines in the fifth stanza rhyme. While the verses vary considerably in length, there is a sprinkling of octosyllables, decasyllables, and alexandrines.

With one exception, "1909" is written entirely in the imperfect tense. Jean Richer's theory that it was mainly intended to be read after Apollinaire's death is thoroughly unconvincing (as is his numerological analysis).[45] However, since Apollinaire recounts events that occurred in the past, the poem must have been composed after 1909—probably in the following year. Although the title is maddeningly precise, it does not seem to refer to a specific event. Nothing in the work evokes F. T. Marinetti's *Futurist Manifesto*, for example, or the first flight across the Channel, both of which received lots of publicity that year. Perhaps Apollinaire simply chose the title because, as Etienne-Alain Hubert intimates, the word "neuf" (new) occurs twice in the text.[46] Whatever the explanation, the poem opens with a portrait of a fashionably dressed woman:

> La dame avait une robe
> En ottoman violine
> Et sa tunique brodée d'or
> Etait composée de deux panneaux
> S'attachant sur l'épaule.

> (The lady wore a dress
> Made of violet ottoman fabric
> And her tunic embroidered with gold
> Was composed of two panels
> Attached at the shoulder.)

Dazzled as much by the woman's beauty as by her sudden appearance, Jean-Claude Chevalier calls her a "femme de féerie [qui] se dévoile comme irréelle" ("fairy woman who turns out to be unreal").[47] Benefiting from an experienced feminine eye, Laurence Campa describes the woman as "classique, harmonieuse, elegante et froide comme un médaillon" ("classical, harmonious, elegant, and cold as a medallion").[48]

Also known as "grogram" (*grosgrain* in French), ottoman is a ribbed fabric, like corduroy, made either of silk or of cotton and silky yarn. It is mostly worn on formal dress occasions. Citing the relevant line from "1909," *Le Petit Robert* defines the adjective *violine* as "de couleur violet pourpre" ("purplish violet"). Apparently influenced by Richer's article, Madeleine Boisson believes this color symbolized Apollinaire's fear of dying in 1909.[49] However, as Hubert has demonstrated, there is nothing sinister about the color or about the woman's dress.[50] Like the ottoman fabric and the tunic with two panels, the colors mauve and plum were all the rage in 1909. Similarly, no evidence exists that Apollinaire believed he might die that year. As Décaudin was the first to suggest, the woman in the poem was probably modeled on a fashion illustration.[51] Apollinaire probably found the original picture in a magazine or on a calendar, which would explain why the portrait is so precise. While the first stanza describes the woman's clothes, the second focuses on her face:

> Les yeux dansants comme des anges
> Elle riait elle riait
> Elle avait un visage aux couleurs de France
> Les yeux bleus les dents blanches et les lèvres très rouges
> Elle avait un visage aux couleurs de France.

> (Her eyes dancing like angels
> She laughed she laughed

> She had a face with French colors
> Blue eyes white teeth and very red lips
> She had a face with French colors.)

Interestingly, the first three verses were taken almost verbatim from another poem entitled "L'Anguille."[52] The initial image establishes the poem's mood and, without really meaning to, demonstrates Apollinaire's surprising erudition. Since angels do not normally indulge in frivolous pursuits, the fact that they are dancing is surprising. Apollinaire knew from his studies of angelology, however, that angels are called "dance masters" in the Talmud. As Scott Bates indicates, this is probably the source of the angels in "1909," who can be found in other texts as well.[53] Nevertheless, paintings of dancing angels also exist that, despite their rarity, could also have influenced Apollinaire. The Musée Condé possesses a canvas by Giovanni di Paolo di Grazia (1403–1483), for example, entitled *Five Angels Dancing Before the Sun*. In contrast to the first stanza, which is completely static, the second is filled with flirtatious activity. While the woman may be narcissistic, as Apollinaire implies, she is certainly not as cold as a medallion. Despite her initial appearance, she turns out to be quite vivacious. The fact that she was so attractive presented a problem initially, since Apollinaire wanted his readers to laugh at her rather than admire her. Ultimately, to be sure, his remarks are aimed at the class to which she belongs—the *haute bourgeoisie*. To overcome this problem, he adopted two ingenious strategies: senseless repetition and patent absurdity. The former is exemplified by the second line "Elle riait elle riait," which represents two bursts of laughter. The latter is represented by the third line, which compares the woman's face to the French flag. Employed simultaneously in the last verse, these strategies create a humorous effect that is simply devastating. The source of this humor is the unrelenting banality that pervades the stanza. It sounds as if a child or a simpleton is speaking. Citing the reference to the French flag, Pierre Brunel suggests the scene might take place the night before Bastille Day, which is certainly possible.[54]

The next stanza is composed of only three lines:

> Elle était décolletée en rond
> Et coiffée à la Récamier
> Avec de beaux bras nus.

> (She wore a scoop-neck dress both front and back
> And her hair in the style of Mme Récamier
> With beautiful bare arms.)

Focusing on the woman's body, the description closely resembles the famous portrait of Mme Récamier by Jacques-Louis David (Figure 4.1). Like Mme Récamier, the woman is wearing a low-cut dress that reveals her creamy skin and shapely arms. Like her, she is wearing a golden headband that barely contains her loosely styled curls. Despite these striking similarities, "1909" is the product of a completely different time and place. For some reason, the woman in the poem is wearing clothes that have been out of fashion for more than a century. Thanks to some excellent detective work by Hubert, we finally know the reason why.[55] The winter of 1908 witnessed a widespread revival of Directory and Empire fashions, which appealed to a whole new audience. Like velvet and ottoman fabric, tunics with multiple panels were suddenly back in style. Women not only began to dress like Mme Récamier but also adopted her distinctive hairstyle. Like "1909," another poem written at the same time incorporates the latest clothing styles. Probably written for Louise Lalanne, Apollinaire's imaginary alter ego, it concludes with two fashionable alexandrines: "Ma robe est aujourd'hui en velours raisiné / Et ma longue jaquette est genre Directoire" ("My dress today is of blood-red velvet / And my long jacket is in Directory style").[56]

Figure 4.1. Jacques-Louis David, *Madame Récamier*
Musée du Louvre/Angèle Dequier—M. Bard.

The next stanza in "1909" consists of a single line, which abruptly interrupts the previous description: "N'entendra-t-on jamais sonner minuit" ("Will midnight never sound").Writing in 1963, Décaudin suggested the verse refers to New Year's Eve, when people everywhere eagerly wait for the clock to strike twelve.[57] Eventually, he expanded his hypothesis to include two additional bits of information. The scene takes place on December 31, 1908, he insisted, and the anonymous woman represents the new year, which is ready to arrive.[58] Since this interpretation was the only one available for a great many years, critics have tended to accept it at face value. Unfortunately, upon closer examination, it appears to be seriously flawed. The scene does not take place on New Year's Eve, and the woman does not represent 1909. She is simply a narcissistic clothes horse whom Apollinaire enjoys ridiculing. Among other things, as we will see, this completely changes the way the conclusion has been interpreted. And once New Year's Eve has been ruled out, there is no reason to think that "1909" was inspired by "Recueillement" as Décaudin suggests.

If the single verse stanza does not refer to the fashionable woman, to whom does it refer? Who else is waiting anxiously for midnight to sound? The answer is almost certainly Cinderella, whose time at the ball is quickly running out. Apollinaire's question, "N'entendra-t-on jamais sonner minuit," is practical applied to the New Year's Eve situation but purely rhetorical applied to Cinderella's situation, where it has metaphorical overtones. Assuming that everyone is impatient for 1909 to dawn, as the first scenario claims, what exactly would the woman's role be? What does she really have to contribute other than her physical presence? Unfortunately, there is no indication anywhere in the poem. There is no reason to suspect that 1909 would be any better or any worse than 1908. At this point, the question loses most of its interest, and the New Year's Eve scenario self-destructs. Assuming that the question refers to Cinderella, it becomes an accusation. Uttered in an incredulous voice, it acquires the force of an exclamation: "Will you look at those airs she is putting on!" Or alternatively, "Who does she think she is?" Once again the woman is subjected to ridicule. Dressed in her latest finery, she resembles Cinderella dressed for the ball. Each woman is a bogus princess. Viewed in this perspective, Apollinaire's question can be rephrased as, "Won't she ever give up this nonsense?" To be sure, the answer is inevitably no. Unlike Cinderella, who knows her time is limited, the woman plans to keep up her pretense indefinitely. The next stanza describes her clothing in more detail:

> La dame en robe d'ottoman violine
> Et en tunique brodée d'or
> Décolletée en rond

Promenait ses boucles
Son bandeau d'or
Et traînait ses petits souliers à boucles.

(The Lady wearing a dress of violet ottoman
And a tunic embroidered with gold
Scooped low both front and back
Shook her curls
Her golden headband
And dragged her little buckled slippers.)

Although there are no outrageous statements this time, there is considerable repetition again. Borrowed from previous stanzas, the first three lines strike a hollow note, one after the other, as the reader descends the page. Not surprisingly, the sense of *déjà vu* (or *déjà entendu*) is intense. Among other things, one finally realizes why some of the lines are rhymed. In order to heap even more ridicule on the woman, Apollinaire employs two sets of *rimes banales*: "d'or" / "d'or" and "boucles" / "boucles." As before, the reader feels like he or she is the butt of some mysterious joke. The banality is almost overpowering. As Hubert has shown, golden headbands and tiny slippers with buckles were very popular at the time. The more stylish slippers came in gold or silver colors. Judging from the last three lines, the woman is dragging her slippers as she walks, stopping from time to time to show off her headband, her curls, and her earrings. These stylized actions may also have been dictated by fashion. Whatever the explanation, she obviously enjoys attracting attention to herself. Ironically, Apollinaire confides in the next stanza, "Elle était si belle / Que tu n'aurais pas osé l'aimer." Despite her best efforts to appear attractive, men hesitate to approach her. Why this should be is difficult to say. Perhaps her narcissism drives men away. Perhaps she is so beautiful that men don't think they stand a chance with her.

The final stanza introduces another kind of woman altogether:

J'aimais les femmes atroces dans les quartiers énormes
Où naissaient chaque jour quelques êtres nouveaux
Le fer était leur sang la flamme leur cerveau
J'aimais j'aimais le peuple habile des machines
Le luxe et la beauté ne sont que son écume
Cette femme etait si belle
Qu'elle me faisait peur.

(She was so beautiful
That you wouldn't have dared love her

> I have loved awful women in vast quarters
> Where each day new beings were born
> Iron was their blood flame their brain
> I loved I loved the people skilled with machines
> Luxury and beauty are only froth to them
> That woman was so beautiful
> She frightened me.)

Without any warning, the scene shifts abruptly from the center of town to the outskirts. All of a sudden the reader is transported to a grimy industrial area. Additional changes are evident as well. Whereas the poem's first half was dominated by octosyllabic rhythms, the second half consists entirely of alexandrines. The last two verses simply need to be combined. More importantly, Apollinaire switches from impersonal third person narration to the first person. The change in rhythm and perspective prepares the reader for some intimate revelations. However, the most important change concerns the "dame" in the first part, who is replaced by several "femmes" in the second part. The change in terminology is significant. There is nothing ladylike about the women who work with machinery. In fact, as the poet himself tells us, they are "atroces." What this means is not completely clear, but it is not a flattering portrait. *Le Petit Robert* gives the following synonyms: "abominable, affreux, effroyable, épouvantable, horrible, monstrueux" ("abominable, awful, frightening, terrible, horrible, monstrous"). If the fashionable lady flaunts her beauty, the industrial women have no beauty to flaunt. A similar ambiguity characterizes the "quartiers énormes" where the women live, which may be either very large, extraordinary, or monstrous. Donald Revell translates the expression as "awful places," William Meredith chooses "monstrous places," and Anne Hyde Greet opts for "crowded slums."[59] What matters is that they do not live in one of *les beaux quartiers* like the first woman. They have been working with machines for so long that they have nearly become machines themselves. Since their world is dominated by iron and fire, luxury and beauty hold few attractions. They are not nearly as exciting as industrial modernity.

Ironically, although the fashionable lady is very attractive, Apollinaire prefers the other women because they are more down to earth. Like Cinderella's prince, who chooses to marry a scullery maid, he values integrity more than superficial appearance. Despite their unconventional look, the industrial women possess a beauty of their own—a purely modern beauty. As Décaudin declares, "1909" is structured around a binary opposition between "[la] beauté luxueuse de la femme et [la] beauté nouvelle . . . de la vie industrielle" ("[the] luxurious beauty of the lady and [the] new beauty . . .

of industrial life).[60] Luxury is contrasted with poverty, sterility with fertility, order with adventure, and so forth. The list can be extended indefinitely. Among other things the poem serves as an excellent *ars poetica*. In art as in life, Apollinaire rejects the artificial in favor of the genuine, the superficial in favor of the authentic, and the imitation in favor of the real. While the beautiful "dame" is more attractive, the industrial "femmes" are more approachable, more in touch with life. "This represents a further stage in Apollinaire's progression towards a preoccupation with the presence of the city," Garnet Rees notes, "which is clearly described in 'Vendémiaire.'"[61] It is also another indication that the poem was composed in 1909 or 1910. Scott Bates detects an important political dimension that has escaped notice until now. In his opinion, the lady and the women represent different visions of the French nation, which has turned its back on the proletariat: "From a rough beauty fashioned by the hands of workers, France has become a very chic Marianne indeed with her elegant ottoman gown."[62] Perhaps there will be a workers' uprising, he adds, when the clock strikes twelve.

Originally intended for "Vendémiaire," the final stanza was conceived while Apollinaire was flirting with Unanimism. In particular, it seems to have grown out of his plans to create a revolutionary calendar in verse. Embodying the Unanimist philosophy, the stanza stresses the importance of fraternity and solidarity. This is why Apollinaire speaks of atrocious women in general. This is why he praises "le peuple habile des machines." His affection is only directed at them insofar as they constitute a group, and it reflects his sympathy for workers everywhere. While their world is harsh, brutal, and vulgar, Jean-Charles Gateau explains, it contains great poetic potential, "Le rôle du poète est de le mettre au jour" ("the poet's role is to reveal it").[63] Thus the last stanza represents a kind of manifesto. For the very first time, Apollinaire announces his intention to speak for modern society, to incorporate modern aesthetics into his poetry. However, as Renaud has shown, this brave new stance was preceded by considerable ambivalence.[64] A rough draft reveals that Apollinaire viewed the factory workers at first as threats. His task was to protect poetry from the workers rather than to celebrate them. Nor did Apollinaire show any interest in becoming a modern poet. At the time, he was merely trying to establish himself as a serious poet. Bridging the gap between his initial efforts and the finished stanza required him to undergo an immense transformation. Apollinaire needed to completely reconceptualize what he was doing.

Hubert suspects the poet still continues to lust after the beautiful lady when the poem ends. The last two lines "sonnent comme le retour obstiné de l'ambivalence insurmontable entre la crainte et le désir qu'inspire la femme" ("sound like the stubborn return of the insurmountable ambivalence between fear and desire that the woman inspires").[65] In a similar vein, Anna Boschetti evokes Apollinaire's "peur fascinée de la femme" ("fascinated fear of the woman").[66] Guillaume Robichez even goes so far as to suggest that Apollinaire may have been suffering from a castration complex.[67] Although the verses were originally set off from the preceding stanza, Apollinaire decided to join them together for *Alcools*. Unfortunately, this has caused a certain amount of confusion. Both Brunel and Chevalier appear to believe the two lines describe one of the atrocious women.[68] Admittedly, the situation is complicated by the fact that the text says "cette femme" instead of "cette dame," but there is only one possible antecedent: the beautiful lady. In addition, the two lines closely paraphrase an earlier stanza: "Elle était si belle / Que tu ne l'aurais pas osé l'aimer." To be sure, the attraction Apollinaire experiences for her is quite different from that which he feels for the other women. While the first is simply lust, the second expresses his sympathy and admiration. Although the lady has basically taught him nothing, the women have taught him to appreciate modern industrial beauty. Thanks to their knowledge of machinery, moreover, they are destined to transform the world. In the last analysis, they are the ones who really incarnate 1909.

Notes

1. Margaret Davies, *Apollinaire* (New York: St. Martin's, 1964), 88.

2. Philippe Renaud, *Lecture d'Apollinaire* (Lausanne: L'Age d'Homme, 1969), 63.

3. Marie-Jeanne Durry, *Guillaume Apollinaire: "Alcools,"* Vol. 3 (Paris: SEDES, 1964), 40.

4. Pierre Laforgue, "'L'Emigrant de Landor Road': poète cou coupé," *Apollinaire: Revue d'Etudes Apollinariennes*, No. 11 (June 2012), 53.

5. LeRoy C. Breunig, *Guillaume Apollinaire* (New York: Columbia University Press, 1969), 23–24.

6. Michel Décaudin, *Le Dossier d'"Alcools,"* rev. ed. (Paris: Minard, 1965), 169.

7. Durry, *Guillaume Apollinaire*, 2:144.

8. Gilberte Jacaret, *La Dialectique de l'ironie et du lyrisme dans "Alcools" et "Calligrammes" de G. Apollinaire* (Paris: Nizet, 1984), 84.

9. André Breton, "Entretiens 1913–1952," repr. in *Oeuvres complètes*, Vol. 3, ed. Marguerite Bonnet et al. (Paris: Gallimard, 1999), 438.

10. Renaud, *Lecture d'Apollinaire*, 63.

11. Laforgue, "'L'Emigrant de Landor Road,'"45.

12. Claudine Gothot-Mersch, "'L'Emigrant de Landor Road' de Guillaume Apollinaire," *Cahiers d'Analyse Textuelle*, No. 8 (1966), 25.

13. Durry, *Guillaume Apollinaire*, 3:37.

14. I. Merlin, "Poésie contemporaine. Guillaume Apollinaire: 'L'Emigrant de Landor Road,'" *L'Ecole des Lettres*, Vol. 60, No. 10 (February 15, 1969), 501.

15. Laforgue, "'L'Emigrant de Landor Road,'" 45.

16. L. C. Breunig, "Apollinaire et Annie Playden," *Mercure de France*, April 1, 1952, 650.

17. Merlin, "Poésie contemporaine," 502.

18. Anne Hyde Greet, tr. *"Alcools." Guillaume Apollinaire* (Berkeley: University of California Press, 1965), 249.

19. Renaud, *Lecture d'Apollinaire*, 64.

20. Scott Bates, *Guillaume Apollinaire*, rev. ed. (Boston: Twayne, 1989), 47.

21. Roger Lefèvre, *Apollinaire. "Alcools"* (Paris: Nouveaux Classiques Larousse, 1965), 68 n3. Gothot-Mersch comes to the same conclusion in "'L'Emigrant de Landor Road,'" 29.

22. Durry, *Guillaume Apollinaire*, 3:37, and Merlin, "Poésie contemporaine," 502.

23. Laurence Perfézou, *"Alcools." Apollinaire* (Paris: Bordas, 1988), 11.

24. Claude Morhange-Bégué and Pierre Lartigue, *"Alcools." Apollinaire* (Paris: Hatier, 1991), 15.

25. Guillaume Apollinaire, *Oeuvres poétiques*, ed. Marcel Adéma and Michel Décaudin (Paris: Gallimard, 1965), 332.

26. Gothot-Mersch, "'L'Emigrant de Landor Road,'" 32.

27. Ibid., 33.

28. See Durry, *Guillaume Apollinaire*, 2:69.

29. Robert Faurisson, "Notes sur *Alcools*," *L'Information Littéraire*, No. 1 (January–February 1967), 41.

30. Laforgue, "'L'Emigrant de Landor Road,'" 42.

31. Morhange-Bégué and Lartigue, *"Alcools." Apollinaire*, 48.

32. Laforgue, "'L'Emigrant de Landor Road,'" 43.

33. Apollinaire, *Oeuvres poétiques*, 556.

34. See Durry, *Guillaume Apollinaire*, 2:69–70.

35. Laforgue, "'L'Emigrant de Landor Road,'" 50.

36. Gothot-Mersch, "'L'Emigrant de Landor Road,'" 38.

37. Renaud, *Lecture d'Apollinaire*, 65.

38. Michel Décaudin, discussion following the paper by Marc Poupon in note 38, 151.

39. Marc Poupon, "'Lul de Faltenin,' et l'etymologie," *Du Monde européen à l'univers des mythes*, ed. Michel Décaudin (Paris: Minard, 1970), 140.

40. Ibid.; Bates, *Guillaume Apollinaire*, 47; and Madeleine Boisson, *Apollinaire et les mythologies antiques* (Paris: Nizet, 1989), 62.

41. For a brief analysis, see Willard Bohn, *Apollinaire on the Edge: Modern Art, Popular Culture, and the Avant-Garde* (Amsterdam: Rodopi, 2010), 71–72.

42. "La Cinquième Vente de la Bibliothèque Jacques Guérin," *QueVlo-Ve?: Bulletin International des Etudes sur Apollinaire*, 2nd series, No. 29 (January–March 1989), 26.

43. Décaudin, *Le Dossier d'"Alcools,"* 224–25.

44. Ibid., 210. J. G. Clark suggests "1909" is modeled on Théophile Gautier's "Ballade II," but again the resemblance is slight ("De fil en aiguille: complément à une étude," *Revue des Lettres Modernes*, Nos. 576–581 [1980], 40).

45. Jean Richer, "Une Prémonition d'Apollinaire: '1909,'" *French Review*, Vol. 39, No. 4 (February 1966), 491–95.

46. Etienne-Alain Hubert, "Scolies sur *Alcools*," *Littératures Contemporaines*, No. 2 (1996), 253. Jean-Charles Gateau points out that the title can also be pronounced "dis neuf, sang neuf" and "dits neufs, sang neuf" ("'1909': entre la vamp, l'aéroplane et l'anarchie" in *"Alcools" en corps, Lectures et situation du recueil d'Apollinaire*, ed. Jean-Yves Debreuille [Grenoble: Université Stendhal-Grenoble 3, 1998], 130).

47. Jean-Claude Chevalier, *"Alcools" d'Apollinaire: Essai d'analyse des formes poétiques* (Paris: Minard, 1970), 226.

48. Laurence Campa, *Guillaume Apollinaire* (Paris: Gallimard, 2013), 311.

49. Boisson, *Apollinaire et les mythologies antiques*, 357.

50. Hubert, "Scolies sur *Alcools*," 252–53.

51. Michel Décaudin, "Obscurité et composition chez Apollinaire," *Cahiers de l'Association Internationale des Etudes Françaises*, Nos. 14–15 (March 1963), 123.

52. Apollinaire, *Oeuvres poétiques*, 356.

53. Scott Bates, "Notes sur 'Simon Mage' et Isaac Laquedem," *Revue des Lettres Modernes*, Nos. 123–26 (1965), 68.

54. Pierre Brunel, *Apollinaire entre deux mondes: Mythocritique II* (Paris: Presses Universitaires de France, 1997), 126–27.

55. Hubert, "Scolies sur *Alcools*," 253.

56. Apollinaire, *Oeuvres poétiques*, 855.

57. Décaudin, "Obscurité et composition chez Apollinaire," 123.

58. See, for example, Michel Décaudin, *"Alcools" de Guillaume Apollinaire* (Paris: Gallimard, 1993), 48 and 96–97.

59. Donald Revell, tr., *Poems by Guillaume Apollinaire."Alcools"* (Middletown, CT: Wesleyan University Press, 1995), 147; William Meredith, tr., *Guillaume Apollinaire. "Alcools": Poems 1898–1913* (Garden City, NY: Doubleday, 1965), 203; Greet, tr.,*"Alcools." Guillaume Apollinaire* (Berkeley: University of California Press, 1965), 185.

60. Décaudin, *Le Dossier d' "Alcools,"* 210.

61. Garnet Rees, ed., *Guillaume Apollinaire: "Alcools"* (London: Athlone, 1975), 173.

62. Bates, *Guillaume Apollinaire*, 63.

63. Gateau, "'1909,'" 134.

64. Renaud, *Lecture d'Apollinaire*, 86–87.

65. Hubert, "Scolies sur *Alcools*," 253.

66. Anna Boschetti, *La Poésie partout: Apollinaire homme-époque (1898–1918)* (Paris: Seuil, 2001), 109.

67. Guillaume Robichez, "Note sur quelques égarements d'Apollinaire dans *Alcools*," *Revue des Lettres Modernes*, Nos. 450–55 (1976), 126–27.

68. Brunel, *Apollinaire entre deux mondes*, 127, and Chevalier, *"Alcools" d'Apollinaire*, 226.

~

CHAPTER FIVE

Discovery and Renewal

The two poems here, "Lul de Faltenin" and "Le Brasier," show Apollinaire at his most hermetic but also reveal him to be a dedicated visionary. Following a period of deep discouragement and sterility, about which we know very little, he felt the need to develop a new style, a more difficult style whose complexity reflected the multifaceted nature of reality. In turn, the new poetic style he was seeking necessitated the discovery of a new poetic language. If some of Apollinaire's earlier poems recall Verlaine, those that he wrote during his next phase remind one of Mallarmé. Influenced to some extent by a group of neo-Symbolists in Paris, he began to view each poem as an autonomous object. To a considerable extent, it was left to the reader to decide how each should be interpreted.

"Lul de Faltenin"

"L'un des poèmes les plus hermétiques d'*Alcools*" ("One of the most hermetic poems in *Alcools*") according to Marc Poupon, "Lul de Faltenin" was published in *La Phalange* on November 15, 1907, with a dedication to poet and critic Louis de Gonzague Frick.[1] In return, the latter dedicated a poem to him on the following page. Formerly students at the College de Saint-Charles in Monaco, they had recently run across each other in Paris. The only known manuscript of "Lul de Faltenin," dated November 5, 1907, was discovered by LeRoy C. Breunig.[2] Since it is written on the back of four sheets of stationary from the Hôtel zu den Vier Jahreszeiten in Munich, the manuscript could theoretically date from Spring 1902—like the manuscript of "Automne malade" (see Chapter 2). Judging from the numerous words and sentences that have been crossed out, it is the original manuscript. Although Apollinaire could have added the date when he sent it to *La Phalange*, Frick told Breunig he saw the poet working on it in 1907. Thus the date on the manuscript is probably the date it was composed. The poem itself is written in octosyllabic quintains with *rimes croisées*. As so often in his poetry, Apollinaire alternates masculine and feminine rhymes. In keeping with the poem's experimental nature, however, many of the rhymes are extremely daring. Thus "langue" is paired with "anges," "merveille" with "orgueil," and "aime" with "naine."

Although the Symbolist movement was in the process of disappearing, a few individuals were trying hard to revive it. One of these was Jean Royère, a poet and the editor of *La Phalange*, who headed a neo-Symbolist circle and who idolized Mallarmé. Since the latter was famous for his deliberate obscurity, convinced that poetry must be wrapped in mystery to remain sacred, Apollinaire set out to write a poem that would be equally hermetic. His strategy seems to have worked perfectly. Royère published "Lul de Faltenin" and two other works shortly thereafter. Because the poem is so enigmatic, so impossibly obscure, it has attracted a tremendous amount of attention—perhaps even more than "Les Colchiques." Scholars have vied with each other for years to find a key that would unlock its hidden meaning, with only partial success. That the poet was influenced by Mallarmé seems indisputable. Struck by references to a shipwreck, a broken mast, and a Siren, a number of critics have singled out "A la nue accablante tu" in particular as evidence of this. However, as Alexander Dickow has recently argued, Mallarmé's influence on Apollinaire was considerably broader than that.[3] In addition, Antoine Fongaro thinks "Lul de Faltenin" was influenced by Théophile Gautier's "Tristesse en mer," which was included in *Emaux et camées*.[4] The fact that Gautier's poem includes several references to seven swords piercing the Virgin Mary's heart makes it especially interesting (see below).

The first stumbling block confronting anyone seeking to interpret "Lul de Faltenin" is its puzzling title. Those readers who are familiar with "La Chanson du mal-aimé" will recognize it as the third sword in the section entitled "Les Sept Epées":

> La troisième bleu féminin
> N'en est pas moins un chibriape
> Appelé Lul de Faltenin
> Et que porte sur une nappe
> L'Hermès Ernest devenu nain.

(The third a feminine blue
Is nevertheless a chibriape
Called Lul de Faltenin
That a dwarf Hermes Ernest
Carries on a cloth.)

According to Scott Bates, "chibriape" is a neologism created by combining two slang words for "penis": "chibre" and "priape."[5] Similarly, according to André Fonteyne, "lul" is a common (though vulgar) Dutch and Flemish word for "penis."[6] Unlike a phallus, he adds, a "lul" is not necessarily erect. Since "Faltenin" is generally thought to be a contraction of the Latin *phallum tenens*, one wonders how a phallus can hold another phallus. Fonteyne explains that "lul" can also describe a person who is incompetent or useless—a person who spends his time masturbating. A similar expression exists in English. Unfortunately, nothing in the poem indicates that Apollinaire was aware of this meaning. The likelihood grows even more remote if, as Bates and Jean-Claude Chevalier believe, he adopts Lul de Faltenin as a pseudonym in the poem.[7] Nevertheless, Madeleine Boisson points out, the title can still be understood in two different ways: as a reference either to masturbation or to castration.[8] Indeed, the image of someone holding a detached phallus in his hand recalls "L'Hermès Ernest devenu nain," who is carrying one on a cloth. Scholars generally believe he carries his own phallus and thus that he has been castrated.

The next problem confronting the reader is to identify the poem's protagonist, who at the same time is also the narrator. All we know is that he is a sailor who, presumably lured by the song of the legendary Sirens, jumps overboard and swims to shore. Not surprisingly, since so many people have written about "Lul de Faltenin," there are a great many possibilities. Since the setting appears to be ancient Greece, Margaret Davies has suggested that he is Odysseus, Orpheus, Dionysos, and/or Heracles.[9] Other critics have proposed Jason, Icarus, Ixion, the Argonaut Butes, the sun, and Apollinaire himself. Unfortunately, there are two difficulties with this kind of approach: none of these heroes is obviously a better candidate than the others, and none of them is entirely problem-free when one attempts to plug them into the poem. Thus, we cannot say for certain that any one of them is the protagonist. As Dickow observes, the poem's irreducible ambiguities prevent the protagonist from being identified with any particular mythological character.[10] After all, "Lul de Faltenin" was conceived as a poem, not as a *roman à clef*.

In view of this unfortunate situation, it is time to consider a new approach, one for which several critics have laid the groundwork. Analyzing the poem in 1956, Breunig conflated the sailor's story with the poet (Apollinaire) and the setting sun "dans le moi du narrateur" ("in the narrator's ego").[11] Refuting a proposal to make Icarus the protagonist, Davies insisted in 1972 that the poem incorporates a "mythe composite" and that the sailor wears a succession of masks. In her view, the masks are all "transformations de ce dieu-soleil à qui le poète s'assimule dans le but . . . de rivaliser avec Dieu" ("transformations of the sun-god with whom the poet assimilates himself with the aim of . . . rivaling God").[12] Taking a walk with Louise Faure-Favier in 1913, for example, Apollinaire assumed precisely this persona: "Attendons ici, devant ce décor fluvial, le lever du soleil. Vous verrez comment je renais à l'aurore. Car je suis le cours du soleil. Je m'éteins à son coucher, je m'éveille à son lever. Je suis solaire" ("Let's wait here for the sunrise, before this river landscape. You will see how how I am reborn at dawn. For I follow the course of the sun. I go to sleep when it sets, I wake up when it rises. I am solar").[13]

It has become increasingly clear, therefore, that "Lul de Faltenin" does not have a single protagonist. On the contrary, it seems to contain a number of protagonists, traces of whom are scattered throughout the poem. Instead of focusing on a particular myth, Apollinaire seems to have decided, in the best Symbolist tradition, to create a mythological *état d'âme*. Following Mallarmé's advice to "peindre, non la chose, mais l'effet qu'elle produit" ("depict, not the thing, but the effect that it produces"), he set out to evoke the world of Greek mythology. And since he believed (or affected to believe) that he was a solar hero himself, he decided to populate his poem with other solar heroes. Because Apollinaire was simply interested in creating a mythological atmosphere, "Lul de Faltenin" only includes glimpses of these characters. Although scholars claim to have discerned different stories at different levels, except for the central plot, these are all fragmentary. The only story that really has a beginning, a middle, and an end is that of the sailor and the Sirens. Instead of employing parallel plots that take place at different levels, Apollinaire adopts a syncretic approach. Despite their lack of continuity, he blends all the different mythological strands together to form a single poem. Poupon refers to this process as "hypostasis,"[14] which is basically the same thing. Since the fragmentary stories all involve solar heroes, they basically complement each other. As the reader attempts to make sense of the central plot, different characters appear in different places depending on their familiarity with classical mythology.

> Sirènes j'ai rampé vers vos
> Grottes tiriez aux mers la langue
> En dansant devant leurs chevaux

Puis battiez de vos ailes d'anges
Et j'écoutais ces choeurs rivaux.

(Sirens I have crawled toward your Grottos
You were sticking out your tongues at the seas
While dancing before their horses
Then you flapped your angel wings
And I listened to those rival choirs.)

As the first stanza demonstrates, "Lul de Faltenin" was conceived as a dramatic monologue. Written in the past tense, it describes events that occurred sometime before the poem's narration. Although the first few words recall a verse from Gérard de Nerval's "El Desdichado"—"J'ai rêvé dans la grotte où nage la sirène" ("I have dreamed in the grotto where the siren swims")—the resemblance ends there.[15] At most, the poem might have given Apollinaire the idea of situating the action in the Sirens' grotto. And while it is tempting to compare "Lul de Faltenin" to *The Odyssey*, as several critics have done, the resemblance is largely superficial. Although Odysseus spent some time as Circe's captive, he never actually encountered the Sirens. Stuffing his crew's ears with wax and lashing himself to the mast, he sailed right by the Sirens without yielding to their song. John Wesley Cameron argues that the sailor is actually Jason, who has set sail in search of the Golden Fleece.[16] According to the *Argonautika*, however, Jason was protected by Orpheus during the voyage so he was able to safely bypass the Sirens.

By contrast, Boisson is convinced that the sailor represents Butes, the only one of the Argonauts who succumbed to the Sirens' song and jumped into the water.[17] Unfortunately, Butes was rescued by Aphrodite, who carried him off to Sicily and became his lover. Like the profiles of Odysseus and Jason, his does not really match the sailor's either. Similarly, Léon Cellier believes that the sailor is Icarus, who has just fallen into the sea—as Brueghel painted him and as W. H. Auden would later describe him.[18] Cellier believes that the first five stanzas evoke his ascent toward the sun and the last four his fall into the sea. Jean-Claude Chevalier agrees with Cellier but insists that the sailor also represents Ixion, who was bound to a fiery spinning wheel for all of eternity.[19] Once again, these tentative identifications work for a few stanzas but fail to cover the entire poem. On a more promising note, Bates, Poupon, and Phlippe Renaud think the sailor is Apollinaire himself, who in his role as poet is the ultimate narrator.[20] Nevertheless, the fact that Apollinaire is the author of "Lul de Faltenin" does not automatically make him the protagonist. The most that can be said is that his personal story parallels that of the sailor from time to time. As mentioned earlier, all of the foregoing identifications are temporarily valid. Each one appears to work for a limited amount of time, which is what makes them attractive. However, the sailor is the only character who will make it through all nine stanzas to the end.

Apparently responding to the Sirens' song, the speaker in "Lul de Faltenin" previously jumped into the sea and swam toward them. As he drew nearer, he relates, he could see the Sirens dancing "before their horses" and sticking out their tongues at the sea. For some reason, Apollinaire deleted the subject pronouns that would normally accompany "tiriez" and (in the next line) "battiez." Although there could be a metrical explanation for this, he was probably attempting to create an archaic effect as if he were writing in Old French. While "leurs chevaux" is clearly a metaphor, it is unfortunately rather ambiguous. Comparing the stanza to a similar stanza by Gautier, Antoine Fongaro concludes that it refers to the waves ("les chevaux de la mer").[21] However, it is equally possible that Apollinaire is alluding to a group of seahorses (*chevaux marins*) cavorting in the sea. Fongaro goes on to explain that the "ailes d'anges" mentioned in the next line belong to the Sirens. Although they are angels, he continues, they are "anges du mal" rather than "anges du paradis." Unlike Roman Sirens, who closely resembled mermaids, Greek Sirens were portrayed as birds with the head and bust of a woman (Figure 5.1).

Figure 5.1. A Greek Siren
Georg Weicher, *Der Seelenvogel in der alten Litteratur une Kunst* (1902).

The stanza concludes with two rival choruses, the sea and the Sirens, attempting to drown each other out. According to Boisson's scenario, which as noted is problematic, the rivalry is between Orpheus and the Sirens:

> Une arme ô ma tête inquiète
> J'agite un feuillard défleuri
> Pour écarter l'haleine tiède
> Qu'exhalent contre mes grand cris
> Vos terribles bouches muettes
>
> Il y a là-bas la merveille
> Au prix d'elle que valez-vous
> Le sang jaillit de mes otelles
> A mon aspect et je l'avoue
> Le meurtre de mon double orgueil.
>
> (A weapon O my troubled head
> I shake a blossomless branch
> To fan the tepid breath away
> That your terrible mute mouths
> Exhale against my loud cries
>
> The marvel is down there
> What are you worth compared to it
> Blood spurts from my heraldic wounds
> At my approach and I confess
> The murder of my double pride.)

The remainder of the poem is written in the dramatic present. Thus, the action takes place at the same time as its narration. As the reader soon learns, the adventurous sailor suffers from a number of fresh wounds. Perhaps his shipmates attempted to prevent him from jumping overboard, or perhaps he injured himself when he jumped. Feeling feverish in any case, he searches for a weapon and seizes a bare branch—not with the intention of performing an exorcism, as Poupon suggests, but in order to defend himself.[22] Not only are the monstrous Sirens frightening to look at, but also their breath is unbelievably foul. Whereas they have finally stopped singing, the sailor is yelling at the top of his lungs—whether from fear or from anger is hard to say. Several critics have wondered why the Sirens suddenly fall silent. Once they have managed to seduce the sailor, Cellier explains, they do not need to sing anymore.[23] Their song has accomplished its objective. According to Boisson's own scenario there is a musical rivalry between Orpheus and the Sirens.

Although the Sirens have succeeded in attracting the sailor, he remains curiously defiant. Unexpectedly, his best defense turns out to be his sharp tongue. Compared to "la merveille" ("the marvel"), he tells the bird-women, they are completely worthless. The identity of this mysterious entity has preoccupied scholars for years. According to Cameron's version, it is the Golden Fleece. According to Boisson's, it is Orpheus and his sailors, winners of a singing contest with the Sirens. The best guess is probably by Renaud, who proposes that the second great love of Apollinaire's life, Marie Laurencin, is "la merveille."[24] Since Apollinaire met her the same year he composed "Lul de Faltenin," she could also be "l'attentive et bien-apprise," who figures in the seventh stanza. Davies has a different take altogether. Like the stars and the fire in later stanzas, she declares, "la merveille" represents the sailor's poetic ambitions: "The poem represents the conflict that the young swimmer (Odysseus) experiences when he is attracted on the one hand by the sirens, and on the other by poetry and glory."[25] Bates also thinks that the stars and the swimmer are symbols of aspiration, but in his opinion "la merveille" alludes to masturbation.[26] This is the only interpretation that attempts to account for the poem's title. However, Poupon has a more provocative explanation. In his opinion, the Sirens are prostitutes, the sailor is a patron, and "la merveille" is the sun.[27] Although Bates and Renaud agree that the Sirens are prostitutes, they believe the sailor represents Apollinaire, which, of course he does from time to time.[28] As noted earlier, however, the references to Apollinaire are sporadic and unsystematic.

Viewed in this light, the Sirens' irresistible song turns out to be a metaphor for sexual attraction. Their "terribles bouches" ("terrible mouths") seem to be their vulvas, which, among other things, explains why they are "muettes" ("mute"). In fact, "Lul de Faltenin" is filled with sexual references (like the title) and with sexual symbols (like the very first sentence). The fact that the poem was composed in 1907 makes this interpretation all the more attractive. Earlier in the year, Picasso had completed *Les Demoiselles d'Avignon* and had shown it to Apollinaire.[29] There is good reason to believe that Apollinaire decided to do in poetry what his friend was doing in painting. Galvanized by *Le Bordel d'Avignon*, as it was originally called, he chose to depict a similar scene in a style that would be as impenetrable as the painting. He could call the prostitutes "Sirens," and nobody would suspect who they really were. This, then, is one of the reasons that "Lul de Faltenin" is so difficult to penetrate. A significant amount of the poem serves essentially as camouflage. The poem was influenced not only by Mallarmé but also by Picasso. Since there was a sailor in earlier versions of the painting, which

Apollinaire had doubtless seen, he decided to include him in the poem as well. One wonders if he ever told Picasso about his ambitious project. What all this means, finally, is that "la merveille" must be a woman rather than an object or a concept. The reason she is so superior to the Sirens, one begins to realize, is because she represents pure, unsullied love. Sex is not a commercial transaction for her but rather the highest expression of a noble emotion. It begins to look more and more like Apollinaire was thinking of Marie Laurencin, with whom he had recently fallen deeply in love. Since he had a new lover, it is hard to believe, as Bates and Poupon both assert, that he loses himself in masturbation.

Bleeding copiously from his mysterious wounds, the sailor confesses to the murder of his "double orgueil" ("double pride"). What this means is anybody's guess. Since it could conceivably refer to his testicles, some critics have inferred that Apollinaire suffered from impotence or from a castration complex. Coming after his personal crisis in 1906, the expression could also allude to the absence of love and inspiration that had plagued him until recently. Adopting a slightly broader perspective, Marie-Jeanne Durry suggests it evokes the many personal defeats in Apollinaire's life and his regret at not yet having written a masterpiece.[30] Fortunately, by the middle of 1907 he had entered a brand new period in his life and had put these memories behind him. With Marie Laurencin at his side, Apollinaire approached the challenges that faced him with gusto and with a renewed self-confidence. These qualities are evident in the next two stanzas:

> Si les bateliers ont ramé
> Loin des lèvres à fleur de l'onde
> Mille et mille animaux charmés
> Flairent la route à la rencontre
> De mes blessures bien-aimées
>
> Leurs yeux étoiles bestiales
> Eclairent ma compassion
> Qu'importe ma sagesse égale
> Celle des constellations
> Car c'est moi seul nuit qui t'étoile.
>
> (If the boatmen have rowed far
> Away from the lips near the water's surface
> Thousands of charmed animals
> Smell the trail after encountering
> My beloved wounds

Their eyes bestial stars
Illumine my compassion
What does it matter my wisdom
Equals that of the constellations
For it is I alone night who fills you with stars.)

The "bateliers" (boatmen) mentioned in the first stanza are undoubtedly Lul's fellow sailors, who have decided to row further out to sea. The fact that they are rowing at all suggests that they are the victims of a maritime disaster. As far as can be ascertained, the ship they were on seems to have sunk. This impression is confirmed by the next verse, which explains that they are fleeing because of some mysterious "lèvres" (lips) in the water. Fortunately, we know the line originally referred to reefs that were hidden just below the surface of the water. Apollinaire deliberately changed "récifs" to "lèvres" to make the allusion more difficult to follow.[31] Although Poupon thinks it refers to Scylla and Charybdis, the latter were rocks inhabited by two monsters not by the Sirens.[32] Apollinaire's original term was historically (mythologically) accurate. The Sirens were surrounded by impassible reefs that destroyed any ship that tried to reach them. That was how they lured sailors to their death, and that is exactly what happened to the sailor's ship. That may very well be how he received his wounds. Perhaps he calls them "bien-aimées" ("beloved") simply because he escaped with his life. Whatever the explanation, their odor attracts thousands and thousands of charmed animals. Although Poupon thinks they are carnivorous fish, the sailor must surely be standing on land by now.[33] Where else would he have obtained the bare branch in the second stanza?

While Renaud suspects Apollinaire is referring to constellations that have animal names, the animals are far too numerous to be constellations.[34] Their number alone practically guarantees that they are stars. Or rather, as the next stanza reveals, they are celestial animals each of which has two stars for eyes. Since the stars do not produce enough light to provide much illumination, Poupon suggests that *éclairer* (illuminate) should be understood as something like *surveiller* ("watch") or *éspionner* ("spy on").[35] Noting that the stars illuminate the sailor's "compassion," Bates suggests that he takes pity on the prostitutes. However, as Poupon has discovered, in certain instances *compassion* can also mean "agony," as it does here.[36] Ignoring his suffering for a moment, the sailor boasts that he is as wise as the heavens. As proof, he confides that he is the one who populates the sky with stars every night. Although this statement is certainly puzzling, it is not impossible to explain. As we have seen, the poem is filled with solar heroes, who make a brief appearance from time to time. Since the sailor is also a solar hero, he assumes the sun's identity here in addition to his own. Unexpectedly, there turn out to be two complementary explanations for this. As soon as the solar disc disappears below the horizon, Durry explains, the stars gradually begin to appear. While they have been there all along, they have not been visible. In addition, she continues, in his poetic capacity Apollinaire himself possesses the ability to "semer de constellations . . . le firmament poétique" ("sow the poetic firmament . . . with constellations").[37]

> Sirènes enfin je descends
> Dans une grotte avide J'aime
> Vos yeux Les degrés sont glissants
> Au loin que vous devenez naines
> N'attirez plus aucun passant
>
> Dans l'attentive et bien-apprise
> J'ai vu feuilloler nos forêts
> Mer le soleil se gargarise
> Où les matelots désiraient
> Que vergues et mâts reverdissent.
>
> (Sirens at last I descend
> Into an eager grotto I love
> your eyes The steps are slippery
> Turned into dwarves far away
> You no longer attract passers-by
>
> In the attentive and well-taught
> I have seen our forests leaf out
> Sea the sun is gargling
> Where the sailors desired
> The yards and masts to come alive again.)

From here until the end of the poem, two dramas take place simultaneously: that of the sailor and that of the sun. If we accept Cellier's proposal to include Icarus, despite its flaws, there are actually three dramas. The sailor descends into the Sirens' grotto, the sun sinks into the sea, and Icarus falls into the water, where he drowns.[38] That the sailor should suddenly embrace the Sirens after insulting them is not only unlikely but also extremely surprising. Nevertheless, the references to the "grotte avide" ("eager grotto") and the "degrés glissants" ("slippery stairs") leave little doubt that sexual activity is taking place between them. Although it requires some critical acrobatics, another possibility exists. Since the second verse says "une grotte" instead of "votre grotte," the sailor could have evicted the Sirens from their nest and invited "la merveille" to join him. This interpretation is supported by the fourth verse, which seems to describe the Sirens diminishing in size as they walk away. As the sun sets in the west, Poupon adds, the fact that the stairs are slippery suggests that it suddenly accelerates.[39]

The first verse in the second stanza has attracted a number of explanations. According to Chevalier, "l'attentive et bien-apprise" refers to one of the Siren-prostitutes as "en qui refleurit le sexe du poète" ("in whom the poet's penis flourishes anew").[40] As so often in Apollinaire, the first term involves a play on words. She is "attentive" not because she knows how to pay attention but because she knows how to wait (*attendre*). Davies thinks she could be Lea, who is evoked in "Zone" and who could possibly represent the night.[41] However, several critics believe the expression refers to the sea, which is "attentive" in the sense that it waits every day for the sun to immerse itself in its cooling waters. The image of the sun gargling with salt water provides some momentary comic relief. "J'ai vu feuilloler nos forêts" ("I have seen the forests leaf out") presents a problem only because it is supposed to take place in the middle of the water. In retrospect, however, it confirms the critics' impression that the first verse alludes to the sea. Apollinaire appears to be referring to forests that have been converted into ships. Indeed, the last two lines recall the shipwreck evoked at the beginning of the poem. Apollinaire jokes that the sailors would have liked to reverse the process described in the first two lines. If the ship had been converted back into forest, they would find themselves on dry land.

Je descends et le firmament
S'est changé très vite en méduse
Puisque je flambe atrocement
Que mes bras seuls sont les excuses
Et les torches de mon tourment

Oiseaux tiriez aux mers la langue
Le soleil d'hier m'a rejoint
Les otelles nous ensanglantent
Dans le nid des Sirènes loin
Du troupeau d'étoiles oblongues.

(I descend and the firmament
Has quickly changed into a jellyfish
Since I flame atrociously

And my arms alone are the excuses
And the torches of my torment

Birds stick your tongue out at the seas
Yesterday's sun has rejoined me
The heraldic wounds stain us with blood
In the Sirens' nest far
From the flock of oblong stars.)

As Breunig declares, the last two stanzas constitute an allegorical description "du coucher du soleil sur la mer" ("of the sunset on the sea").[42] On an admittedly lesser scale, they also enable us to follow the sailor's activities. The first stanza charts the sun's continuing descent and the last few minutes before it sinks into the sea. According to Durry, the first two lines describe the sea "où se reflète le firmament empourpré, et qui se colle au plongeur comme une meduse" ("where the purple firmament is reflected, which sticks to the diver like a jellyfish").[43] The last two lines describe the flaming sun as it prepares to plunge into the water. The statement "je flambe atrocement" ("I flame atrociously") applies to the sailor as well as to the sun. The former cherishes his suffering, Durry asserts, because he is locked in the last throes of a sexual embrace. As Poupon also recognizes, his flaming torment is purely orgasmic.[44] Meeting yesterday's sun beneath the waves, the dying sun bathes the two lovers in its last bloody rays. Curled up together in the Sirens' former nest, they watch the oblong stars slowly appear.

"Le Brasier"

Initially entitled "Le Pyrée," "Le Brasier" first appeared in *Gil Blas* on May 4, 1908.[45] Besides a manuscript fragment, two rough drafts exist that also bear this title. Since Apollinaire was particularly fond of the composition, he published it twice more before including it in *Alcools*. It appeared in *L'Heure qui sonne* in January 1913, with a dedication to Paul-Napoleon Roinard, and in the *Anthologie des poètes nouveaux* at the beginning of the same year, where it was finally entitled "Le Brasier." Roinard was a Symbolist poet who had previously invited Apollinaire to lecture on contemporary poetry at the Salon des indépendants. Together with "Les Fiançailles," to which it is closely related, "Le Brasier" marks an important step in the evolution of Apollinaire's poetry. As he wrote Ange Toussaint Luca on May 11, 1908, his initial goals were relatively modest: "Je ne cherche qu'un lyrisme neuf et humaniste à la fois" ("I'm only searching for a new, humanist lyricism").[46] Little did he suspect that his efforts would result in the creation of a new poetic language with far-reaching ramifications. Adopting a visionary perspective bordering on the messianic, Apollinaire spoke with new conviction and with new authority. Writing to Madeleine Pagès on July 30, 1915, he confided that "Le Brasier" and "Les Fiançailles" were his two best poems.[47]

"Le Brasier" itself is divided into three sections of unequal length, which were originally numbered. Each of these possesses its own distinctive features. Composed of five octosyllabic quintains with alternating rhymes, the first section is entirely traditional in appearance. While Apollinaire rhymes "feu" with "feu," it obeys all the Classical rules. Combining alexandrines and *vers libres*, rhymed and unrhymed verses, the rest of the poem looks entirely different. The second section possesses three stanzas that seem to grow progressively shorter. While the longest line possesses eighteen syllables, the shortest has six. The third section is longer than the other two and is much more spatialized. Most of the lines are either alexandrines or modeled on alexandrines. At one point, three sentences seem to be suspended in midair, isolated by white spaces before and after them.

It is important for English speakers to realize that a *brasier* is not the same thing as a brazier (which in French is a *brasero*). *Le Petit Robert* defines it as follows: "masse d'objets ou de matières en complète ignition du fait d'un incendie" ("a mass of objects or other matter fully ignited by a fire"). Instead of a container for a blazing fire, therefore, *brasier* refers to the blazing fire itself. This accords with the original title "Le Pyrée," which although Durry associates it with the Zoroastrian fire altar, derives from the Greek and Latin word *pyra* (< pyr = "fire").[48] Like the original title, ironically, *brasier* is best translated into English as "pyre." In the poem, Margaret Davies explains, the pyre is a metaphor for "l'imagination du poète qui est allumée par le feu de l'idéal" ("the poet's imagination lit by the fire of the ideal").[49] According to Anne Hyde Greet, the composition describes "three different aspects of a glowing passion for a life, a new vision, that consumes the poet."[50] Scott Bates provides headings for each of the three sections: Renunciation, Renewal, and Elevation.[51] After consigning his past to the flames, Apollinaire purifies himself in the fire and eventually witnesses his own apotheosis. Thus the poem basically reenacts the drama of the Phoenix. Convinced that the anonymous narrator is Heracles on Mt. Etna, Madeleine Boisson pursues an alternate line of investigation.[52]

> J'ai jeté dans le noble feu
> Que je transporte et que j'adore
> De vives mains et même feu
> Ce Passé ces têtes de morts
> Flamme je fais ce que tu veux

Le galop soudain des étoiles
N'étant que ce qui deviendra
Se mêle au hennissement mâle
Des centaures dans leurs haras
Et des grand'plaintes végétales

Où sont ces têtes que j'avais
Où est le Dieu de ma jeunesse
L'amour est devenu mauvais
Qu'au brasier les flammes renaissent
Mon âme au soleil se dévêt.

(I have thrown in the noble fire
That I transport and that I adore
Living hands and even fire
This past these decapitated heads
Flame I do what you want

The sudden gallop of the stars
Only being what will happen
Mingles with the male whinnying
Of the centaurs in their stud farms
And with the great vegetable complaints

Where are those heads I had
Where is the God of my youth
Love has grown bitter
Let the flames flare up in the brazier
My soul strips bare in the sun.)

Like "Cortège" and "Lul de Faltenin," "Le Brasier" is essentially a dramatic monologue. Recalling Rimbaud's mission in "Une Saison en enfer," it recounts, in language that is nearly as hallucinatory, how Apollinaire transformed his poetry by subjecting himself to the torments of Hell. Struck by the poet's new confidence, Robert Champigny calls the first three stanzas "peut-être les meilleures qu'il ait jamais écrites" ("perhaps the best he ever wrote").[53] Determined to free himself from the past, Apollinaire set out to destroy every conceivable impediment. In practice, that meant consigning traditional thoughts, memories, and practices into the "noble fire" of mental oblivion. Because the fire has a purificatory role in most of the poem, Apollinaire calls it noble. However, its initial role is purely destructive. Everything in the first three stanzas is destined to be incinerated. The image of the "vives mains" ("living hands") recalls similar hands in "Rhénane d'automne" and "L'Emigrant de Landor Road." "Ces têtes de morts" ("These decapitated heads") refers to all of the people who have figured in the poet's past. Erasing previous poetry and previous acquaintances from his memory, Apollinaire confides that he is simply obeying the fire's commands. Although he seems to be an active agent, his actions are dictated by his visionary inspiration.

In the second stanza, the list of things to eliminate includes cosmic, mythological, and vegetable motifs. The first two lines evoke the stars' ability to influence human destiny, evoked in "La Tzigane" and elsewhere. Since centaurs appear here and there in his poetry, Apollinaire jokes that the males should be confined to stud farms like racehorses. And although the "plaintes végétales" are initially puzzling, George Schmits suggests the phrase refers to various plant noises[54]—for example, the branches rubbing against each other in "Le Vent nocturne." Beginning with the *ubi sunt* motif, the third stanza concentrates on Apollinaire himself. At first glance, he seems to regret that he no longer possesses certain things from his youth. However, since he is drawing up a list of items to be thrown on the fire, this is clearly impossible. Sometimes interpreted to indicate nostalgia, the *ubi sunt* motif is actually a meditation on the transitory nature of life. According to Champigny, the "têtes" in the first line are previous masks the poet assumed at one time or another.[55] Although Roger Lefèvre believes the second line refers to previous love affairs, like the third line, the fact that "Dieu" is capitalized suggests it evokes Apollinaire's loss of religious faith.[56] Stripped of these useless memories, he bares his soul, prepared for purification and rebirth. As Lefèvre points out, the last line recalls Rimbaud's "Alchimie du verbe": "J'aimai le désert, les vergers brûlés . . . et les yeux fermés, je m'offris au soleil, dieu du Feu" ("I loved the desert, the burnt orchards . . . and with closed eyes I offered myself to the sun, god of Fire").[57]

> Dans la plaine ont poussé des flammes
> Nos coeurs pendent aux citronniers
> Les têtes coupées qui m'acclament
> Et les astres qui ont saigné
> Ne sont que des têtes de femmes
>
> Le fleuve épinglé sur la ville
> T'y fixe comme un vêtement
> Partant à l'amphion docile
> Tu subis tous les tons charmants
> Qui rendent les pierres agiles.
>
> (On the plain flames have sprung up
> Our hearts hang from the lemon trees

The severed heads that acclaim me
And the stars that have bled
Are only women's heads

The river pinned on the town
Holds you like a piece of clothing
You inflicted all your charming tones
Tones that make the stones agile
On docile Amphion.)

The first stanza portrays an apocalyptic landscape worthy of Salvador Dali. Destruction reigns everywhere—from the flaming plain to the hearts and heads hanging from the trees to the wounded stars, which rain down blood upon the proceedings. While this is simply a metaphorical description of the pyre in action, it is extremely effective. The fire consumes everything connected to Apollinaire's past. The hearts represent former loves, the decapitated heads memories, and the bloody stars painful events. Since these are all associated with women he has known, they are subsumed under the heading "têtes de femmes." References to lemon trees occur in other poems by Apollinaire, where they represent memories of Italy and the Côte d'Azur. The second verse is more fully realized, for example, in "Les Fiançailles": "Et parmi les citrons leurs coeurs sont suspendus" ("And their hearts are hanging from the lemon trees"). Marie-Claude Rampant believes the poet borrowed the idea from the Jewish liturgy, where the heart is represented by a lemon.[58] Bates claims the lemons are the Virgin Mary's fruit and thus symbolize the golden hearts he had once seen hanging in a chapel.[59]

Up until now, the poem has been narrated in the past tense. The second stanza introduces the present tense and a lovely metaphor. Apollinaire compares a river winding through a city to a ribbon pinned on a gown. Although there are no indications of this, Bates assumes the city is Paris and the river the Seine.[60] Following the initial metaphor, the reader learns that the ribbon is pinned so tightly that it inhibits the wearer's movements. Unfortunately, we have no idea who that wearer is. Durry and A. E. Pilkington both conclude that "tu" refers to the flame mentioned in the very first stanza.[61] Peter Fröhlicher thinks it designates either the anonymous woman implied in the expression "nos coeurs" ("our hearts") or else Apollinaire himself.[62] Bates believes it evokes Paris pinned to the earth by its bridges.[63]

Jumping ahead to the poem's third section, Schmits focuses on two verses (64–65) that employ the same clothing vocabulary as the verse in question: "Terre / O Déchirée que les fleuves ont reprisée" ("O Torn / Earth that the rivers have mended"). Based on this comparison, there would appear to be little doubt—the anonymous ribbon-wearer is almost certainly the earth. Although Lefèvre assumes that "partant" in the next line is a present participle, most critics believe it means "thus" or "therefore."[64] Amphion was a Greek musician who was so gifted that the sound of his lyre caused stones to move by themselves and build the walls of Thebes. This reference anticipates the construction of the theater in the third section.

> Je flambe dans le brasier à l'ardeur adorable
> Et les mains des croyants m'y rejettent multiple
> > innombrablement
> Les membres des intercis flambent auprès de moi
> Eloignez du brasier les ossements
> Je suffis pour l'éternité à entretenir le feu de mes délices
> Et des oiseaux protègent de leurs ailes ma face et le soleil

> (I flame in the brazier's adorable heat
> And the hands of the believers throw me back innumerable times
> Limbs of torn martyrs flame near me
> Remove the bones from the brazier
> I suffer for eternity to maintain the fire of my delights
> And birds protect my face and the sun with their wings.)

Freed from the burden of the past, Apollinaire seeks to purify himself in the flames. Ironically, the fire that has consumed so many unwanted thoughts, memories, and practices becomes his own funeral pyre. Hoping to be reborn like the Phoenix, he actually welcomes his immolation. The first line contains an interesting play on words centered around the word "adorable." In addition to being "delightful," the fire is the object of religious veneration. Just as with the ancient Zoroastrian rite, the faithful are invited to come and worship (adorer) the blazing pyre. Thus, as Davies observes, Apollinaire "seems to see himself if not as a god then at least as a saint and martyr."[65] Since poetry is sacred in his view, he happily assumes the persona of a martyred holy man. Because the blaze itself is also sacred, each time he falls out of the fire his faithful disciples push him back in. Observing the dismembered bodies of other martyrs who have been added to the pyre, Apollinaire orders his disciples to pull their remains away, presumably so his glory will remain unsullied. By himself, he boasts, he offers enough food to keep the fire burning forever. Indeed, his face has become so bright that its intensity rivals that of the sun. In order to protect each one from the other, mysterious birds have interposed their extended wings. Durry speculates that

Apollinaire may have taken this image from the legend of King Solomon or from the representation of an Egyptian pharaoh.[66] In theory at least, the birds could also be angels.

> O Mémoire Combien de races qui forlignent
> Des Tyndarides aux vipères ardentes de mon bonheur
> Et les serpents ne sont-ils que les cous des cygnes
> Qui étaient immortels et n'étaient pas chanteurs
> Voici ma vie renouvelée
> De grands vaisseaux passent et repassent
> Je trempe une fois encore mes mains dans l'Océan
>
> Voici le paquebot et ma vie renouvelée
> Ses flammes sont immenses
> Il n'y a plus rien de commun entre moi
> Et ceux qui craignent les brûlures.
>
> (O Memory How many races descend
> From the Tyndarids to the ardent vipers of my happiness
> And the serpents are they only the necks of swans
> That were immortal and were not singers
> Here my life is renewed
> Great ships pass back and forth
> I dip my hands in the Ocean once again
>
> Here is the steamer and my life renewed
> Its flames are immense
> I no longer have anything in common
> With those who are afraid of burns.)

As Fröhlicher remarks, the invocation of Mnemosyne introduces a reflection on the degenerative nature of the flames enveloping Apollinaire.[67] The Tyndarids were born of a mythological triangle involving Leda, Tyndareus, and Zeus. Castor and Pollux were mighty warriors. Helen committed adultery with Paris and sparked the Trojan War. Clytemnestra committed adultery with Aegisthus and murdered her husband Agamemnon. Reading between the lines, Davies deduces that Apollinaire regrets the use of myth in his earlier works. In retrospect, he realizes that it led him to neglect the true sources of poetry.[68] Searching for a metaphor to describe the flames, Apollinaire chooses a pun involving a writhing mass of vipers. The reptiles are "ardent" not only because they eagerly pursue him but also because they are actually on fire. The snakes' sinuous curves remind the poet, in turn, of the neck of a swan—not just any swan but the shape Zeus assumed in order to impregnate Leda. Since swans sing before they die, according to Plato, and since Zeus himself is immortal, the swan in question is destined to remain mute forever. Fortunately, this does not describe Apollinaire, who, like the Phoenix before him, emerges from the fire unscathed and with renewed vigor. Symbolizing his new vitality, powerful steamships pass back and forth as he dips his hands into the ocean of life. Inured to the immense flames all around him, he scoffs at those who are afraid to get burned:

> Descendant des hauteurs où pense la lumière
> Jardins rouant plus haut que tous les ciels mobiles
> L'avenir masqué flambe en traversant les cieux.
>
> Nous attendons ton bon plaisir ô mon amie
> J'ose à peine regarder la divine mascarade
>
> Quand bleuira sur l'horizon la Désirade.
>
> (Descending from the heights where the light thinks
> Gardens wheeling higher than all the mobile skies
> The masked future flames as it crosses the skies
>
> We await your good pleasure O my love
>
> I scarcely dare to watch the divine masquerade
> When will La Desirade turn blue on the horizon.)

In 1970, when Pilkington was writing the notes for his edition of *Alcools*, he complained that the poem's final section defied "adequate comment."[69] Since that date, fortunately, Apollinaire scholars have painstakingly investigated this section and have solved a number of problems. The initial scene, Schmits explains, incorporates an ancient cosmological model according to which the universe consists of a series of concentric spheres.[70] The highest point is traditionally that of the Empyrean Heaven, which, according to Christian tradition, is the dwelling place of God and the source of light and creation. Evoked in the first verse, the celestial beings who accompany him are so divine that they are made of nothing but light. Antoine Fongaro argues convincingly that the first two verses were inspired by *The Divine Comedy*.[71] In particular, the whirling gardens resemble the immense rose wheel that concludes the latter work. In the last analysis, therefore, Apollinaire shares Dante's vision of Paradise. The "ciels mobiles" are the seven lower spheres governed by the Moon,

Mercury, Venus, the Sun, Mars, Jupiter, and Saturn according to the medieval worldview. The eighth level, where the celestial gardens are located, is that of the Empyrean. Masquerading as a comet or a shooting star, the "avenir" (future) leaves a flaming trail behind as it plummets toward the earth. Since only God can know the future in advance, it is forced to wear a disguise.

Like the first three lines, the next three are also alexandrines. Isolated from the rest of the text, they are relatively impenetrable. Speculating about the identity of "mon amie," who is apparently refusing to be rushed, Durry suggests she is either Marie Laurencin or the Muse.[72] Since neither one appears elsewhere in the text, however, "la lumière" (light) would appear to be a much better candidate. Like divine grace, which must be earned over time, divine illumination is bestowed at the Creator's discretion. "La divine mascarade" in the next verse continues the theme of divinity and expands the implicit references to *The Divine Comedy*. Referring back to "l'avenir masqué," it prolongs the theatrical metaphor and evokes events that are yet to be experienced. The last line was taken from a sketch Apollinaire wrote around 1899.[73] La Désirade is a tropical island in the French West Indies belonging to Guadeloupe. In contrast to the realm "où pense la lumière" ("where the light thinks"), it represents an earthly paradise.

> Au-delà de notre atmosphère s'élève un théâtre
> Que construisit le ver Zamir sans instrument
> Puis le soleil revint ensoleiller les places
> D'une ville marine apparue contremont
> Sur les toits se reposaient les colombes lasses
>
> Et le troupeau de sphinx regagne la sphingerie
> A petits pas Il orra le chant du pâtre toute la vie
> Là-haut le théâtre est bâti avec le feu solide
> Comme les astres dont se nourrit le vide.
>
> (Beyond our atmosphere rises a theater
> Constructed by the worm Zamir without tools
> Then the sun returned to brighten the squares
> Of a seaside city positioned against the mountain
> Weary doves rested on the rooftops
>
> And the flock of sphinxes return to the sphinxery
> Slowly they will hear the shepherd's song all their lives
> Up there the theater is constructed with solid fire
> Like the stars that nourish empty space.)

As Schmits and Fongaro have both shown, the divine amphitheater was also inspired by Dante.[74] Like its counterpart in *The Divine Comedy*, it presents another view of paradise. Since Apollinaire's structure is situated in the Empyrean, which by definition is a realm of pure fire, it is constructed with "feu solide" ("solid fire") like the stars.[75] The worm Zamir, who built the Temple of Jerusalem without using tools, according to Jewish legend, is another of Apollinaire's marvelous discoveries.[76] Like Amphion, who was charged with erecting the Theban walls, he is able to accomplish great things without actually doing anything. Nor, one suspects, did the homonymy between *ver* and *vers* ("verse" and "worms") go unnoticed. As Apollinaire exclaimed one month later, "Quelle saisissante image du poete!" ("What a splendid image of the poet!").[77] Like his mythological counterparts, the poet constructs marvelous edifices with no instrument but his imagination. The last three lines of the first stanza were taken from an earlier poem entitled "Le Printemps."[78] The subject of the first verse was originally "le jour" (the day) rather than "le soleil" (the sun). Although Schmits complains that the two parts of the stanza are discontinuous, Fongaro insists there is a logical transition between them introduced by "Puis."[79] The seaside town was not borrowed from *The Divine Comedy*, like the theater, but was invented by Apollinaire for "Le Printemps." According to clues elsewhere in the composition, Fongaro concludes that the town was originally Monaco.

The reference to a group of sphinxes in the second stanza is surprising to say the least. Although sphinxes are solitary beasts with ferocious reputations, these troop across the page as if they were a flock of sheep. One wonders whom they are following and where their "sphingerie" is located. This word is a neologism coined by Apollinaire on the model of *bergerie* (or perhaps *ménagerie*).[80] Since 1964, when Durry despaired of ever learning the identity of the sphinxes and their shepherd, several explanations have been proposed.[81] Jean Richer claims the sphinxerie is in fact the constellation Libra because the sphinxes were guardians of the Equinox.[82] Schmits points out that sphinxes were originally associated with the ancient Egyptian god Harmakhis, who, as a personification of the rising sun, symbolized resurrection and eternal life.[83] Instead of identifying the anonymous shepherd with Harmakhis, however, he concludes that the shepherd represents Orpheus. Fongaro points out that the sphinxes' action (returning to the sphinxerie) depends syntactically on the sun's return,[84] from which he deduces that they must represent stars. Since the sphinxes like to pose enigmas and since the stars that determine human fate are enigmas themselves, he explains, there is a logical connection.

Convinced, finally, that the shepherd's song is the "chant du firmament" mentioned in the "Chanson mal-aimé" (stanza 50), Fongaro deduces that the shepherd himself is the firmament. So far, however, no one has convincingly identified both the shepherd and his flock. The key to finally unlocking the poem's symbolism is furnished by two works: Apollinaire's first novel and Boisson's massive study of his use of ancient mythology.[85] At one point in Apollinaire's *L'Enchanteur pourrissant*, published in 1909, the god Pan appears "jouant de la flûte qu'il a inventée [et] menant un troupeau de jolis sphinx" ("playing the flute that he invented [and] leading a flock of lovely sphinxes").[86] The sphinxes resemble a group of schoolgirls rather than ferocious animals. At first glance, the shepherd in "Le Brasier" would appear to be Pan, who, for some reason, is leading a flock of stars. However, the symbolism continues unabated, for according to two mythology specialists consulted by Boisson, Pan himself represents the sun. "En tant que soleil," she concludes, "il conduit les étoiles."[87] Ultimately, therefore, the shepherd and the sphinxes represent the dawn, when the sun rises and the stars disappear. Boisson fails to make the connection with "Le Brasier" because she believes the protagonist is Heracles rather than Pan. Among other things, this interpretation explains why the troupe of sphinxes returns to the sphinxerie "à petits pas" (slowly). Since it is early morning, they don't want to wake anyone up.

> Et voici le spectacle
> Et pour toujours je suis assis dans un fauteuil
> Ma tête mes genoux mes coudes vain pentacle
> Les flammes ont poussé sur moi comme des feuilles
>
> Des acteurs inhumains claires bêtes nouvelles
>
> Donnent des ordres aux hommes apprivoisés
> Terre
> Ô Déchirée que les fleuves ont reprisée
>
> J'aimerais mieux nuit et jour dans les sphingeries
> Vouloir savoir pour qu'enfin on m'y devorât.
>
> (Behold the show
> And I have taken a theater seat forever
> My head my knees my elbows vain pentacle
> Flames have sprouted on me like leaves

> Inhuman actors bright new beasts
>
> Give orders to tamed men
>   Earth
> O Torn Earth that rivers have mended
>
> Night and day in the sphinxeries I would rather
> Desire to know in order to be devoured there.)

Where there is a theater, sooner or later someone will put on a performance. Eager to watch the divine masquerade in the fiery amphitheater—which consists of the same substance as the stars—Apollinaire takes a front row seat. As Fongaro points out, the first two lines here contain a playful reference to Musset's poem *Un Spectacle dans un fauteuil*.[88] Waiting for the performance to begin, Apollinaire notices that, in keeping with the celestial setting, his head, knees, and elbows form a five-pointed star, or "pentacle." The resemblance between the magic charm and the human body, Fröhlicher notes, is part of the esoteric tradition.[89] Interestingly, Bates reports that the pentacle is also the symbol of Pan.[90] Although it symbolizes the dominion of the spirit over the elements of nature, it fails to prevent the poet's immolation in the next line. This explains why he calls the pentacle "vain." Not surprisingly, since Apollinaire is surrounded by fire on every side, he soon bursts into flame. Besides being perfectly logical, this development conforms to one of the pentacle's alternate names: "flaming star." In addition to possessing the shape of a pentacle, therefore, Apollinaire finally becomes one. Or rather, since we are witnessing his apotheosis, he is transformed into an actual star. Seated in his chair and blazing away, Apollinaire focuses his attention on the mysterious "acteurs inhumains" who are performing on stage. Schmits rightly connects these individuals to a preface Apollinaire wrote for an art exhibition, published one month before "Le Brasier."

> Avant tout, les artistes sont des hommes qui veulent devenir inhumains.
> Ils cherchent péniblement les traces de l'inhumanité, traces que l'on ne
>   rencontre nulle part dans la nature.
> Elles sont la vérité et en dehors d'elles nous ne connaissons aucune réalité.
>
> (Above all, artists are people who want to become inhuman.
> They painstakingly search for traces of inhumanity, traces that are found
>   nowhere else in nature.
> They are truth and outside of them we know no reality.)[91]

In Apollinaire's vocabulary, therefore, being "inhumain" is actually a good thing. It encourages artists and writers to abandon realism, to experiment with abstraction, and to focus on higher truths. Poetry and art should abandon tradition in favor of invention and imagination. Drawing on Apollinaire's discussion, José Ortega y Gasset would publish an influential essay entitled "The Dehumanization of Art" thirteen years later.[92] Since Apollinaire praises the role of instinct in the preface quoted above, Schmits explains, he calls the actors "bêtes nouvelles" ("new beasts"). What makes these stellar beings so superior to ordinary mortals—and thus gives them the right to order the latter around—is their commitment to aesthetic adventure. In contrast to traditional artists and writers, who resemble tame pets, those who embrace the new aesthetics are portrayed as wild animals. Viewed in this light, the actors' performance is essentially allegorical. Its principles and conclusions apply to life in general. Not only is all the world a stage, but their stage is all the world. Accordingly, the next two lines focus on the earth: "Terre / Ô Déchirée que les fleuves ont reprisée." Glimpsing the earth far below, Apollinaire revives a lovely metaphor introduced in the first section. Since the globe is covered with winding rivers, he compares it to an article of clothing that has been torn and mended.

Although the final stanza is deliberately enigmatic, it is not impossible to decipher. Writing in 1964, Davies found the conclusion to be ironic. Having ascended to the highest point in the universe, she claimed, Apollinaire was forced to descend and confront "the small, gnawing secrets of real life."[93] According to what we have seen, however, there is no reason to think he has come back to Earth. On the contrary, since he has become a star, he is destined to remain in the sky forever. Twenty years later, the same author suggested that "vouloir savoir" gave Apollinaire the courage to confront the divine masquerade of language.[94] While this is an interesting hypothesis, it is unfortunately impossible to verify. Nevertheless, the reference to sphinxeries implies that Pan and his troupe are somehow involved. Indeed, the sphinxes were famous for devouring people who could not answer their riddles. For some reason, the situation is the opposite in "Le Brasier." While the sphinxes still threaten to devour Apollinaire, or seem to, he is the one who is asking the questions. "J'aimerais mieux vouloir savoir," of course can be translated as "I would prefer to satisfy my curiosity" as well as "I would prefer to search for knowledge." Bates speaks of Apollinaire being "devoured by knowledge" rather than by the sphinxes, which does not seem entirely accurate.[95] He believes the poet is attracted to the sphinxeries by the opportunity to hear Pan's music for the rest of his life.

Two additional critics offer to translate Apollinaire's words into prose. Lefèvre produces an allegorical translation that takes a little too much for granted: "La conquête poétique doit être une perpétuelle recherche qui consume l'être" ("Poetic conquest must be a perpetual search that consumes the searcher").[96] However, one wonders if Apollinaire is really talking about poetry. Schmits' translation is short and sweet: "Je voudrais tout savoir, quitte à en mourir" ("I would like to know everything, even if it kills me").[97] Unfortunately, this translation fails to account for the cause-and-effect relationship implied by *pour que*. Nevertheless, another possibility exists that seems to avoid the foregoing problems. As far as can be ascertained, the two lines describe a celestial drama. As we have seen, the sphinxerie is situated in the sky rather than on the ground (possibly in the constellation Libra). As we have also seen, the sphinxes are stars rather than bloodthirsty monsters. Since Apollinaire is a star as well, it is highly unlikely that other stars would want to devour him. In any case, the fact that he is destined to spend the rest of his existence among them rules out such a scenario. He needs to stay alive at all costs. However, several questions remain. How can Apollinaire possibly survive being eaten? And by whom is he willing to be consumed if not the sphinxes? According to all indications, the answer appears to be the sun. As noted earlier, the stars follow the sun in the sense that they appear when it sets and disappear when it rises. Apollinaire looks forward to being "devoured" by the sun every morning and regurgitated every evening. This is the price he is willing to pay so that he can spend the rest of his life among his fellow stars.

Notes

1. Marc Poupon, "'Lul de Faltenin' et l'étymologie," *Du monde européen à l'univers des mythes*, ed. Michel Décaudin (Paris: Lettres Modernes, 1970), 132; Michel Décaudin, *Le Dossier d' "Alcools,"* rev. ed. (Paris: Minard, 1965), 157.

2. L. C. Breunig, "Le Manuscrit de 'Lul de Faltenin," *Revue des Sciences Humaines*, new ser., Fasc. 84 (October–December 1956), 401–12. A reproduction followed by a transcript appears on 407–10. The transcript is also included in Décaudin, *Le Dossier*, 159–61.

3. Alexander Dickow, "Sur 'Lul de Faltenin': Mallarmé selon Apollinaire," *Symposium*, Vol. 66, No. 4 (2012), 206–12.

4. Antoine Fongaro, "Apollinaire, Gautier et les Sirènes," *Revue des Lettres Modernes*, Nos. 183–88 (1968), 64–71.

5. Scott Bates, *Dictionnaire des mots libres d'Apollinaire* (Sewanee, TN: privately printed, 1991), 129.

6. André Fonteyne, "Lul," *Revue des Lettres Modernes*, Nos. 380–84 (1973), 145.

7. Bates, *Dictionnaire*, p. 191, and Jean-Claude Chevalier, *"Alcools": Analyse des formes poétiques* (Paris: Lettres Modernes, 1970), 154.

8. Madeleine Boisson, *Apollinaire et les mythologies antiques* (Paris: Nizet, 1989), 497.

9. Margaret Davies, "'Lul de Faltenin,'" *Revue des Lettres Modernes*, Nos. 327–30 (1972), 89. She also detects references to Amphion, Zeus, the worm Zamir, and Pan (see 92–93).

10. Dickow, "Sur 'Lul de Faltenin.'" 208.

11. Breunig, "Le Manuscrit," 405.

12. Davies, "'Lul de Faltenin,'" 89, 92–93.

13. Quoted by Poupon in "'Lul de Faltenin,'" 137.

14. Poupon, "'Lul de Faltenin,'" 133

15. Décaudin, *Le Dossier*, 161.

16. John Wesley Cameron, *Apollinaire and the Painters: His Poetic Orphism* (Ph.D. diss., Indiana University, 1955).

17. Boisson, *Apollinaire et les mythologies*, 488.

18. Léon Cellier, "Lecture de 'Lul de Faltenin," *Revue des Lettres Modernes*, Nos. 327–30 (1972), 74.

19. Jean-Claude Chevalier, *"Alcools": analyse des formes poétiques* (Paris: Lettres Modernes, 1970), 166–80.

20. Bates, "Sur 'Lul de Faltenin,'" *Le Flâneur des Deux Rives*, No. 6 (June 1955), 7–9, and *Guillaume Apollinaire*, rev. ed. (Boston: Twayne, 1989), 48; Poupon, "'Lul de Faltenin,'" 132–46; Philippe Renaud, *Lecture d'Apollinaire* (Lausanne: L'Age d'Homme, 1969), 495–502.

21. Fongaro, "Apollinaire, Gautier et les Sirènes," 67.

22. Poupon, "'Lul de Faltenin,'" 142.

23. Cellier, "Lecture," 76.

24. Renaud, *Lecture d'Apolllinaire*, 499–500.

25. Margaret Davies, *Apollinaire* (New York: St. Martin's, 1964), 132–33.

26. Bates, *Guillaume Apollinaire*, 48, and "Sur 'Lul de Faltenin,'" 7.

27. Poupon, "'Lul de Faltenin,'" 138. He also thinks the sun is the poem's protagonist.

28. Bates, "Sur 'Lul de Faltenin,'" 7, and Poupon, "Sur 'Lul de Faltenin,'" 136.

29. See Peter Read, *Picasso and Apollinaire: The Persistence of Memory* (Berkeley: University of California Press, 2008), 73–76.

30. Marie-Jeanne Durry, *Guillaume Apollinaire: "Alcools,"* Vol. 3 (Paris: SEDES, 1964), 158.

31. Décaudin, *Le Dossier*, 161.

32. Poupon, "'Lul de Faltenin,'" 134.

33. Ibid., 135.

34. Renaud, *Lecture d'Apollinaire*, 495.

35. Poupon, "'Lul de Faltenin,'" 145–46.

36. Ibid., 136–37.

37. Durry, *Guillaume Apollinaire: "Alcools,"* 3:159.

38. Cellier, "Lecture de 'Lul de Faltenin," 74.

39. Poupon, "'Lul de Faltenin,'" 136.

40. Chevalier, "Alcools," 177.

41. Davies, "'Lul de Faltenin,'" 91.

42. Breunig, "Le Manuscrit," 404.

43. Durry, Guillaume Apollinaire: "Alcools," 3:158.

44. Poupon, "'Lul de Faltenin,'" 143.

45. Michel Décaudin, Le Dossier d' "Alcools," rev. ed. (Paris: Minard, 1965), 174–76.

46. Ibid., 175.

47. Ibid.

48. Durry, Guillaume Apollinaire: "Alcools," 3:160.

49. Margaret Davies, "'Le Brasier,'" Etudes autour d''Alcools,'" ed. Anne de Fabry and Marie-France Hilgar (Birmingham: Summa, 1985), 4.

50. Anne Hyde Greet, tr., "Alcools." Guillaume Apollinaire (Berkeley: University of California Press, 1965), 251.

51. Bates, Guillaume Apollinaire, 76.

52. Boisson, Apollinaire et les mythologies, 441–57.

53. Robert Champigny, "Le Temps chez Apollinaire," PMLA, Vol. 67, No. 2 (March 1952), 9.

54. George Schmits, "'Le Brasier,'" Part I, Les Etudes Classiques, No. 35 (January 1967), 40.

55. Champigny, "Le Temps chez Apollinaire," 10.

56. Roger Lefèvre, Apollinaire. "Alcools" (Paris: Nouveaux Classiques Larousse, 1965), 71.

57. Ibid.

58. Marie-Claude Rampant, "A propos de citrons," Revue des Lettres Modernes, Nos. 276–79 (1971), 110–12.

59. Bates, Guillaume Apollinaire, 76.

60. Ibid.

61. Durry, Guillaume Apollinaire, 3:165, and A. E. Pilkington, Apollinaire: "Alcools" (Oxford: Blackwell, 1970), 141.

62. Peter Fröhlicher, "Le Brasier" d'Apollinaire: lecture sémiotique (Paris: Lettres Modernes, 1983), 38.

63. Bates, Guillaume Apollinaire, 76.

64. Lefèvre, Apollinaire. "Alcools," 71.

65. Davies, Apollinaire, 149.

66. Durry, Guillaume Apollinaire, 3:165.

67. Fröhlicher, "Le Brasier" d'Apollinaire, 54.

68. Davies, Apollinaire, 150.

69. Pilkington, Apollinaire: "Alcools", 141.

70. George Schmits, "'Le Brasier,' Part II," Les Etudes Classiques, April 1967, 156.

71. Antoine Fongaro, Apollinaire poète: Exegèses et discussions 1957–1987 (Toulouse: Presses Universitaires du Mirail-Toulouse, 1988), 166–68. Schmits detects numerous similarities between Dante and Apollinaire. See note 27.

72. Durry, *Guillaume Apollinaire*, 3:151.

73. Décaudin, *Le Dossier*, 176.

74. Schmits, "'Le Brasier,'" Part II, 162; Fongaro, *Apollinaire poète*, 168.

75. For a discussion of Empedocles and the concept of solid fire in Apollinaire's work, see Lionel Follet, "Encore Empédocle," *Revue des Lettres Modernes*, Nos. 677–81 (1983), 136–39.

76. See Durry, *Guillaume Apollinaire*, 3:160–62.

77. Guillaume Apollinaire, "André Salmon," *Vers et Prose*, June–August 1908. Repr. in Apollinaire, *Oeuvres en prose complètes*, Vol. 2, ed. Pierre Caizergues and Michel Décaudin (Paris: Gallimard, 1991), 1007.

78. Guillaume Apollinaire, *Oeuvres poétiques*, ed. Marcel Adéma and Michel Décaudin (Paris: Gallimard, 1965), 558.

79. Schmits, "'Le Brasier,'" Part II, 162; Fongaro, *Apollinaire poète*, 170.

80. See Claude Debon, *Apollinaire: Glossaire des oeuvres complètes* (Paris: Sorbonne Nouvelle, 1988), 117.

81. Durry, *Guillaume Apollinaire*, 3:168.

82. Jean Richer, "Le Destin comme matière poétique," *Revue des Lettres Modernes*, Nos. 166–69 (1967), 18.

83. Schmits, "'Le Brasier,'" Part II, 166.

84. Fongaro, *Apollinaire poète*, 173.

85. Guillaume Apollinaire, *Oeuvres en prose*, Vol. 1, ed. Michel Décaudin (Paris: Gallimard, 1977), 19; Boisson, *Apollinaire et les mythologies*, 422–23.

86. Bates also evokes Pan and the sphinxes—and even relates them to "Le Brasier"—but he believes they represent art and erotic knowledge (*Guillaume Apollinaire*, 77).

87. Boisson, *Apollinaire et les mythologies*, 422.

88. Fongaro, *Apollinaire poète*, 164.

89. Fröhlicher, *"Le Brasier" d'Apollinaire*, 81.

90. Bates, *Guillaume Apollinaire*, 77.

91. Schmits, "'Le Brasier,'" Part II, 171; Guillaume Apollinaire, "Les Trois Vertus plastiques," *Catalogue de la Troisième Exposition du Cercle de l'Art Moderne du Havre*, June 4, 1908. Reprinted as the first chapter of *Méditations esthétiques: Les Poètes cubistes* (Paris: Figuière, 1913) in *Oeuvres en prose complètes*, 2:8.

92. See Willard Bohn, *Apollinaire and the International Avant-Garde* (Albany: State University of New York Press, 1997), 222.

93. Davies, *Apollinaire*, 151.

94. Margaret Davies, "'Le Brasier,'" in *Etudes autour d'"Alcools*,*" ed. Anne de Fabry and Marie-France Hilgar (Birmingham: Summa, 1985), 12.

95. Bates, *Guillaume Apollinaire*, 78.

96. Lefèvre, *Apollinaire. "Alcools*,*"* 74.

97. Schmits, "'Le Brasier,'" Part II, 173.

CHAPTER SIX

~

Easter Sunday

One of Apollinaire's longer, more ambitious works, "Les Fiançailles" nevertheless rewards those who carefully consider the poet's words. Covering the period 1901 to 1908, it is divided into nine sections, some of which were written considerably earlier and incorporated into the finished poem. As such, it charts Apollinaire's development from the short limpid verses of the "Rhénanes"—which, although beautiful, seemed terribly old-fashioned to his friends in 1908—to his contemporary experiments with hermetic and visionary poetry. The parallels with what Picasso, his best friend, was doing at the same time are fascinating. Both men were carefully feeling their way toward a revolutionary new way of viewing and representing the world around them. In order to accomplish these goals, they set out to create a radical new language. Like Picasso's first tentative efforts, the poem is clearly associated with the beginnings of Cubism.

Like "Le Brasier," which in many ways it resembles, "Les Fiançailles" occupies a crucial stage in Apollinaire's poetic development. Not only were both works conceived simultaneously, but also verses from each poem ended up in the other while they were taking shape.[1] Writing to Madeleine Pagès on July 30, 1915, Apollinaire confided: "[Le poème] le plus nouveau et le plus lyrique, le plus profond ce sont ces 'Fiançailles' dédiées à Picasso dont j'admire l'art sublime . . . nul doute qu'avec le 'Brasier' il ne soit mon meilleur poème si non le plus immédiatement accessible" ("[My] newest, most lyrical, and most profound [poem] is 'Les Fiançailles' dedicated to Picasso, whose sublime art I admire . . . no doubt that with 'Le Brasier' it is my best poem if not the most immediately accessible").[2] Published in November 1908, "Les Fiançailles" appeared initially in *Pan* but without a dedication to Picasso, which was added on to the proofs for *Alcools*. To some observers, the dedication suggests that the poet was experimenting with Cubist techniques. Indeed, LeRoy C. Breunig argues that the poem is Apollinaire's *Demoiselles d'Avignon*. He and Laurie Edson have both detected a number of stylistic similarities between the two works.[3] Anne Hyde Greet believes "Les Fiançailles" reveals the kinship that existed between Apollinaire and Picasso, since it is concerned with "artists who must find in themselves totally new forms of expression."[4]

Writing to Ange Toussaint Luca on May 11, 1908, Apollinaire insisted he was merely trying to create "un lyrisme neuf et humaniste à la fois ("a new, humanist lyricism").[5] Like "Le Brasier," however, "Les Fiançailles" far surpassed his modest expectations. Like the former, it introduced a brand new poetic language, one that presented exciting new possibilities. Combining structural ellipsis, parataxis, and free association, it was also much more demanding. The poem not only seems to be impenetrable to many readers, but, as Marie-Jeanne Durry remarks, it is "sans cesse imprévisible" ("ceaselessly unpredictable").[6] It proceeds by discontinuous leaps and bounds rather than by logical progression. "Les Fiançailles" marks an important change in Apollinaire's attitude toward the writing of poetry. Instead of continuing to write about love, Greet explains, he attempts to convey an "almost mystical experience of life."[7] A number of pronouncements have a visionary quality about them. Since "Les Fiançailles" is a confessional poem, moreover, much of it is also autobiographical. Viewed from this angle, it contains two notable "firsts." For the first time, Breunig declares, Apollinaire openly reveals his joys and sufferings as a poet.[8] For the first time, as S. I. Lockerbie points out, he uses images of daily life to express his own aspirations.[9]

"Les Fiançailles" is divided into nine unequal sections, each of which occupies a single page. The first section was borrowed from an earlier poem entitled "Le Printemps," which seems to have been composed in May 1902.[10] Although the first stanza consists of only three verses, it was originally a quatrain like the next two stanzas. Apollinaire deleted the fourth line and switched some of the rhymes around. Even at the beginning of his career, he dared to combine *rimes embrassées* with *rimes croisées* and to rhyme "bleu" with "bleues." Although the first section utilizes classical alexandrines and alternates masculine and feminine rhymes, some of the latter are rich ("eglantines" / "destine"), some are sufficient ("giroflées" / "Paraclet"), and some are only approximative ("venues" / "suspendus"). Whether or not one decides to pronounce a mute "e" depends on the situation. As Michel Décaudin notes, "Le compte des syllabes est soumis à l'oreille bien plus qu'à la règle. . . . Apollinaire a le sens de la poésie parlée, il *entend* le vers" ("The syllable count is governed by the ear more than by rules. . . . Apollinaire is sensitive to spoken poetry, he *hears* the verse").[11] Composed of three classical quatrains, the final section provides a symmetrical conclusion to the poem. Although it consists of alexandrines like the first section, it uses an alternating rhyme scheme throughout. Framed by the first and last sections, the remainder of the poem combines free verse with regular verse in varying proportions. With one exception, every section has at least two verses that rhyme. A few have four or five rhymes.

A Picasso

Le printemps laisse errer les fiancés parjures
Et laisse feuilloler longtemps les plumes bleues
Que secoue le cyprès où niche l'oiseau bleu

Une Madone à l'aube a pris les églantines
Elle viendra demain cueillir les giroflées
Pour mettre aux nids des colombes qu'elle destine
Au pigeon qui ce soir semblait le Paraclet

Au petit bois de citronniers s'énamourèrent
D'amour que nous aimons les dernières venues
Les villages lointains sont comme leurs paupières
Et parmi les citrons leurs coeurs sont suspendus.

(Springtime lets foresworn lovers wander
And blue feathers leaf out at length
Which the cypress shakes from the bluebird's nest

A Madonna picked the wild roses at dawn
She will come tomorrow to pick the stock
To line the nests of the doves she destines
For the pigeon that seemed the Paraclete tonight

In the little lemon grove the newcomers
Fell in love with the passion we adore
The distant villages are like their eyelids
And their hearts are hanging among the lemons.)

The first two sections of "Les Fiançailles" are fragments of two long poems that were composed in 1902: "Le Printemps" and "Les Paroles étoiles."

Unlike the second composition, which draws its inspiration from an urban environment, the first depicts an idyllic spring landscape. Since we are expecting to encounter an engagement, or perhaps even an engagement party, the image of two lovers strolling hand-in-hand does not seem unusual until we reach the end of the first line—at which point the scene suddenly implodes. Susan Harrow's reaction is typical: "[Il y a une] contradiction entre la promesse d'union annoncée par le titre et la réalité d'une déception amoureuse ("[There is a] contradiction between the promise of a union announced by the title and the reality of an unhappy love affair").[12] Although the lovers are (or were) engaged to be married, they have apparently been lying to each other—just as Apollinaire has been lying to us. What looked like a conventional scene seems to be an aporia. As both Greet and Harrow point out, the fact that *errer* means both "to wander" and "to be mistaken" leaves the reader in a quandary.[13] Which one is it? Greet wonders if the foresworn lovers wander together or separately. "Is their mistake one of betrayal," she asks, "or one of an attempted reconciliation?" While the stanza's apparent undecidability leads Timothy Mathews to speak of "a deconstructed Spring," Breunig adopts a philosophical approach.[14] In his view, the stanza "announces the theme of falsehood as an aesthetic problem, which will come to the fore in part seven."[15]

Although Apollinaire deleted a reference to "Prince Charmant" in the original poem, presumably because it was too obvious, all three verses are clearly inspired by Madame d'Aulnoy's *L'Oiseau bleu* (1697). While several critics have suggested the poem's bluebird could refer to Picasso and his blue period, Apollinaire evokes a specific event in the fairy story. Transformed into a bluebird by the wicked fairy godmother Mazilla, King Charming manages to visit his beloved Florine, who is imprisoned in a tower, and bring her gifts of precious jewels. When the wicked queen finds out, she orders the cypress tree in which the bird perches to be covered with knives and other sharp instruments. The next time the bluebird arrives, he cuts his feet and wings and mistakenly concludes that Florine is responsible. Florine is heartbroken when the bluebird fails to appear and mistakenly concludes that he has abandoned her. Created by Apollinaire, who uses it in at least a dozen texts, the neologism *feuilloler* normally means "to leaf out."[16] On this occasion, it describes the injured bird's feathers falling to the ground like leaves. The same image occurs in "La Tzigane," where it is likewise associated with the theme of thwarted love (see Chapter 2). Fortunately, Madame d'Aulnoy's story has a happy ending. Rescued by a wizard, the king and Florine get married and live happily ever after. According to all indications, the story is evoked in the first stanza of "Les Fiançailles." Apollinaire calls the lovers "parjures" because each thought the other had betrayed them. The term expresses their mistaken opinion of each other, therefore, not Apollinaire's opinion. The stanza itself portrays the happy couple after they have been reunited. Unexpectedly, what looked initially like a sad occasion turns out to be a cause for celebration.

Unfortunately, the preceding discussion sheds no light whatsoever on the next two stanzas. Since the second contains references to a Madonna and the Holy Spirit, it seems vaguely religious and vaguely sacrilegious. Greet believes the Madonna is primarily a spring deity who presides over the flowers and the animals.[17] However, the fact that she is raising a flock of (female) doves to present to a (male) pigeon makes one wonder about her motives. Why does the Holy Spirit need a harem? Understandably, Mathews concludes that Apollinaire is trying to undermine the Christian symbolism.[18] The third stanza is only slightly more intelligible than the second. To be sure, the lemon trees situate the scene on the Côte d'Azur, where Apollinaire grew up, but who are "les dernières venues" ("the newcomers"), and what are they doing there? As it appeared originally in "Le Printemps," the verse read: "D'amour que nous aimons les filles éperdues." By substituting a less specific phrase, Apollinaire made the line more suggestive but also more hermetic. Greet and William Meredith associate the "dernières venues" with the doves in the previous stanza, and while Donald Revell avoids the problem altogether, Oliver Bernard mentions girls.[19] As Bernard astutely deduces, the term must refer to the distracted girls mentioned in the original poem. Who would compare distant villages to doves' eyelids? Assuming, perhaps rightly, that the comparison involves a common color, he provides the following translation: "Blue as their eyelids are the distant hamlets." The reason the girls are so distracted, clearly, is because they are falling in love—apparently with each other. What form their mutual affection takes is left to the reader's imagination.

According to "Le Printemps," however, the whole orchard is palpitating with love: "Tout l'horizon palpite ainsi que leurs paupières" ("The entire horizon palpitates like their eyelids"). The fourth line recalls a verse from "Le Brasier": "Nos coeurs pendent aux citronniers." Like someone who "wears his heart upon his sleeve" in English, the French girls have hung their hearts among the lemons. As noted previously, Marie-Claude Rampant believes that Apollinaire borrowed the comparison from the Jewish liturgy, where a lemon is sometimes used to represent the heart.[20] However, the key is provided by Scott Bates, who explains that lemons are associated with the Virgin Mary. As such, he continues, they recall the golden hearts the poet had once seen hanging in a chapel.[21] One assumes that these were votive offerings. Apollinaire appears to have worked backward from the initial equation—between golden hearts and lemons—to construct the rest of the stanza.

As a number of critics have pointed out, the first section of the poem is extremely mannered. By 1908, when Apollinaire was putting the finishing touches on "Les Fiançailles," it was also rather old-fashioned. The poet himself had changed dramatically during the six years since the verses were originally composed. He had recovered from his adventure with Annie Playden, had fallen in love with Marie Laurencin, and had developed a radical new style. The world of poetry had evolved as well. When Apollinaire read his poetry to his friends, so the story goes, they would cry "encore trop symboliste!" ("still too Symbolist!"). This experience is evoked at the beginning of the second section:

> Mes amis m'ont enfin avoué leur mépris
> Je buvais à pleins verres les étoiles
> Un ange a exterminé pendant que je dormais
> Les agneaux les pasteurs des tristes bergeries
> De faux centurions emportaient le vinaigre
> Et les gueux mal blessés par l'épurge dansaient
> Etoiles de l'éveil je n'en connais aucune
> Les becs de gaz pissaient leur flamme au clair de lune
> Des croque-morts avec des bocks tintaient des glas
> A la clarté des bougies tombaient vaille que vaille
> Des faux cols sur des flots de jupes mal brossées
> Des accouchées masquées fêtaient leurs relevailles
> La ville cette nuit semblait un archipel
> Des femmes demandaient l'amour et la dulie
> Et sombre sombre fleuve je me rappelle
> Les ombres qui passaient n'étaient jamais jolies.

> (My friends have finally confessed their disdain
> I drank in the stars by the glassful
> While I was sleeping, an angel exterminated
> The lambs the shepherds the sad sheepfolds
> Some false centurions carried off the vinegar
> And beggars falsely wounded by spurge were dancing
> I have never seen a warning star
> Gas lamps pissed their flame in the moonlight
> Undertakers clinked their mugs of beer
> By the light of candles for better or worse false collars
> Fell on waves of badly brushed skirts
> New mothers in masks celebrated the church ceremony

The city seemed an archipelago that night
Women demanded love and adoration
And dark dark river I recall
The shadows that passed by were never pretty.)

Beginning with the second section, Apollinaire abandons the omniscient third person in favor of first-person narrative, which continues for the remainder of the poem. The section itself is divided into two distinct halves. In contrast to the first half, which evokes Apollinaire's previous poetry, the second illustrates his latest style. Switching into a confessional mode, he describes what has happened to him since he wrote "Le Printemps." Initially, he admits in the second line, he set his poetic sights too high. His dreams and his ambition knew no bounds. More specifically, as he confides in "Les Paroles étoiles," he dreamed of "poèmes si grandioses que j'ai dû les laisser inachevés" ("poems so ambitious that I had to leave them unfinished"). A period of "engourdissement" ("numbness") followed (the term is Décaudin's) during which Apollinaire essentially lost his way. He says that the period lasted three years on one manuscript and five years on another. During this period, which he refers to as "sleeping," his poetry underwent a profound transformation.

Most commentators assume that the next four lines describe a series of dreams, but they could also represent an elaborate allegory. An angel arrives first and exterminates every pastoral image in Apollinaire's memory. Next, disguised as Roman centurions, several men who destroy all of the Christian images in his memory bank appear. Although some critics assume Apollinaire is parodying the Crucifixion, the false centurions, who brought vinegar for Jesus to drink (mentioned by St. Luke), are carrying it away from Calvary Hill rather than toward it. Like the centurions, the beggars are also false. Apollinaire calls them "mal blessés" because they use sap from the spurge plant—similar to poison ivy—to simulate wounds and excite pity. Why they are dancing in the poem is not immediately clear. Whatever the explanation, the massive celebration apparently leaves Apollinaire free to adopt a different style.

The rest of the stanza provides a dramatic contrast to the idyllic scenes portrayed in the first section. Although they introduce Apollinaire's new style, which initially appears to be realistic, they also depict big city life at its worst. Images of urban industrial decay at night are everywhere. Everything is vice-ridden, filthy, and ugly, including the people who inhabit this Sodom and Gomorrah. The gas jets piss flame, undertakers sit around clinking funereal glasses of beer, and prostitutes walk the streets demanding to be loved and respected.

Since "dulie" denotes the kind of respect normally paid to saints, the last comment is meant to be ironic. As Garnet Rees observes, the scene furnishes "a glimpse of life bereft of friendship, love, or beauty."[22] Much of what passes for acceptable behavior takes place by candlelight. Although "faux col" may be slang for a head of beer, as A. E. Pilkington remarks, here it denotes a celluloid collar—like those lying on top of a heap of wrinkled skirts.[23] The conclusion is inescapable: a bunch of naked people are having an orgy. The next line is equally scandalous and even more ironic than before. *Le Petit Robert* defines "relevailles" as a "rite chrétien par lequel une accouchée vient [à l'église] remercier Dieu" ("a Christian rite for which a new mother comes [to church] to thank God"). However, these new mothers have decided to celebrate the blessed event in a brothel. The fact that they are wearing masks assures their anonymity and increases the general kinkiness of the scene. Greet provides a trenchant description: "Death lacks dignity, love has become sordid, and birth a masquerade."[24] No wonder Apollinaire compares the quarter initially to an isolated archipelago and finally to Hades. As Pierre Brunel points out, the "sombre sombre fleuve" ("dark dark river") is obviously the Acheron, and the mysterious "ombres" ("shadows") are the souls of the dead.[25]

> Je n'ai plus même pitié de moi
> Et ne puis exprimer mon tourment de silence
> Tous les mots que j'avais à dire se sont changés en étoiles
> Un Icare tente de s'élever jusqu'à chacun de mes yeux
> Et porteur de soleils je brûle au centre de deux nébuleuses
> Qu'ai-je fait aux bêtes théologales de l'intelligence
> Jadis les morts sont revenus pour m'adorer
> Et j'espérais la fin du monde
> Mais la mienne arrive en sifflant comme un ouragan.

> (I don't even pity myself anymore
> And cannot explain my tormented silence
> All the words I was intending to say became stars
> An Icarus tries to reach each of my eyes
> And bearing suns I burn in the center of two nebulae
> What have I done to the theological beasts of the mind
> Formerly the dead returned to adore me
> And I awaited the end of the world
> But mine arrives whistling like a hurricane.)

Leaving the nightmarish city behind, Apollinaire resumes his intimate confession in the third section. A certain amount of disagreement exists about the meaning of the first three lines. Some scholars believe they refer to the period of "engourdissement," when Apollinaire found himself unable to write. Others think he is experiencing problems adapting to his radical new style. "Having rejected the past," Greet states, "the poet does not . . . immediately feel liberated but, at first, bankrupt, incapable of achieving his new poetry."[26] However, this interpretation appears to be contradicted by the first verse: "Je n'ai plus même pitié de moi-même" ("I don't even pity myself anymore"). The statement implies that there was an earlier period when Apollinaire did pity himself. Although this experience is still too painful to discuss, he confides, he no longer feels sorry for himself. The problem, as we saw previously, was that he was much too ambitious. His words were all reserved for grandiose projects ("étoiles") ("stars").

At this point, Apollinaire suddenly has a vision of himself transformed into an enormous cosmic deity. Positioned between two nebulae, he watches as an Icarus ascends toward each one of his eyes, which have been transformed into suns. Presumably because the figure is burning brightly, Henri Scepi suggests that he represents Lucifer.[27] The next line, with its reference to theological beasts of the mind, remains obscure. Greet believes the beasts are probably allegories of cardinal sins such as the Leopard (lust), the Lion (pride), and the Wolf (covetousness).[28] Margaret Davies thinks they could be the Beasts of the Apocalypse: the Calf, the Lion, the Eagle, and the Human.[29] In addition, they could conceivably represent the three theological virtues: Faith, Hope, and Charity. What the verse means is equally obscure. Davies has suggested that Apollinaire wonders why his customary cleverness has deserted him and, in a later article, why allegory itself has disappeared.[30] Although the antepenultimate verse is also puzzling, it turns out to be associated with his status as a deity. Apollinaire scribbled the following lines on the manuscript of "Les Paroles étoiles":

La Fête

Ce jour là pour fêter ma divine puissance
Tous les morts revenant adorèrent ma vie
Un ouragan de glace en sifflant les suivit.

(That day to celebrate my divine power
The returning dead all adored my life
An icy whistling hurricane followed them.)

Thus the dead all came to worship Apollinaire because they had adopted him as their god. Like them, the icy hurricane also issued from the underworld. The fact that Apollinaire expected the world to end that day is interesting to say the least. For when the Last Judgment arrives, every grave will supposedly open, the living and the dead will be judged, and the Earth will cease to exist. Did Apollinaire believe that day had come? Did he actually think he was Jesus? If so, the fact that the world did not disappear must have been quite a shock. Surprisingly, despite his divine status, Apollinaire does not seem to be immortal. As we glimpse him for the last time, he is waiting for the deadly wind to carry him away.

> J'ai eu le courage de regarder en arrière
> Les cadavres de mes jours
> Marquent ma route et je les pleure
> Les uns pourrissent dans les églises italiennes
> Ou bien dans de petits bois de citronniers
> Qui fleurissent et fructifient
> En même temps et en toute saison
> D'autres jours ont pleuré avant de mourir dans des tavernes
> Où d'ardents bouquets rouaient
> Aux yeux d'une mulâtresse qui inventait la poésie
> Et les roses de l'électricité s'ouvrent encore.

> (I have had the courage to look back
> The corpses of my days
> Mark my route and I mourn them
> Some are rotting away in Italian churches
> Or else in the little lemon groves
> That flower and bear fruit
> Simultaneously and in every season
> Other days shed tears before expiring in taverns
> Where ardent bouquets circled
> Before the gaze of a mulatto girl who invented poetry
> And the electric roses still blossom
> In the garden of my memory.)

After the previous convoluted exercises, the fourth section seems refreshingly straightforward. Having miraculously escaped the fate reserved for him in the preceding section, Apollinaire takes a moment to look back over his life. Since this process turns out to be highly emotional for him, Mathews relates it to the hurricane that "swept through [his] consciousness in the previous line."[31] As elsewhere in his poetry, Apollinaire does not hesitate to borrow from himself. The wonderfully evocative "cadavres de mes jours" ("corpses of my days") were taken from "L'Emigrant de Landor Road," which borrowed them in turn from "Printemps" (see Chapter 4). The first seven lines here are concerned with nostalgic memories related to Apollinaire's boyhood in Italy and his adolescence on the Côte d'Azur. Since lemon trees flower and bear fruit at the same time, lemons are associated with miracles once more in the poem. The last five lines evoke all the time Apollinaire wasted on drinking and general dissipation. Although he was twenty-eight years old, he had remarkably little to show for it. Davies suggests that the mulatto girl in the tavern is Dante's Beatrice, Rees that she is Baudelaire's mistress Jeanne Duval, and Greet that she represents Marie Laurencin.[32] Although any of the three could have "invented poetry" by serving as their poet's muse, Apollinaire is almost certainly referring to Marie.

As Harrow remarks, the section ends with "admirables synthèses de la fleur et de la flamme bien-aimée" ("admirable syntheses of the flower and the beloved flame").[33] Similarly, Mathews calls it "a breath-taking manipulation of image."[34] However, much more is involved than the simple comparison of fire and flower. Greet thinks the "ardents bouquets" may refer to witty conversations, poems, laughter, or declarations of love.[35] Mechtild Cranston believes they are actual flowers: "Le rouge des fleurs évoque le feu, le feu appelle l'alcool, l'alcool la taverne" ("The flowers' red color evokes fire, fire evokes alcohol, and alcohol the tavern").[36] In reality, the sequence was probably the reverse of what is stated. Apollinaire decided to create a tavern first and then set about furnishing it. Judging from his description, moreover, the "ardents bouquets" appear to be electric chandeliers decorated with imitation roses. They are "blazing" all right but with light rather than fire. Whether or not they are actually revolving is hard to say. Apollinaire could conceivably be referring to a type of chandelier called a "girandole" (< Latin *gyrare* = "to turn"). "Chandelier à plusieurs branches disposées en pyramide" ("A chandelier with several branches forming a pyramid") according to *Le Petit Robert*, it was also available as a table lamp or as a sconce mounted on the wall.

> Pardonnez-moi mon ignorance
> Pardonnez-moi de ne plus connaître l'ancien jeu des vers
> Je ne sais plus rien et j'aime uniquement
> Les fleurs à mes yeux redeviennent des flammes
> Je médite divinement
> Et je souris des êtres que je n'ai pas créés
> Mais si le temps venait où l'ombre enfin solide
> Se multipliait en réalisant la diversité formelle de mon amour
> J'admirerais mon ouvrage.
>
> (Pardon my ignorance
> Pardon me for no longer knowing the ancient game of verse
> I no longer know anything and I am only able to love

In my eyes the flowers are transformed back into flames
I meditate divinely
And I smile at beings I haven't created
But if the time came when the finally solidified shadow
Multiplied and increased my love's formal diversity
I would admire my achievement.)

The fifth section adopts an interesting rhetorical strategy: it begins with a mock apology. Although Apollinaire pretends to be ashamed of his poetic ignorance, in reality he is proud of what he has accomplished. Indeed, as it appeared in "Les Paroles étoiles," the first line originally read: "Pardonnez-moi d'avoir reconquis mon ignorance" ("Pardon me for having reconquered my ignorance"). It is something he has worked hard to achieve. Tired of his friends' scornful comments, he has abandoned the kind of poetry found in the first section and has developed an entirely different style. Although Apollinaire insists on his ignorance again in the third line, Mathews notes, it is with a marked feeling of liberation.[37] In a very real sense, ignorance turns out to be bliss. The second hemistich counterbalances the first by juxtaposing the presence of love with the absence of knowledge. The latter encompasses a much greater sphere than Apollinaire's affection for Marie Laurencin. In Mathews' opinion, it is a love affair with the world—with existence itself.[38] For Breunig, "it is the all-embracing *agapé* of divine inspiration which can transfigure everything it beholds."[39]

The next two verses illustrate this principle in action. Apollinaire reverses the cause-and-effect relationship between initial inspiration and the effect it produces. Thus, flowers are transformed into flames in the fourth line, and, as Pilkington intuits, "the poet meditates quietly, waiting for inspiration" in the fifth line.[40] Some of the images that come to him are so amusing that he is forced to smile. As it first appeared in "Les Paroles étoiles," the mysterious shadow in the antepenultimate line was described as "l'ombre de ma substance." Thus, the verse refers to Apollinaire's own shadow, not to some shadowy figure. Etienne-Alain Hubert has shown that it was originally suggested by a passage in Fabre d'Olivet's *La Langue hébraïque restituée*.[41] As adopted by Apollinaire, Pilkington explains, the shadow suggests "the potential creative power which he hopes to turn into concrete achievement in the 'formal diversity' of poems yet unwritten."[42] The final line sounds strangely familiar: "J'admirerais mon ouvrage." Eventually the realization dawns on the reader that Apollinaire is casting himself in a role like that of God. The echoes of Genesis are unmistakable: "And God saw everything that he had made, and, behold, it was very good" (King James Version).

J'observe le repos du dimanche
Et je loue la paresse
Comment comment réduire
L'infiniment petite science
Que m'imposent mes sens
L'un est pareil aux montagnes au ciel
Aux villes à mon amour
Il ressemble aux saisons
Il vit décapité sa tête est le soleil
Et la lune son cou tranché
Je voudrais éprouver une ardeur infinie
Monstre de mon ouïe tu rugis et tu pleures
Le tonnerre te sert de chevelure
Et tes griffes répètent le chant des oiseaux
Le toucher monstrueux m'a pénétré m'empoisonne
Mes yeux nagent loin de moi
Et les astres intacts sont mes maîtres sans épreuve
La bête des fumées a la tête fleurie
Et le monstre le plus beau
Ayant la saveur du laurier se désole.

(Sunday I observe the day of rest
And I praise idleness
How how to reduce
The infinitely little knowledge
That my senses impose on me
One is like mountains in the sky
Like cities like my love.
It resembles the seasons
It lives decapitated its head is the sun
And the moon its sliced throat
I would like to feel an infinite ardor
Monster of my hearing you roar and you cry
Thunder serves as your hair
And your claws repeat the birds' song
Your monstrous touch has penetrated me and poisons me
My eyes swim far from me
And the intact stars are my unproven masters
The vaporous beast has a flowery head
And having the taste of laurel the most beautiful monster
is grieving.)

Continuing the blasphemous fantasy with which the preceding section concludes, Apollinaire chooses to rest on Sunday like the Creator. The reason that he praises idleness is because it provides him with time to think about poetry and also for inspiration to strike. As Brunel remarks, the sixth section is "la section la plus inquietante."[43] Not only is it extraordinarily complex, but also there is relatively little agreement about what takes place in it. Apollinaire sets the stage by posing what looks like an absurd question: how can the minute amount of knowledge imparted by the senses be reduced? In the first place, the senses provide an enormous amount of information, not a little. In the second place, if the amount of information they furnish is inadequate, why reduce it further? The problem, Greet explains, is that the senses continually interrupt Apollinaire's aesthetic meditations with reports from the outside world.[44] Eliminating these distractions, Davies adds, will help him "retrouver le macrocosme de l'imaginaire" ("find the macrocosm of the imaginary again").[45] For these reasons, Apollinaire prefers cerebral knowledge to sensory impressions and thoughts to physical sensations. Ironically, while Bates considers the loss of his senses to be a terrible sacrifice, Apollinaire actually wants to sacrifice them.[46] Only then will he be free to re-create the world according to the dictates of his imagination, without fear of contradiction.

Brunel calls the sixth verse a syntactic monstrosity: "L'un est pareil aux montagnes au ciel."[47] Where is the corresponding "l'autre"? he asks, which the construction normally demands. And what exactly does it refer to? If to one of the senses, as seems probable, then to which one? And although the verse introduces a series of comparisons, these are "fort peut clair[es]" ("very unclear"). Like the rest of the section, Breunig declares, they represent an immediate reply to the question about reducing the senses.[48] They illustrate exactly how to proceed. The best way to diminish sensory influence, Davies interjects, is by exploiting resemblance, analogy, and correspondence.[49] In other words, by comparing one of the senses to mountains, the sky, cities, love, or the seasons. Translating this sense into human terms, Apollinaire goes even further. Abandoning comparisons altogether, he asserts that the decapitated head of the first sense is the sun and its bloody neck the moon. Metaphor works even better than simile.

The remainder of the poem consists of "a metamorphosis of all the senses,"[50] which, since they are the enemy, are mostly compared to monsters. These imaginary beasts replace the "betes théologales" that Apollinaire lost in the third section. Although the line "Je voudrais éprouver une ardeur infinie" ("I would like to feel an infinite ardor") anticipates the poem's conclusion, it also seems to describe a sixth sense. Bates and Madeleine Boisson think the latter is sexual, while Breunig and Rees believe it is poetic.[51] Although Brunel and Jean Burgos assert that the remaining lines form a single monstrous body, most critics are convinced that they describe multiple monsters.[52] Because the first monster represents hearing, it roars loudly and is accompanied by thunder. Associated with touch, the second monster penetrates Apollinaire's body and somehow poisons him. Ironically, although the third monster represents sight, it is nowhere to be seen. Instead, Apollinaire contributes a definition of the act of seeing: "Mes yeux nagent loin de moi" ("My eyes swim far from me"). Although it remains to be proved, he adds, the stars supposedly control human destiny. Since the monster connected with the sense of smell has a "tête fleurie" ("flowery head"), Greet wonders if it isn't a fruit tree. Perceiving a pun on "laurier," finally, Bates and Greet both believe the most beautiful monster is Marie Laurencin.[53] It remains to mention another interpretation that is impossible to prove or to disprove: pursuing her mythological investigations, Boisson argues that the speaker in this section is Heracles rather than Apollinaire. According to her, the last half depicts his battle against the legendary Hydra of Lerna, whose six heads are actually his own six senses.[54]

> A la fin les mensonges ne me font plus peur
> C'est la lune qui cuit comme un oeuf sur le plat
> Ce collier de gouttes d'eau va parer la noyée
> Voici mon bouquet de fleurs de la Passion
> Qui offrent tendrement deux couronnes d'épines
> Les rues sont mouillées de la pluie de naguère
> Des anges diligents travaillent pour moi à la maison
> La lune et la tristesse disparaîtront pendant
> Toute la sainte journée
> Toute la sante journée j'ai marché en chantant
> Une dame penchée à sa fenêtre m'a regardé longtemps
> M'éloigner en chantant.

> (In the end lies no longer frighten me
> There's the moon cooking like a fried egg
> This necklace of drops of water will adorn the drowned woman
> Behold my bouquet of Passion flowers
> Which tenderly offer two crowns of thorns
> The streets are wet from the recent rain
> Some diligent angels work for me at home
> The moon and sadness will disappear during
> The whole blessed day
> The whole blessed day I walked around singing
> For a long time a woman leaning out the window watched me
> Continue on my way singing.)

As several critics have remarked, the seventh section begins with a mood of supreme confidence. It also returns to the theme of falsehood as an aesthetic problem, introduced at the beginning of the poem. Indeed, it is because Apollinaire has finally solved this problem that he is able to be so confident. The first line announces his breakthrough: "A la fin les mensonges ne me font plus peur" ("In the end lies no longer frighten me"). As Rees notes, this recalls a similar statement by Apollinaire in *La Phalange* in January 1908.[55] Celebrating the poetry of Jean Royère, he boldly proclaimed, "La fausseté est une mère féconde" ("Falsity is a fertile mother").[56] Since Apollinaire's new style distorts reality in the service of a higher, poetic truth, by definition it constitutes a "lie." Instead of being a liability, however, it possesses numerous advantages. In particular, it allows him to say things that cannot be said any other way. Now that Apollinaire is no longer afraid of lies, he ventures to tell a few himself. The image of the moon sizzling in space like a fried egg, Edson declares, is "a humorous example of the contradiction between what our senses tell us and what we know to be true."[57] Although it is really spherical, the moon appears to be flat. Similarly, although we recognize drops of water as such, under certain circumstances they can appear to be diamonds.

While most critics regard these two examples as lies illustrating Apollinaire's new poetics, they are also striking metaphors. Falsehood is elevated to the level of an aesthetic principle. According to Breunig, the third line reminds some people of Ophelia, drowned and lying lifeless on the riverbank. In his opinion, however, the false necklace is better suited to the sister of Narcissus.[58] The next two lines, with their references to passion flowers, are taken from "Le Printemps." They re-utilize "l'ancienne image des passiflores dans 'L'Ermite'" ("the former image of passion flowers in 'L'Ermite,'"), Davies observes, "mais en transformant leur 'saint cruauté' en tendresse nouvelle" ("but by transforming their 'holy cruelty' into a new tenderness").[59] Since passion flowers grow on a vine, in reality they would make a terrible bouquet. Their presence here is due both to their appearance and to their symbolic value. According to all indications, the day the poet has chosen to rest is Easter Sunday. The theme of crucifixion encountered in the second section is renewed accordingly, but the false centurions have been replaced by tender flowers. Their "thorns" are completely harmless. Reflecting Apollinaire's optimistic mood, the remaining verses contain pleasing images. Cleansed by the recent rain, the streets feel as if they have been baptized. The exterminating angels encountered earlier have become diligent helpers. Madness and sadness promise to disappear as well during the joyous holiday. Apollinaire finds himself in such a good mood that he bursts into song "the whole blessed day." The lighthearted pun on "sainte" (blessed) provides a final touch of humor.

Au tournant d'une rue je vis des matelots
Qui dansaient le cou nu au son d'un accordéon
J'ai tout donné au soleil
Tout sauf mon ombre

Les dragues les ballots les sirènes mi-mortes
A l'horizon brumeux s'enfonçaient les trois-mâts
Les vents ont expiré couronnés d'anémones
O vierge signe pur du troisième mois.

(At a turn in the street I saw some sailors
Dancing bare-necked to an accordion
I have given everything to the sun
Everything but my shadow

The dredges the bales of goods the half-dead sirens
A three-masted ship disappeared on the misty horizon
Crowned with anemones the winds have expired
O Virgin pure sign of the third month.)

The eighth section continues the journey that Apollinaire began at the end of the previous section. Still singing to himself, he wanders down to the docks to see what is going on. There he finds several boisterous sailors who, happy to have the day off, are dancing to the sound of an accordion. Since it is a sunny day, they are wearing T-shirts and trousers. As Breunig observes, the sailors' joyous dance sets the tone for the whole section.[60] Already in an expansive mood, Apollinaire surrenders to the sun without compunction. Bates thinks he even strips off his shirt.[61] Not only is the sun an old friend, but Pilkington suspects it also symbolizes Apollinaire's new inspiration.[62] The reason that he has given it everything except his shadow is because the latter is not his to give away. His shadow is created by the sun in the first place. Since darkness is the absence of light, in any event, the two could never exist together. In addition, Durry explains, "l'ombre est ce double du poète, ce *Doppelgänger*, qui dure autant que lui" ("the shadow is the poet's double, a Doppelgänger, that lasts as long as he does").[63] In order to get rid of it Apollinaire would have to die.

Looking around absentmindedly, Apollinaire notices several dredges in the harbor, piles of bales on the dock, and, curiously, some half-dead sirens—creatures with the head of a bird and the body of a fish. Greet speculates that they are gasping and flopping around because they have recently been netted.[64] In retrospect, the "dragues" may not be dredges after all but rather trawlers (another meaning of *drague*), in whose nets the sirens had become entangled. Or alternatively, she adds, they could represent the poet's use of traditional imagery, which he is abandoning. As in "L'Emigrant de Landor Road," finally, Apollinaire could be referring to ships' sirens. That they are "mi-mortes" (half-dead) would suggest that they are some distance away. And indeed, partially obscured by the haze, several three-masted ships are about to disappear over the horizon. The verb *s'enfoncer* suggests they are actually sinking into the ocean. Like the subject of the earlier poem, Bates assumes that Apollinaire has booked passage on one of the ships. Since *anemos* is Greek for "wind," the next-to-last line contains a play on words. Having subsided, the winds are finally crowned with "windflowers." Since the poet will perish in the next section, Breunig suspects that "ombre" also refers to his "shade."[65] At least the half-dead sirens, the sinking ships, and the dying wind combine to create an atmosphere of death. Slightly modified, the last verse is borrowed from "Le Printemps." Addressed to the Virgin Mary, it embraces the constellation Virgo, as well. As Apollinaire notes, Virgo is the third sign following the summer solstice, lasting from approximately September 17 to October 17. Since he was born on September 26, Virgo is also his sign. Having just celebrated Easter, however, he must wait five more months to celebrate his birthday.

> Templiers flamboyants je brûle parmi vous
> Prophétisons ensemble ô grand maître je suis
> Le désirable feu qui pour vous se dévoue
> Et la girande tourne ô belle ô belle nuit.
>
> Liens déliés par une libre flamme Ardeur
> Que mon souffle éteindra O Morts à quarantaine
> Je mire de ma mort la gloire et le malheur
> Comme si je visais l'oiseau de la quintaine
>
> Incertitude oiseau feint peint quand vous tombiez
> Le soleil et l'amour dansaient dans le village
> Et tes enfants galants bien ou mal habillés
> Ont bâti ce bûcher le nid de mon courage.
>
> (Flaming Templars I burn among you
> Let us prophesize together O grand master I am
> The desirable fire that devotes itself to you
> And the pinwheel turns O lovely O lovely night
>
> Bonds undone by a free flame Ardor
> That my breath will extinguish O Dead during Lent

With my death I take aim at glory and suffering
As if I aimed at the bird of the quintain.

Uncertainty painted pretend bird when you fell
The sun and love danced in the village
And your gallant children well or badly dressed
Built this pyre the nest of my courage.)

Although the final section is composed of three rhymed quatrains like the first section, its tone could scarcely be more different. Instead of a lovely spring garden, the setting resembles the flaming interior of a volcano. Recounting the poet's martyrdom and betrothal, his death and resurrection, the section is "one of the most obscure passages in Apollinaire" in Bates' opinion.[66] Members of a military order founded in Jerusalem during the Crusades, the Knights Templar were famed for their gallantry, courage, and moral fiber. Accused of heresy at the beginning of the fourteenth century, they were condemned by King Philippe le Bel to be burned at the stake. Although many knights were executed earlier, Apollinaire focuses on the execution of Jacques de Molay, the Templars' Grand Master, together with his deputy Geoffroi de Charnai on March 18, 1314. From the beginning, it is evident that Apollinaire considers himself to be their equal and a martyr as well. Among other things, Greet detects the traditional theme of the artist's persecution.[67] In Pilkington's opinion, Apollinaire uses the image of the Templars to confer "a quasi-mythical quality upon his own experience."[68] The fact that the knights swore allegiance to only one mistress, the Virgin Mary, links this section to the invocation at the end of the preceding section. That Apollinaire invites the Grand Master to prophesize with him is unexpected to say the least. However, one of the things that made Jacques de Molay a legendary figure, besides his refusal to yield to authority, was the prophecy he issued as the flames shot up around him. Not only would Pope Clement V be dead within forty days, he supposedly predicted, but the king himself would also die before the end of the year. Miraculously, both predictions came true.

Bates suggests that the second line refers to Picasso, whose band of followers, like the Templars before them, were determined to defend the temple (of art), to serve (Beauty), and to purify the world (with their ardor).[69] Apollinaire's next statement is equally surprising: "Je suis / Le désirable feu qui pour vous se dévoue" ("I am / The desirable fire that devotes itself to you"). As in "Le Brasier," Greet explains, fire represents inspiration and fertility as well as purification and death. In this context, she opts for an allegorical interpretation: "my spirit is as ardent as the flame that destroyed you."[70] By contrast, Breunig adopts a more literal approach. He believes that Apollinaire sees himself not only as a martyr but also as the fire itself. "It is thanks to him," he writes, "that the others will achieve their rebirth through death."[71] Thus, Apollinaire will be both the instrument and the result of his own regeneration. Of course, it is also possible that *suivre* means "to follow," in which case he would adopt a more passive role.

The fourth verse seems to have generated considerable scholarly confusion: "Et la girande tourne ô belle ô belle nuit" ("And the girandole turns O lovely night"). For example, Durry imagines "une gerbe de fusées qui s'envolent du bûcher et font . . . un tourbillon embrasé" ("a sheaf of rockets that burst from the pyre and create . . . a fiery whirlwind").[72] Unfortunately, she transforms not only a single *girande* into a whole pyrotechnical display but also one type of firework into another. Unlike a rocket, which shoots straight up in the air, a pinwheel is stationary and simply spins around and around. Greet and Breunig suggest two possible scenarios. Either the burning martyrs become celestial bodies, or the bonfires that consume them become imitation suns.[73] Nevertheless, a third possibility exists that seems much more likely. According to all indications, the relationship between the first hemistich and the second hemistich is one of equivalence. In other words, the night sky seems to be revolving like a pinwheel. Significantly, Apollinaire employed the very same metaphor two years later. Describing a painting at the Salon des Artistes Français, he declared: "Des étoiles semblent tourner au loin ainsi que les girandes aux feux d'artifice" ("Some far away stars seem to turn like pinwheels during fireworks displays").[74]

At the beginning of the second stanza, both of the Templars are dead. Although Apollinaire was burning along with them in the previous stanza, somehow he seems to have escaped their fate. While not technically "déliés" (untied), the knights have been freed from their bonds by the fire that consumed them. That they were tied to a stake while the flame itself was "libre" (free) is ironic. That they had to die before they could be freed is even more ironic. "Ardeur / Que mon souffle éteindra" ("Ardor / That my breath will extinguish") can be interpreted in several ways. At the most banal level, Apollinaire apparently promises to blow out the few remaining flames. Or perhaps his breath is so powerful that it will extinguish the whole conflagration. According to Breunig, the phrase is often interpreted as predicting the poet's death and with it his inspiration.[75] However, this conclusion is not supported by the phrase's grammatical construction, which presupposes a cause-and-effect relationship. Apollinaire has to be alive in order to extinguish the "ardor" with his breath.

"O Morts à quarantaine" has also generated considerable discussion. Since the second word is capitalized, it almost certainly refers to the Templars. However, as Bates remarks, the last two words could mean "during Lent," "at the age of forty," "in forty days," "in a group of forty," or "in quarantine."[76] Although several critics think the second suggestion works best, Jacques de Molay and Geoffroi de Charmai were well over fifty at the time. Since they were executed during Lent, the best translation is clearly the first one. Judging from line 7, Apollinaire has not escaped the fire after all. He is still tied to the burning stake and about to succumb to the flames. While his death will obviously be a calamity, his subsequent rebirth will be glorious.

The "quintaine" is a medieval jousting game in which a knight on horseback demonstrates his skill with a lance. Not surprisingly, it is also a metaphor for sexual intercourse—as Apollinaire discovered by reading the Italian author Pietro Aretino. According to Boisson, the "oiseau" in "Les Fiançailles" is a piece of painted wood shaped like a bird. "Servant de cible dans les jeux d'une fête de village" ("serving as a target in village games during a celebration"), it also represents the Holy Spirit.[77] Because it is difficult to hit a small target with a lance, Apollinaire makes the bird a symbol of uncertainty in the final stanza. Although Greet relates this concept to the poet's love life, it almost certainly refers to his aesthetic uncertainty—to that period of "engourdissement" when he ceased to write (or at least to publish) poetry. She also detects a certain amount of wordplay between "feint" ("artificial") and "fin" (either "fine" or "clever").[78] As Breunig points out, the wooden bird illustrates the stanza's central theme: that fulfillment can emerge only from destruction.[79] Indeed, this is the central theme of the entire poem. When the anonymous jouster in line 9 finally knocks the target down, the village stages an impromptu celebration—joined by the sun, which is a surprisingly good dancer. A similar scene occurs in "Merlin et la vieille femme," where "le soleil en dansant remuait son nombril" ("the dancing sun moved its navel"). As Apollinaire well knew, the sun only dances on one day a year: Easter, which, not coincidentally, is when the poem takes place. Boisson reports that Apollinaire gleaned this piece of arcane information from Colin de Plancy's *Dictionnaire infernal.*[80]

However, the most important celebration takes place in the poet's mind rather than in the village square. With the loss of his uncertainty, he is free to create a different kind of poetry—illustrated by "Les Fiançailles." In addition to his new aesthetics, the latter embodies his newly found confidence. Although "tes" (your) in the next to last line is hopelessly vague, it probably refers to the village's inhabitants. It is they who have built Apollinaire's pyre and who watch as the flames slowly consume him. Unexpectedly, the poem ends on a triumphant note. Since the pyre also serves as the poet's nest, he will rise again from his ashes like the Phoenix. Breunig argues that Apollinaire has learned not only to live with uncertainty but also to value it. It is no longer a vice but "a cherished virtue."[81] However, this interpretation requires us to ignore the central development in the last stanza. By the end of the quatrain, the bird of uncertainty has been replaced by the courageous bird in the last line. The "oiseau de la quintaine" has been replaced by the Phoenix. No longer wracked with doubt and insecurity, Apollinaire finally possesses the courage to forge ahead.

Notes

1. Michel Décaudin, *"Alcools" de Guillaume Apollinaire* (Paris: Gallimard, 1993), 91. The existing manuscripts are reproduced in Décaudin, *Le Dossier d'"Alcools,"* rev. ed. (Paris: Minard, 1965), 201–8.

2. Guillaume Apollinaire, *Tendre comme le souvenir* (Paris: Gallimard, 1952), 74.

3. LeRoy C. Breunig, "Apollinaire's 'Les Fiançailles,'" *Essays in French Literature*, November 1966, 1–32; Laurie Edson, "A New Aesthetic: Apollinaire's 'Les Fiançailles,'" *Symposium*, Vol. 36, No. 2 (Summer 1982), 115–28.

4. Anne Hyde Greet, tr., *"Alcools." Guillaume Apollinaire* (Berkeley: University of California Press, 1965), 267.

5. Décaudin, *Le Dossier*, 175. Henri Scepi examines the former in "'Un lyrisme neuf': Le Cas des 'Fiançailles' dans *Alcools* d'Apollinaire," *Apollinaire: Revue d'Etudes Apollinariennes*, No. 13 (September 2013), 13–28.

6. Marie-Jeanne Durry, *Guillaume Apollinaire: "Alcools,"* Vol 3 (Paris: SEDES, 1964), 175.

7. Greet, tr., *"Alcools,"* 267.

8. LeRoy C. Breunig, *Guillaume Apollinaire* (New York: Columbia University Press, 1959), 25.

9. S. I. Lockerbie, "*Alcools* et le symbolisme," *Revue des Lettres Modernes*, Nos. 85-89 (Fall 1963), 21.

10. Décaudin, *Le Dossier*, 204. Guillaume Apollinaire, *Oeuvres poétiques*, ed. Marcel Adéma and Michel Décaudin (Paris: Gallimard, 1965), 556. Michel Décaudin, "Compléments à un dossier," *Revue des Lettres Modernes*, Nos. 69–70 (Spring 1962), 59.

11. Quoted in Garnet Rees, ed., *Guillaume Apollinaire: "Alcools"* (London: Athlone 1975), 27.

12. Susan Harrow, "'Les Fiançailles': cristallisation d'un amour," *Revue des Lettres Modernes*, Nos. 805–11 (1987), 121.

13. Ibid., 121–22, and Greet, tr., *"Alcools,"* 267.

14. Timothy Mathews, *Reading Apollinaire: Theories of Poetic Language* (Manchester: Manchester University Press, 1987), 54.

15. Breunig, "Apollinaire's 'Les Fiançailles,'" 21.

16. See Claude Debon, *Apollinaire: Glossaire des oeuvres complètes* (Paris: Sorbonne Nouvelle, 1988), 44.

17. Greet, tr., "*Alcools*," 268.

18. Mathews, *Reading Apollinaire*, 57.

19. Greet, tr., "*Alcools*," 171; William Meredith, tr., *Guillaume Apollinaire. "Alcools." Poems 1898–1913* (Garden City, NY: Doubleday, 1965), 191; Oliver Bernard, tr., *Apollinaire: Selected Poems* (Harmondsworth, UK: Penguin, 1965), 34; Donald Revell, tr., *Alcools: Poems by Guillaume Apollinaire* (Middletown, CT: Wesleyan University Press, 1995), 137.

20. Marie-Claude Rampant, "A propos de citrons," *Revue des Lettres Modernes*, Nos. 276–79 (1971), 110–12.

21. Scott Bates, *Guillaume Apollinaire*, rev. ed. (Boston: Twayne, 1989), 76.

22. Rees, ed. *Guillaume Apollinaire*, 170.

23. A. E. Pilkington, ed. *Apollinaire: "Alcools"* (Oxford: Blackwell, 1970), 150.

24. Greet, tr., "*Alcools*," 270.

25. Pierre Brunel, *Apollinaire entre deux mondes: Mythocritique II* (Paris: Presses Universitaires de France, 1997), 78.

26. Greet, tr., "*Alcools*," 270.

27. Scepi, "'Un lyrisme neuf,'" 22.

28. Greet, tr., "*Alcools*," 270.

29. Margaret Davies, "Image d'hier, image d'aujourd'hui," *Essays in French Literature*, No. 17 (November 1980), 84.

30. Ibid., 83, and Margaret Davies, *Apollinaire* (New York: St. Martins, 1964), 152.

31. Mathews, *Reading Apollinaire*, 63.

32. Davies, "Image d'hier," 84; Rees, ed. *Guillaume Apollinaire*, 170; and Greet, tr., "*Alcools*," 271.

33. Harrow, "'Les Fiançailles,'" 132.

34. Mathews, *Reading Apollinaire*, 64.

35. Greet, tr., "*Alcools*," 271.

36. Mechtild Cranston, "Sortir d'Orkenise: Réflexions sur 'Onirocritique,' 'Le Brasier,' et 'Les Fiançailles,'" *Revue des Lettres Modernes*, Nos. 166–69 (1967), 57.

37. Mathews, *Reading Apollinaire*, 65.

38. Ibid., 65–66.

39. Breunig, "Apollinaire's 'Les Fiançailles,'" 15.

40. Pilkington, ed., *Apollinaire: "Alcools*," 152.

41. Etienne-Alain Hubert, "Erudition d'Apollinaire: quatre exemples," *Revue des Lettres Modernes*, Nos. 530–36 (1978), 84–85. As he demonstrates, "ombre" in this instance means "image."

42. Pilkington, ed., *Apollinaire: "Alcools*," 152.

43. Brunel, *Apollinaire entre deux mondes*, 78.

44. Greet, tr., "*Alcools*," 272.

45. Davies, "Image d'hier," 85.

46. Bates, *Guillaume Apollinaire*, 82.

47. Brunel, *Apollinaire entre deux mondes*, 79.

48. Breunig, "Apollinaire's 'Les Fiançailles," 22.

49. Davies, "Image d'hier," 85.

50. Breunig, "Apollinaire's 'Les Fiançailles,'" 22.

51. Bates, *Guillaume Apollinaire*, 82; Madeleine Boisson, *Apollinaire et les mythologies antiques* (Paris: Nizet, 1989), 436; Breunig, "Apollinaire's 'Les Fiançailles,'" 22; Rees, ed., *Alcools*, 171.

52. Brunel, *Apollinaire entre deux mondes*, 79, and Jean Burgos, "Sur les sentiers de la creation," in Jean Burgos, Claude Debon, and Michel Décaudin, *Apollinaire, en somme* (Paris: Champion, 1998), 209.

53. Bates, *Guillaume Apollinaire*, 82, and Greet, tr., "*Alcools*," 273.

54. Boisson, *Apollinaire et les mythologies antiques*, 436–40.

55. Rees, ed., *Guillaume Apollinaire*, 171.

56. Guillaume Apollinaire, "Jean Royère," *La Phalange*, January 1908. Reprinted in Apollinaire, *Oeuvres en prose complètes*, Vol. 2, ed. Pierre Caizergues and Michel Décaudin (Paris: Gallimard, 1991), 1006.

57. Edson, "A New Aesthetic," 23–124.

58. Breunig, "Apollinaire's 'Les Fiançailles,'" 23.

59. Davies, "Image d'hier," 85.

60. Breunig, "Apollinaire's 'Les Fiançailles,'" 25.

61. Bates, *Guillaume Apollinaire*, 93.

62. Pilkington, ed., *Apollinaire: "Alcools,"* 153.

63. Durry, *Guillaume Apollinaire*, 3:196. See 191–231 for the various roles *ombre* plays in Apollinaire's works.

64. Greet, tr., "*Alcools*," 275.

65. Breunig, "Apollinaire's 'Les Fiançailles,'" 25.

66. Bates, *Guillaume Apollinaire*, 63.

67. Greet, tr., "*Alcools*," 276

68. Pilkington, ed. *Apollinaire: "Alcools,"* 153.

69. Bates, *Guillaume Apollinaire*, 80 and 84.

70. Greet, tr., "*Alcools*," 276 and 277.

71. Breunig, "Apollinaire's 'Les Fiançailles,'" 26.

72. Durry, *Guillaume Apollinaire*, 3:203.

73. Greet, tr., "*Alcools*," 277, and Breunig, "Apollinaire's 'Les Fiançailles,'" 26.

74. Guillaume Apollinaire, "Promenades au Grand Palais," *L'Intransigeant*, May 3, 1910. Reprinted in *Oeuvres en prose complètes*, 195.

75. Breunig, "Apollinaire's 'Les Fiançailles,'" 27.

76. Bates, *Guillaume Apollinaire*, 84.

77. See Boisson, *Apollinaire et les mythologies antiques*, 277.

78. Greet, tr., "*Alcools*," 277.

79. Breunig, "Apollinaire's 'Les Fiançailles,'" 27.

80. Boisson, *Apollinaire et les mythologies antiques*, 78.

81. Breunig, "Apollinaire's 'Les Fiançailles,'" 27–28.

CHAPTER SEVEN

A Thirst for Life

"Cortège" is one of the more daring compositions in *Alcools* and also one of the more challenging. Written in response to an existential crisis, it traces Apollinaire's experience as he embarks on a voyage of self-discovery. Conceived primarily as an investigation, it follows the poet as he explores both his personal and his poetic identity. Since the poem is basically a work in progress, Apollinaire carefully feels his way as he proceeds, occasionally drawing on Walt Whitman and the French Unanimist poets. Assembling the building blocks of his personal and professional life one-by-one, he eventually arrives at an understanding of his mission in life. In "Vendémiaire," Apollinaire takes a similar journey, although in this poem it is the destinations themselves that do the talking and are distilled into a wine that leaves him thirsty for more experiences.

"Cortège"

Published in *Poème et Drame* in November 1912, "Cortège" haunted Apollinaire for at least six years as he experimented with several different ideas. Three fragmentary manuscripts of the poem exist: a single page that is difficult to date, twenty-five verses dating from the beginning of 1906, and twenty verses entitled "Brumaire."[1] Since the latter was included in *L'Année Républicaine*, during his flirtation with Unanimism, it dates from around 1909. Like so many of Apollinaire's poems, therefore, the final version is a patchwork creation. Léon Bailby, to whom the work is dedicated, was the editor of *L'Intransigeant*, for which Apollinaire wrote a column entitled "La Vie Artistique." "L'un de ses plus grands poèmes" ("One of his greatest poems"),[2] in Philippe Renaud's opinion, "Cortège" apparently grew out of a *crise de foi* that enveloped the poet in 1906. For an entire year, he wrote little and published virtually nothing. Although this year is almost a complete blank, it must have been a difficult time for him. Apollinaire was still upset about losing Annie, he was trapped in a boring bank job, and, at the age of twenty-six, he was still living at home. The future must have looked pretty bleak. In particular, he undoubtedly wondered whether he should continue to write poetry—the one thing in his life that still had meaning. Since Apollinaire had always lived a relatively rootless life, through no fault of his own, he set out to discover both his identity and his place in the world.

"Cortège" is completely unlike any of the poems we have examined so far. The first section contains three stanzas, each of which is slightly longer than its predecessor, which are written in free verse with an occasional rhyme. The second section follows the same haphazard rhyme scheme and is approximately twice as long. Containing only two quatrains, the third section is surprisingly brief. Each stanza is composed of classical alexandrines rhyming two-by-two. Reflecting the composition's disparate origins, each of the three sections employs a totally different style. The first section is deliberately hermetic, the second adopts a colloquial tone, and the third conforms to the classical model. This is the most daring poem we have encountered so far. In several ways it is also one of the most demanding. Throwing caution to the wind, Apollinaire assails the reader with obscure references, abrupt transitions, and outrageous statements. And yet, as Richard Stamelman notes, "Cortège" possesses a surprising unity: "a desire for self-knowledge informs and unites the entire poem."[3]

> Oiseau tranquille au vol inverse oiseau
> Qui nidifie en l'air
> A la limite où notre sol brille déjà
> Baisse ta deuxième paupière la terre t'éblouit
> Quand tu lèves la tête
>
> Et moi aussi de près je suis sombre et terne
> Une brume qui vient d'obscurcir les lanternes
> Une main qui tout à coup se pose devant les yeux
> Une voûte entre vous et toutes les lumières
> Et je m'éloignerai m'illuminant au milieu d'ombres
> Et d'alignements d'yeux des astres bien-aimés

Oiseau tranquille au vol inverse oiseau
Qui nidifie en l'air
A la limite où brille déjà ma mémoire
Baisse ta deuxième paupière
Ni à cause du soleil ni à cause de la terre
Mais pour ce feu oblong dont l'intensité ira s'augmentant
Au point qu'il deviendra un jour l'unique lumière.

(Tranquil bird with inverted flight bird
Who nests in the air
At the limit where our planet shines
Lower your second eyelid earth dazzles you
When you raise your head

And close up I too am somber and dull
A mist that has just obscured the lanterns
A hand that suddenly covers the eyes
A vault between you and all the lights
and I will depart
shining in the midst of shadows
And of rows of the beloved stars' eyes

Tranquil bird with inverted flight
Who nest in the air
At the limit where my memory shines
Lower your second eyelid
Neither because of the sun nor because of the earth
But for this oblong fire whose intensity will increase
Until one day it is the only light.)

The poem begins with an apostrophe addressed to a marvelous bird Apollinaire discovered during his omnivorous reading. The bird that flies upside down was first described by Jean Mocquet in his *Voyages en Afrique, Asie, Indes Orientales et Occidentales* (1617). Originally recounted to Mocquet by a sailor, the tale of the bird was later included in Ferdinand Denis' *Le Monde enchanté, cosmographie et histoire naturelle fantastiques du Moyen Age* (1843), which is where Apollinaire found it.[4] According to Mocquet, the fabulous bird remains aloft all its life, never landing on the ground. When it comes time to nest, it flies so high that its eggs have time to hatch before they hit the ground! The bird in "Cortège" flies so far above the earth that, illuminated by the sun's rays, the planet shines like the moon. Since the bird is flying upside down, it must lift its head (move its head downward) to look at the earth below.[5] And when it does so, it must lower a specialized eyelid to protect its eye from the dazzling sight. Apollinaire mistakenly calls it a second eyelid. In addition to lower and upper lids, many birds have a semi-transparent nictating membrane that serves as a *third* eyelid. That there is some kind of connection between the bird in "Cortège" and Apollinaire seems fairly clear. Claude Morhange-Bégué and Pierre Lartigue postulate a metaphorical or symbolic link, Robert Champigny thinks the bird represents Apollinaire's "conscience lucide," and Marie-Jeanne Durry believes it represents the poet himself.[6] According to the "Brumaire" manuscript, however, as Stamelman points out, the bird symbolizes "une nouvelle réalité."[7]

The second stanza focuses on the poet. Interestingly, Apollinaire compares himself to the planet Earth rather than to the marvelous bird. Like Earth, he insists, he appears to be somber and dull when viewed close up. This statement is followed by three metaphors intended to serve as illustrations. Apollinaire is like a fog cloaking the streetlights, a hand clapped over someone's eyes, and a ceiling that obscures the stars. And yet, like the earth, he is dazzling when viewed at a distance surrounded by black space and countless stars. The third stanza repeats most of the first stanza but with a few important differences. In particular, Apollinaire commands the bird to close its extra eyelid, not because of the sun or the earth, but because of a mysterious "feu oblong" that grows brighter and brighter. Or rather, since he uses the future tense, the oblong flame *will* grow brighter and brighter, until it eventually shines more brightly than everything else.

The identity of the "feu oblong" has intrigued scholars for many years. Stamelman thinks that it symbolizes Apollinaire's memory, Anne Hyde Greet that it represents some kind of savior, and A. E. Pilkington that it embodies Apollinaire's power to "illuminate reality."[8] However, the last two lines develop and expand an image that was introduced in the previous stanza: "Et je m'éloignerai m'illuminant au milieu d'ombres" ("And I will depart shining in the midst of shadows"). In other words, they describe Apollinaire continuing on his upward path. As Scott Bates declares, "The poet becomes a kind of comet as he goes off into space."[9] In the last analysis, his upward trajectory coincides with his apotheosis. As Madeleine Boisson explains, he is "métamorphosé après sa mort en étoile" ("transformed into a star after his death").[10] The "feu oblong" represents Apollinaire all right but Apollinaire transformed into a star. Significantly, the stars in "Lul de Faltenin" are also oblong (see Chapter 5).[11] Although Durry attributes "l'unique lumière" to a fusion of light and shadow, the poet has to leave the shadowy earth before his star can shine.[12] This observation brings us back to the third line: "A la limite où brille déjà ma mémoire" ("At the limit where my memory shines"), which unfortunately is ambiguous. While Stamelman assumes the line describes Apollinaire's power of recollection, it refers to something else entirely: his future reputation. "Sa mémoire," Renaud comments, "est la mémoire que l'on conservera de lui [après sa mort]" ("His memory is the memory that people will retain of him [after his death]").[13] Thus, the poet's voyage away from his home planet turns out to be an optimistic metaphor. In every sense of the word, it depicts his rising star. Although his journey is expressed in spatial terms, in reality it is a journey over time.

Un jour
Un jour je m'attendais moi-même
Je me disais Guillaume il est temps que tu viennes
Pour que je sache enfin celui-là que je suis
Moi qui connais les autres
Je les connais par les cinq sens et quelques autres
Il me suffit de voir leurs pieds pour pouvoir refaire ces gens à milliers
De voir leurs pieds paniques un seul de leurs cheveux
Ou leur langue quand il me plaît de faire le médecin
Ou leurs enfants quand il me plaît de faire le prophète
Les vaisseaux des armateurs la plume de mes confrères
La monnaie des aveugles les mains des muets
Ou bien encore à cause du vocabulaire et non de l'écriture
Une lettre écrite par ceux qui ont plus de vingt ans
Il me suffit de sentir l'odeur de leurs églises
L'odeur des fleuves dans leurs villes
Le parfum des fleurs dans les jardins publics
O Corneille Agrippa l'odeur d'un petit chien m'eût suffi
Pour décrire exactement tes concitoyens de Cologne
Leurs rois-mages et la ribambelle ursuline
Qui t'inspirait l'erreur touchant toutes les femmes
Il me suffit de goûter la saveur du laurier qu'on cultive
        pour que j'aime ou que je bafoue
Et de toucher les vêtements
Pour ne pas douter si l'on est frileux ou non
O gens que je connais
Il me suffit d'entendre le bruit de leurs pas
Pour pouvoir indiquer à jamais la direction qu'ils ont prise
Il me suffit de tous ceux-là pour me croire le droit
De ressusciter les autres.

(One day
One day as I waited for myself to appear
I said to myself Guillaume it is time that you come
So I will finally know who I am
I who know everyone else
I know them by my five senses and a few others
It is enough to glimpse their feet to recreate thousands of these people
To see their panicked feet a single hair
Or their tongue when I feel like playing doctor
Or their children when I feel like playing prophet
The owners' ships my colleagues' pens
Blind men's coins deaf-mutes' hands
Or even because of the vocabulary not the handwriting
A letter written by people who are older than twenty
It is enough for me to smell the odor of their churches
The odor of the rivers in their towns
The perfume of flowers in their public gardens
O Cornelius Agrippa the smell of a little dog would have sufficed
To identify your fellow citizens of Cologne
Their Wise-Men and the Ursuline swarm
That inspired you with the error regarding all women
It is enough for me to taste a laurel leaf for me to love or scoff
And to touch their clothing
To know for sure if they are cold or not
O people whom I know
It is enough to hear their footsteps
To indicate forever the direction they have taken
All these things are enough to convince me that I have the right
To bring others back to life.)

The central section of "Cortège" is much less abstruse than the first section but a great deal longer. Stamelman calls it "the most prosaic and the most lyrical part of the poem."[14] Abandoning the theme of his own apotheosis, Apollinaire adopts a quieter tone. Among other things, Michel Décaudin remarks, this section recalls certain themes associated with Unanimism and the Abbaye de Créteil. Like them, it is concerned with "la réfraction dans l'individu de tous les autres qui l'entourent et du passé qui l'a créé" ("the refraction in the individual of all the others who surround him and of the past that created him").[15] Greet finds Apollinaire's style reminiscent of Walt Whitman, whom the two groups greatly admired.[16] The first four lines announce his ambitious project: to discover his authentic self. Almost immediately, however, Apollinaire finds himself distracted by other concerns.

Portraying himself as a gifted seer, he boasts that he possesses extraordinary powers of perception. Because of this, he continues, he is able to discover information about people by using his five senses "et quelques autres" ("and a few others"). The simplest clue enables him to reconstruct an entire individual.

The next twenty-one lines illustrate the foregoing remark utilizing sight, smell, taste, touch, and hearing. Apollinaire only needs to see someone's pen, for example, or to smell someone's flowers to imagine what they look like. Addressing the sixteenth-century philosopher and alchemist Corneille Agrippa, who lived in Cologne, he claims he could have imagined the whole city just from smelling a little dog. Since Agrippa was always accompanied by a large black dog, which many people associated with the Devil, the reference to a small dog is puzzling.[17] Renaud speculates that the poet wanted to demonstrate his superiority.[18] Since Apollinaire had visited Cologne, he knew the cathedral contained relics of the Three Wise Men and was acquainted with the legend of Saint Ursula, martyred by the Huns together with her ten thousand handmaidens. "L'erreur touchant toutes les femmes" ("the error regarding all women") is a humorous reference to one of Agrippa's books: *On the Nobility and Excellence of the Female Sex*.[19] The remainder of the catalogue of his abilities contains examples of Apollinaire's unusually perceptive taste, touch, and hearing. Just by touching someone's clothes, for example, he can tell whether that person is unusually sensitive to cold. Once he hears someone's footsteps, he can tell forever which way they have gone. Because Apollinaire possesses this unusual talent, he speaks of "resuscitating" people. With his powerful imagination he is able to bring them to life, at least for a moment.

> Un jour je m'attendais moi-même
> Je me disais Guillaume il est temps que tu viennes
> Et d'un lyrique pas s'avançaient ceux que j'aime
> Parmi lesquels je n'étais pas
> Les géants couverts d'algues passaient dans leurs villes
> Sous-marines où les tours seules étaient des îles
> Et cette mer avec les clartés de ses profondeurs
> Coulait sang de mes veines et fait battre mon coeur
> Puis sur terre il venait mille peuplades blanches
> Dont chaque homme tenait une rose à la main
> Et le langage qu'ils inventaient en chemin
> Je l'appris de leur bouche et je parle encore
> Le cortège passait et j'y cherchais mon corps
> Tous ceux qui survenaient et n'étaient pas moi-même

Amenaient un à un les morceaux de moi-même
On me bâtit peu à peu comme on élève une tour
Les peuples s'entassaient et je parus moi-même
Qu'ont formé tous les corps et les choses humaines.

(One day as I waited for myself to appear
I said to myself Guillaume it is time that you come
And with a lyric step everyone I love came forward
And I was not among them
Giants covered with seaweed entered their underwater
Cities whose towers alone were islands
And this sea with its sparkling lights and its depths
Flowed in my veins like blood and still makes my heart beat
Then on land came a thousand white clans
Each man holding a rose in his hand
And the language they invented along the way
I learned from their mouths and I still speak
The procession passed and I looked for my body
All those who came and who were not myself
Brought pieces of myself one by one
They built me one by one as if erecting a tower
The clans kept coming and I myself appeared
Formed by all the bodies and human qualities.)

At long last, the reader encounters the procession announced in the title. In Durry's opinion, this is the most beautiful part of the poem.[20] Continuing his quest to discover his authentic individuality, which Champigny identifies as the source of his inspiration, Apollinaire watches as a parade of allegorical figures passes by.[21] Since they represent all of human history, the procession begins with the oldest and ends with the most recent. The first to appear are submarine giants covered with seaweed. "Comme la vie est née dans la mer," Renaud explains, "c'est cette mer qui est d'abord évoquée et dont l'onde devient le sang coulant encore dans les veines du poete" ("Since life was born in the sea, the sea is evoked first whose water becomes the blood still flowing in the poet's veins").[22] The giants are followed by innumerable tribes and races, each member of which holds a rose as a token of love. From them, modified by successive generations, Apollinaire receives the language he speaks and with which he composes his poetry. Other ancestors bring additional parts of the poet and reassemble him block-by-block, until he is completely reconstructed. Although he looks just like his old self, he is a changed person. He is aware of all the forces—biological as well as cultural—that have combined over the centuries to make him who he is. This is essentially what he says in the final section:

> Temps passés Trépassés Les dieux qui me formâtes
> Je ne vis que passant ainsi que vous passâtes
> Et détournant mes yeux de ce vide avenir
> En moi-même je vois tous le passé grandir
>
> Rien n'est mort que ce qui n'existe pas encore
> Près du passé luisant demain est incolore
> Il est informe aussi près de ce qui parfait
> Présente tout ensemble et l'effort et l'effet.
>
> (Past time Former generations The gods who shaped me
> I am only passing through just as you passed before me
> And averting my eyes from the vacant future
> I see all of the past magnified in myself
>
> Nothing is dead but that which does not yet exist
> Near the glowing past tomorrow is colorless
> It is formless also next to the perfection that
> Presents effort and effect together.)

After forty-six lines of free verse, the two rhymed quatrains come as quite a surprise. Without exception, the critics are impressed by their Classical purity, which reminds a number of them of Nicolas Boileau. However, the author whom the verses really evoke is not the theoretician of Classicism but rather Pierre Corneille.

As Durry has shown, the last two lines resemble the apostrophe from the Comte de Gomès to Don Diègue in Le Cid:

> Instruisez-le d'exemple et rendez-le parfait,
> Expliquant à ses yeux vos leçons par l'effet![23]
>
> (Instruct him by example and make him perfect,
> Explaining your lessons to him by their effect!)

As Morhange-Bégué and Lartigue remark, the penultimate stanza of "Cortège" begins with a "méditation sur le passage et le passé" ("meditation on passing and the past").[24] For better or worse, Apollinaire has come to realize, everything in life is transitory. Although we live in the present, everything is consigned to the past as soon as it is experienced. It becomes something we have done or something we once did. Since the past plays such a large role in our lives, as Apollinaire has just learned in the poem, he sees no reason to worry about tomorrow. Thus, "Cortège" concludes with a eulogy of the glimmering past as opposed to the colorless future. Since the future does not yet exist, Apollinaire declares, it is as good as dead. By contrast, the past continues to influence human behavior in a great many ways. Although many experiences are finished, they continue to have long-lasting repercussions. "Le passé est plus parfait que l'avenir," Jeanine Moulin explains, "puisqu'il contient à la fois l'espoir et la réalisation, la perspective et l'accomplissement" ("The past is more perfect than the future since it contains both hope and result, perspective and accomplishment").[25] A number of critics believe the last stanza describes poetry in particular, which, if it is really good, can achieve immortality.

"Vendémiaire"

Together with "Cortège," "Vendémiaire" is all that remains of Apollinaire's plan to publish twelve poems based on the Revolutionary French calendar. As noted previously, the project was eventually abandoned when he and Jules Romains drifted apart. Although Apollinaire's flirtation with Unanimism was relatively brief, it inspired him to experiment with new themes and new techniques. As a result, "Vendémiaire" occupies a special place in the evolution of his poetics. As Décaudin declares, "La tentation unanimiste a pris dans ce beau poème la forme d'un lyrisme personnel et chaleureux qui donne à Alcools, ouvert sur la brulante eau-de-vie de 'Zone,' un final d'une généreuse ivresse poétique" ("the Unanimist temptation assumes in this lovely poem the form of a personal and warm lyricism, which provides Alcools, opening with the burning brandy of 'Zone,' with a generous and intoxicating poetic conclusion").[26] Indeed, Apollinaire himself was very fond of the poem. Writing to Madeleine Pagès years later, he confided: "Mais dans Alcools, c'est peut-être 'Vendémiaire' que je préfère" ("But with Alcools, it is perhaps 'Vendémiaire' that I prefer").[27] Published in Les Soirées de Paris in November 1912, "Vendémiaire" was the first of Apollinaire's poems to appear without punctuation. A rough draft also exists that was written in several different colors of ink.[28] Discovered by Georges Schmits, a version based on the latter appeared in La Vie in October 1914.[29] Although Décaudin thinks the poem dates from Fall 1909, LeRoy C. Breunig believes it was composed in 1912. In his opinion, "both the theme and the technique preclude the probability of an earlier year."[30]

Be that as it may, Apollinaire's style is certainly much looser than in any of the poems we have examined so far. Although "Vendémiaire" begins in a traditional manner, the regular rhymes and line lengths yield before long to a desire for more flexibility. Henri Meschonnic has analyzed the poem's prosody in detail.[31] As he has shown, the 174 verses include no fewer than 117 alexandrines. The pattern of their distribution is revealing: the first eighteen verses are alexandrines, followed by groups of alexandrines here and there, and then a pair of alexandrines at the end. A similar pattern characterizes the poem's rhyme scheme. With one exception, the first eighteen lines consist of *rimes plates*. Thereafter, the rhymes grow more and more scattered, and Apollinaire relies more frequently on assonance. Becoming more and more daring, he rhymes "nouvelle" with "écueil" and "univers" with "univers." In several places, he even dispenses with rhyme altogether. A similar irregularity characterizes the length of the verses, which vary from two to seventeen syllables, and that of the stanzas, which contain between one and seventeen lines. This is the greatest liberty Apollinaire has ever known and anticipates his experiments in "Zone." Schmits argues at some length that the poem was influenced by Charles Cros' "La Vision du grand canal royal des deux mers."[32]

Another way in which "Vendémiaire" differs from Apollinaire's previous poetry is in its use of simultaneity. Unlike "Zone," which juxtaposes several different views at the same time, like a Cubist painting, it appears initially to be a linear composition. From his central vantage point, the poet watches as a series of cities pay homage to the French capital one after the other. In "Vendémiaire," "Les Fenêtres," and *L'Enchanteur pourrissant*," he explained in 1914, "on a tenté d'habituer l'esprit à concevoir un poème simultanément comme une scène de la vie" ("I have tried to train the mind to conceive a poem simultaneously like a scene in real life").[33] In other words, although the text is unavoidably sequential, the reader is supposed to construct a mental collage. In theory, the various scenes all take place simultaneously. Incidentally, the fact that Apollinaire associates "Vendémiaire" both with simultaneity and with "Les Fenêtres" tends to support the 1912 date advanced by Breunig. "The truly simultaneous poem in *Alcools* is 'Vendémiaire,'" Richard Stamelman declares, "in which the long enumeration of different cities evoke a feeling of global consciousness and where the cities themselves are portrayed in continual, instantaneous communication."[34]

In 1793, determined to rid the calendar of every religious and royalist trace, the Revolutionary French government bestowed a new name on every month. The first month was Vendémiaire, so named because it was associated with the grape harvest (*vendemia* in Latin). Not surprisingly, therefore, wine plays a central role in the poem, where it quickly assumes mythical proportions. As Renaud declares, "'Vendémiaire' est un grand poème dionysiaque; son thème est la transformation de l'univers en un vin pur offert à Apollinaire" ("'Vendémiaire' is a great Dionysiac poem; its theme is the transformation of the universe into a pure wine offered to Apollinaire").[35] Wine itself serves in turn as a metaphor for historical culture and poetic inspiration. Although "Vendémiaire" is a long poem, its plot is deceptively simple. As in "Zone," the poet walks along the Seine toward Auteuil, beginning in the evening and continuing until dawn the next day. The first four stanzas serve as a prologue:

Hommes de l'avenir souvenez-vous de moi
Je vivais à l'époque où finissaient les rois
Tour à tour ils mouraient silencieux et tristes
Et trois fois courageux devenaient trismégistes

Que Paris était beau à la fin de septembre
Chaque nuit devenait une vigne où les pampres
Répandaient leur clarté sur la ville et là-haut
Astres mûrs becquetés par les ivres oiseaux
De ma gloire attendaient la vendange de l'aube

Un soir passant le long des quais déserts et sombres
En rentrant à Auteuil j'entendis une voix
Qui chantait gravement se taisant quelquefois
Pour que parvînt aussi sur les bords de la Seine
La plainte d'autres voix limpides et lointaines

Et j'écoutai longtemps tous ces chants et ces cris
Qu'éveillait dans la nuit la chanson de Paris.

(Men of the future remember me
I lived during a period when the kings were dying out
One by one they all died silent and sad
And thrice courageous became trismegist.

How lovely Paris was at the end of September
Each night became a grape vine whose branches
Spread their brightness over the city and high above
Pecked by the drunken birds of my glory
Ripe stars awaited the dawn's harvest.

Walking along the dark deserted quays one evening
Returning to Auteuil I heard a deep voice
Singing and occasionally growing silent
So the sound of other distant yet limpid voices
Could reach the banks of the Seine

And for a long time I listened to other songs and cries
That the song of Paris awakened in the night.)

From the very first line, Apollinaire adopts a confident, larger-than-life persona. Not only does he assume that his poetry will have future readers, but he also addresses those readers on behalf of an entire generation. While Renaud describes his voice as "prophétique," Robert Couffignal objects that the poet, like the poem itself, is "trop oratoire."[36] According to him, "la rhétorique joue un role trop voyant de par les énumerations et le prosopopées" ("rhetoric plays a too visible role with all the enumerations and personifications"). As Apollinaire remarked, he and his friends occupied a unique place in time. Thanks to a series of anarchist shootings, stabbings, and bombings, royalty was fast disappearing. Thus, 1898 witnessed the assassination of Empress Elizabeth of Austro-Hungary, 1900 the assassination of King Umberto I of Italy and the attempted assassination of the Prince of Wales, 1902 the attempted assassination of King Leopold II of Belgium, 1906 the attempted assassination of King Alfonso XIII of Spain, 1908 the assassination of King Carlos of Portugal, and 1913 the assassination of King George I of Greece. Interestingly, a rough draft of the poem reveals that the "thrice-great" heroes in verses 3 and 4 were originally the anarchist assassins, not their royal victims.

The second stanza narrows the narrative focus and situates Apollinaire more precisely with regard to space and time. The poem takes place not only in Paris but also at the end of September. And indeed, Vendémiaire began on September 22 and ended on October 21. As Antoine Fongaro points out, the striking image that occupies the rest of the stanza resembles similar passages in the works of Jules Laforgue, Victor Hugo, and F. T. Marinetti.[37] In contrast to these writers, who are basically content to compare the constellations to grapevines, Apollinaire creates a *métaphore filée*. Since it is autumn, the starry vineyard is filled with drunken birds that have been eating fermented grapes. And since the stars disappear when morning dawns, the arrival of morning is compared to a grape harvest. The third stanza narrows the narrative focus still further. Apollinaire situates the action near the section of Auteuil that borders the Seine, where he moved in October 1909. Returning home one evening, he hears a mysterious song that, as we soon learn, belongs to Paris. This is the subject of the next two stanzas.

> J'ai soif villes de France et d'Europe et du monde
> Venez toutes couler dans ma gorge profonde
>
> Je vis alors que déjà ivre dans la vigne Paris
> Vendangeait le raisin le plus doux de la terre
> Ces grains miraculeux qui aux treilles chantèrent

(I am thirsty towns of France and Europe and all the world
Come all of you flow down my deep throat

I saw then that Paris already drunken and standing in the vineyard
Was harvesting the sweetest grapes on earth
Those miraculous grapes singing on their trellises.)

Although each stanza begins with "je," the word is uttered by a different individual in each case. Juxtaposed with the preceding lines, the first case is clearly the "chanson de Paris" announced previously. Although Roger Lefèvre believes the speaker is both Paris and the poet, this seems highly unlikely.[38] Sung by the former, the stanza is set to imaginary music and is surrounded by imaginary quotation marks. If uttered by the latter, the music and quotation marks would both need to be deleted. Because it is impossible for the two formats to coexist, there cannot possibly be two speakers. In any case, Apollinaire is clearly an observer at this stage rather than a participant in the poem. Except for the first line, which uses the imperative, every verb he utters is in the past tense. The second stanza quoted above is a case in point. Although it is early evening, Paris has been drinking for some time. Since the city is so fond of wine, it even possesses its own vineyard—possibly the block of grapevines in Montmartre that still exists today. While waiting for the cities to respond to its song, Paris sets about harvesting the ripe grapes, whose taste is simply "miraculeux." The fact that they also possess the ability to sing is even more miraculous.

Et Rennes répondit avec Quimper et Vannes
Nous voici ô Paris Nos maisons nos habitants
Ces grappes de nos sens qu'enfanta le soleil
Se sacrifient pour te désaltérer trop avide merveille
Nous t'apportons tous les cerveaux les cimetières les murailles
Ces berceaux pleins de cris que tu n'entendra pas
Et d'amont en aval nos pensées ô rivières
Les oreilles des écoles et nos mains rapprochées
Aux doigts allongés nos mains les clochers
Et nous t'apportons aussi cette souple raison
Que le mystère clôt comme une porte la maison
Ce mystère courtois de la galanterie
Ce mystère fatal fatal d'une autre vie
Double raison qui est au-delà de la beauté
Et que la Grèce n'a pas connue ni l'Orient
Double raison de la Bretagne où lame à lame
L'océan châtre peu à peu l'ancien continent.

(And Rennes answered with Quimper and Vannes
Here we are O Paris Our houses our citizens
These clusters of our senses children of the sun
Sacrifice themselves to quench your thirst all too greedy marvel
We bring you all the brains the cemeteries the walls
These cradles full of cries that you will not hear
And from upstream to downstream our thoughts O rivers
The schools' ears and our hands joined together
With extended fingers our hands the bell towers
And we bring you also that supple reason
That mystery closes like the door of a house
That courtly mystery of gallantry
That fatal mystery of another life
Double reason that surpasses beauty
Greece did not know or the Orient
Double reason of Brittany where wave by wave
The ocean gradually castrates the ancient continent.)

As S. I. Lockerbie remarks, the previous seventeen stanzas "renversent la formule du voyage: ce sont les pays et les villes qui viennent à la recherche [de Paris]" ("reverse the voyage formula: it is the countries and the towns that come in search [of Paris]").[39] The first cities to respond to Paris are located in Brittany. "Ces grappes de nos sens qu'enfanta le soleil" ("These clusters of our senses children of the sun") refers to the local grapes, which, transformed into wine, have absorbed all the characteristics of the region. "Raison" is used here in a paradoxical, perhaps even ironic sense to describe a special kind of reasoning—one that is self-validating. As such it evokes two famous "mysteries": courtly love and the quest of the Grail, both of which were celebrated in Breton romances. Thus "double raison" refers to the veneration of woman and of Christianity. The stanza concludes with a stunning bit of wordplay. Since northwest Bretagne is bordered by the ocean, Apollinaire evokes the waves beating against its cliffs, which, since *lame* means "blade," as well as "waves," are slowly castrating the continent.

Et les villes du Nord répondirent gaiement

Ô Paris nous voici boissons vivantes
Les viriles cités où dégoisent et chantent
Les métalliques saints de nos saintes usines
Nos cheminées à ciel ouvert engrossent les nuées
Comme fit autrefois l'Ixion mécanique
Et nos mains innombrables

Usines manufactures fabriques mains
Où les ouvriers nus semblables à nos doigts
Fabriquent du réel à tant par heure
Nous te donnons tout cela.

(And the towns of the North replied gaily

O Paris here we are lively drinks
The virile cities where the metallic saints
Of our sainted factories swear and sing
Our smokestacks in the open air impregnate
The clouds as mechanical Xion did before
And our innumerable hands
Factory fabric manufacturing hands
Where naked workers like our fingers
Fabricate reality at so much an hour
We give you all that.)

The next cities that respond are located in the north of France, which even then was heavily industrialized. As previously in "Les Fiançailles" (see Chapter 6), Apollinaire plays with the multiple meanings of *saint*: "holy-man," "blessed," and "damned." The noisy factories are "viriles" because they possess tall phallic chimneys that impregnate the clouds like Ixion in Greek mythology. Unlike Ixion's coupling with a facsimile Hera, which produced the centaurs, the factory chimneys simply foul the atmosphere with their smoke. The image of naked workers fabricating reality at so much an hour is potentially ambiguous. On the one hand, Apollinaire could be praising the Industrial Revolution's contributions to modern life. On the other, he could be condemning modern society's infatuation with mechanical gadgets. In retrospect, the verse seems heavily ironic and thus expresses the poet's disapproval. As Didier Alexandre observes, "la sacralisation de la machine et de l'usine inverse le rapport de l'homme au divin" ("the sacralisation of machines and factories reverses the relationship between mankind and the divine").[40]

Et Lyon répondit tandis que les anges de Fourvières
Tissaient un ciel nouveau avec la soie des prières

Désaltère-toi Paris avec les divines paroles
Que mes lèvres le Rhône et la Saône murmurent
Toujours le même culte de sa mort renaissant
Divise ici les saints et fait pleuvoir le sang

Heureuse pluie ô gouttes tièdes ô douleur
Un enfant regarde les fenêtres s'ouvrir
Et des grappes de têtes à d'ivres oiseaux s'offrir.

(And Lyon replied while the angels of Fourvieres
Wove a new sky with the silk of prayers

Quench your thirst Paris with the divine words
Murmured by my lips the Rhône and the Saône
Always the same cult of death reborn
Divides the saints here and rains down blood
Blessed rain O tepid drops O sorrow
A child watches the windows open
And clusters of heads offered to drunken birds.)

The first two lines situate the action firmly in Lyon. Perched on top of a hill overlooking the city, the Basilica of Notre-Dame de Fourvières is an important pilgrimage church. Lyon itself has been associated with the silk industry ever since the Middle Ages. Combining the two symbols of the city, Apollinaire imagines angels weaving a silky sky with their prayers. Situated at the juncture of the Rhône and the Saône rivers, Lyon has experienced so much bloodshed over the years that it is hard to interpret the remaining verses. Beginning with the Romans, for example, numerous Christians were beheaded during the reign of Marcus Aurelius. "Toujours le même culte de sa mort renaissant" ("Always the same cult of death reborn") seems to refer to the city's early years, which were characterized by religious heresies and bloody battles. In addition to Gnosticism and Montanism, Marc Poupon reports, there were three religions in which bloodshed was assigned a sacred role: Mithracism, the cult of Cybele, and Christianity. In the first two religions, which eventually blended into one, "la mort et la resurrection d'Attis étaient mimées par un homme qu'on fouetait jusqu'au sang" ("the death and resurrection of Atys were mimed by a man who was whipped until he bled").[41] Poupon thinks the "heureuse pluie" ("blessed rain") in the next two lines may refer to this particular rite. At the same time, he adds, the adjective "renaissant" connects the ancient atrocities to those perpetuated during the Renaissance by the Protestants and the Catholics. Although they were obviously divided by many things, "'il les divise' signifie qu'il les coupe en morceaux, généralement en deux, en les décapitant" ("'it divides them' means that it cuts them into pieces, generally two, while decapitating them"). The "enfant" in the next-to-last line is probably Apollinaire himself, who spent some time in Lyon when he was nineteen.

Les villes du Midi répondirent alors

Noble Paris seule raison qui vis encore
Qui fixes notre humeur selon ta destinée
Et toi qui te retires Méditerranée
Partagez-vous nos corps comme on rompt des hosties
Ces très hautes amours et leur danse orpheline
Deviendront ô Paris le vin pur que tu aimes.

(The towns of the South replied next

Noble Paris sole reason that still exists
Whose destiny determines our mood
And you who retire Mediterranean
Share our bodies as one shares the Host
These exalted loves and their orphan dance
Will become O Paris the pure wine that you love.)

The next response comes from cities in the south of France, who hasten to do the capital's bidding. The reason Paris is the "seule raison qui vi[t] encore" is because it dominates the rest of the country. As Anne Hyde Greet notes, the verse acknowledges the absolute supremacy of the north over the south following the Albigensian crusade, initiated by Pope Innocent III to stamp out a heretical sect in Languedoc.[42] This interpretation is confirmed by the next line, which acknowledges the south's subordinate role. For most scholars, the supremacy of Northern France also explains why the Mediterranean has withdrawn, presumably, from previous civilizations. Athens and Rome have been replaced by Paris as the most important cultural center. However, Poupon raises another intriguing possibility: that the sea has withdrawn in preparation for a tidal wave.[43] As he notes, an immense wave ravaged the Mediterranean coast on December 28, 1908, generated by an earthquake in Sicily. The next reference—to the Eucharist—has attracted the attention of several critics. According to A. E. Pilkington, the fact that the cities are broken and consumed like a Host suggests that "le vin pur" in the last line is holy wine.[44] In a similar vein, Couffignal believes that what the cities are offering Paris is salvation.[45] For better or for worse, the next-to-last verse is hopelessly obscure: "Ces très hautes amours et leur danse orpheline." Garnet Rees explains that the Hussite armies of Bohemia called themselves "Orphelins" and that one of their North African sects, the Adamites, performed naked ritual dances. What this has to do with "Vendémiaire" is anybody's guess.

Et un râle infini qui venait de Sicile
Signifiait en battement d'ailes ces paroles

Les raisins de nos vignes on les a vendangés
Et ces grappes de morts dont les grains allongés
Ont la saveur du sang de la terre et du sel
Les voici pour ta soif ô Paris sous le ciel
Obscurci de nuées fameliques
Que caresse Ixion le créateur oblique
Et où naissent sur la mer tous les corbeaux d'Afrique
Ô raisins Et ces yeux ternes et en famille
L'avenir et la vie dans ces treilles s'ennuyent.

(And an infinite death rattle coming from Sicily
Signified amid beating wings these words

The grapes of our vines have been harvested
And these bunches of dead whose elongated grapes
Taste like blood like earth and like salt
Here they are Paris for your thirst under the sky
Obscured by famished clouds
Caressed by Ixion the oblique creator
Where African crows emerge over the sea
O grapes And these dull familial eyes
The future and life grow weary among these trellises.)

Once the responses start to arrive from cities outside France, they require more than one or two stanzas. The infinite death rattle coming from Sicily is the sound of the earthquake mentioned previously. Transmitted (and translated) by a mysterious "battement d'ailes" ("beating wings"), it will eventually reach Paris. Perhaps the Sirens are tapping out the message in Morse code with their wings. Unfortunately, the harvest mentioned in the next few verses is far from a joyful occasion. In marked contrast to the others we have encountered, it is a harvest of the dead. For the first time in "Vendémiaire," we encounter an example of poetic transubstantiation. Not only have grapes been transformed into dead bodies, but also wine has been transformed into blood. Significantly, this is the second time the poet has explicitly invoked the Eucharist.

Although Greet includes victims of historical bloodshed among the dead offered to Paris, Apollinaire is thinking of the 100,000 people who succumbed to the recent earthquake. At 5:20 in the morning, while everyone was still in bed, the most destructive earthquake in recorded European history struck the Strait of Messina. The shock generated a tidal wave forty feet high that completely destroyed Messina on one side of the straits, and Reggio di Calabria on the other. As Lefèvre remarks, the union between Ixion and the clouds originally produced centaurs rather than crows, but the latter are better suited to the scene's funereal tone.[46] Ixion is called "the indirect creator" because he thought he was making love to Hera when he impregnated the clouds. Since *oblique* also means "underhanded" or "devious," Greet points out, it may also refer to the way in which he murdered his father in law—by luring him onto a bed of burning coals. Surrounded by dead bodies, the speaker in the last two verses laments the terrible fate that has befallen his island.

> Mais où est le regard lumineux des sirènes
> Il trompa les marins qu'aimaient ces oiseaux-là
> Il ne tournera plus sur l'écueil de Scylla
> Où chantaient les trois voix suaves et sereines
>
> Le détroit tout à coup avait changé de face
> Visages de la chair de l'onde de tout
> Ce que l'on peut imaginer
> Vous n'êtes que des masques sur des faces masquées
>
> Il souriait jeune nageur entre les rives
> Et les noyés flottant sur son onde nouvelle
> Fuyaient en le suivant les chanteuses plaintives
> Elles dirent adieu au gouffre et à l'écueil
> A leurs pâles époux couchés sur les terrasses
> Puis ayant pris leur vol vers le brûlant soleil
> Les suivirent dans l'onde où s'enfoncent les astres.
>
> (But where is the luminous gaze of the Sirens
> It deceived the sailors who loved those birds
> It will never return to Scylla's reef
> Where the three suave and serene voices sang
>
> The strait was instantly altered
> Faces of flesh of water of everything
> One can imagine
> You are no more than masks on masked faces
>
> Passing between the two sides the young swimmer smiled
> And the drowned floating in his wake fled the plaintive singers

They bid farewell to the whirlpool and the reef
To their pale spouses lying on the terraces
Then having taken flight toward the burning sun
Followed them into the waves where the stars plunge.)

As J. Patrick Truhn points out, the three Siren stanzas "are sandwiched between the responses of Sicily and Rome in much the same way that . . . the Strait of Messina is sandwiched between Sicily and Italy."[47] Most of the first stanza, which introduces the *ubi sunt* motif—made famous by Francois Villon in "Where are the snows of yesteryear"—was taken from an earlier poem about Ophelia.[48] Unexpectedly, Apollinaire presents a revisionist portrait of the Sirens and their victims. The former are depicted not as cruel harpies who lured sailors to their death but as *femmes fatales* who loved the men they betrayed. According to Apollinaire, the hapless mariners were seduced by the Sirens' beauty instead of by their hypnotic song. And yet, he knew full well that the Sirens were frightening to look at. Like their sisters in "Zone" and "Lul de Faltenin," they are birds with the head and bust of a woman—Greek Sirens rather than Roman Sirens.[49] That they are three in number is attested by Classical mythology. Despite the poet's insistence, nevertheless, the Sirens have nothing to do with Scylla or Charybdis either mythologically or geographically. Protected by impassible reefs that doom unwary ships, their territory lies elsewhere on the island.

As Apollinaire notes, the recent earthquake had a devastating effect on the area surrounding the Strait of Messina. In addition to the appalling casualties recorded in the second stanza, the strait's physical appearance was dramatically altered. The identity of the young swimmer in the third stanza has puzzled more than a few critics. According to Truhn, "Il" is usually assumed to refer either to Orpheus or to Odysseus.[50] Although both figures managed to escape the Sirens' hypnotic song, they had boats and no apparent reason to swim through the Strait of Messina surrounded by dead bodies. As Lefèvre has seen, the fact that the latter are floating on "son onde" ("its wave") suggests that "Il" refers to the Strait itself.[51] Thus, the young swimmer appears to be a metaphor rather than an actual person. Bidding goodbye to Scylla and Charybdis—and to the terraces laden with soggy corpses—the Sirens follow the current as it passes through the Strait.

The last two lines have been the source of a certain amount of confusion as well. Swooping upward toward the sun, the Sirens suddenly plunge into the ocean and disappear. Citing a Classical precedent, several critics are convinced that they have committed suicide. Somewhat bewildered by this turn of events, Truhn believes the Sirens' flight has been confused with the flight of Icarus.[52] Nevertheless, there is a perfectly logical explanation for their behavior, one that is confirmed by the next stanza. According to all indications, the sun is about ready to set. Among other things, this means the Sirens' flight is horizontal instead of vertical. Before they can reach the solar disc, however, it disappears over the horizon, plunging the scene into darkness. Although the text insists that the stars and the Sirens both fall into the ocean, this statement is clearly metaphorical. In actuality, the former are merely reflected in the water, and the latter disappear over the horizon like the sun.

> Lorsque la nuit revint couverte d'yeux ouverts
> Errer au site où l'hydre a sifflé cet hiver
> Et j'entendis soudain ta voix impérieuse
> O Rome
> Maudire d'un seul coup mes anciennes pensées
> Et le ciel où l'amour guide les destinées
>
> Les feuillards repoussés sur l'arbre de la croix
> Et même la fleur de lys qui meurt au Vatican
> Macèrent dans le vin que je t'offre et qui a
> La saveur du sang pur de celui qui connaît
> Une autre liberté végétale dont tu
> Ne sais pas que c'est elle la suprême vertu
>
> Une couronne du trirègne est tombée sur les dalles
> Les hiérarques la foulent sous leurs sandales
> Ô splendeur démocratique qui pâlit
> Vienne la nuit royale où l'on tuera les bêtes
> La louve avec l'agneau l'aigle avec la colombe
> Une foule de rois ennemis et cruels
> Ayant soif comme toi dans la vigne éternelle
> Sortiront de la terre et viendront dans les airs
> Pour boire de mon vin par deux fois millénaire.
>
> (When night returned covered with open eyes
> Wandering on the site where the hydra hissed this winter
> And I suddenly heard your imperious voice
> O Rome
> Stoutly curse my former thoughts
> And heaven where love guides our destinies
>
> Branches that sprouted on the tree of the cross
> And even the lily that dies in the Vatican
> Steep in the wine I am offering you which

Tastes like His pure blood who knows
Another vegetable freedom which unknown
To you is the supreme virtue

A tiara has fallen on the flagstones
The hierarchs trample it under foot
O fading democratic splendor
Let the royal night come when the beasts are slaughtered
The wolf with the lamb the eagle with the dove
A crowd of cruel enemy kings
Thirsting like you for the eternal vine
Will emerge from the earth into the fresh air
To drink my two-thousand-year-old wine.)

Since night has fallen, Apollinaire compares the starry sky to the legendary cowherd Argus, who was covered with a hundred eyes. Slightly changed, the second line was taken from an acrostic poem presented to René Nicosia in 1900.[53] The Hydra of Lerna was a huge water-serpent with nine heads, poisonous breath, and virulent blood. Although the verse originally referred to an earlier earthquake, apparently in August 1894, Apollinaire modified it to reflect the 1908 disaster. Since Rome was the capital of the ancient Roman Empire, the city speaks with a voice that is simultaneously *impérieuse* and *impériale*. However, the Roman emperors have been replaced by the Pope, who immediately denounces Apollinaire's "anciennes pensées" ("former thoughts"). While it is tempting to conclude that he is rebuking the poet for his sinful thoughts, the last line sheds a whole new light on the issue. For the Pope's disapproval is directed not just at Apollinaire but also at "le ciel où l'amour guide les destinées" ("heaven where love guides our destinies"). There are two ways to interpret this incredible statement: either as an attack aimed at Heaven or as an attack aimed at Love, which is what it appears to be. The Pope is criticizing the common opinion (shared by Apollinaire) that love governs the relationship between Heaven and Earth. Thus, as Renaud deduces, the poet's former thoughts are Christian in nature.[54]

The second stanza develops these ideas in more detail. "Rome fait l'éloge du sacrifice," Lefèvre declares, "en présentant au monde son vin eucharistique" ("Rome praises the sacrifice by presenting its Eucharistic wine to the world").[55] According to the Pope, who serves as Rome's mouthpiece, the Crucifixion demonstrates the importance not of love but of sacrifice. Whether this represents the actual position of Pope Pius X is hard to say. Since the latter was famous for opposing attempts to modernize the Catholic Church, he may also have wished to minimize its emphasis on love. Reminiscent of John the Baptist's staff in "Salomé," the new branches sprouting from the cross are a symbol of rebirth and renewal. Paradoxically, the renewal promoted by Pius X took the form of a return to the Church's original values. In contrast to the burgeoning cross, the fleur de lys in the Vatican is practically dead. Greet speculates that it may refer to Charles d'Anjou's dozen years as senator in Rome or to the removal of the popes to Avignon.[56] Pilkington thinks it may allude to the separation of church and state in France in 1905. However, he also points out that Christ is described as "le beau lys" ("the beautiful lily") in "Zone" (v. 33).[57] And since the fleur de lys is an omnipresent symbol in the Vatican, it may represent that establishment as well. In which case, a vibrant, reborn Christianity would be juxtaposed with the moribund institution charged to protect it.

The branches, the fleur de lys, and undoubtedly all of Rome are contained in the wine the Pope eagerly offers Apollinaire. The fact that it "la saveur du sang pur" ("tastes like His [Christ's] pure blood") marks it as Communion wine. Appropriately, Pius X was known as the "Pope of the Eucharist" because he urged people to take Holy Communion frequently, even young children. According to Greet, the last two lines of this stanza comment on how the Church has fallen away from early Christianity.[58] People today, the Pope tells Apollinaire, no longer know the natural liberty that Christ recognized as a supreme virtue. While Truhn perceives a reference to the Second Coming in this stanza, it is far from obvious.[59] And although Renaud believes "le sang du Christ et celui de Dionysos sont confondus dans le vin offert par Rome" ("the blood of Christ and that of Dionysos are mixed in the wine offered by Rome"), his argument is unconvincing.[60] Not only is the wine poured by the Pope himself, but the whole stanza celebrates the miracle of the Eucharist.

Although Lefèvre claims the third stanza is spoken by Apollinaire, the reference to "mon vin" indicates it is still the Pope who is speaking. While he and the poet are sipping the sacramental wine, he suddenly experiences a vision of the future. As a number of critics have observed, his words quickly assume the tone of the Apocalypse. While the details are sketchy, some sort of religious revolution is taking place in the Vatican. A group of religious dignitaries seems to have overthrown the Pope and usurped his power. According to Poupon, the original idea for the poem may have come from a novel by Jean Pauly entitled *Le Faux Pape* (1895).[61] One of the three crowns that constitute the Pope's tiara—not the tiara itself—has fallen to the floor, where it is being trampled underfoot. Poupon thinks it may be the one symbolizing the Church Triumphant (the other two symbolize the Church Militant and the Church Suffering). Since wearing sandals was the traditional mark of the senior clergy, he suspects the dissidents are cardinals who secretly belong to the Freemasons. The next two lines make it clear that they plan to rule with an iron fist and, for some reason, to kill all the animals. As Lefèvre notes, the list of those to be slaughtered is the antithesis of the prophecy of Isaiah, when the wolf shall lie down with the lamb and the leopard with the kid.[62] The rest of the stanza resembles a parody of Judgment Day. Cruel kings will rise from the dead and fly to the Vatican to quench their thirst with wine from the Eternal Vineyard. Couffignal complains that expressions such as "vigne éternelle" ("eternal vine") (borrowed from St. Matthew) and "vin deux fois millénaire" ("two-thousand-year-old-wine") are weary clichés: "Si [Apollinaire] utilise le symbolisme liturgique, c'est pour habiller à sa façon une doctrine à la mode: l'Unanimisme" ("If [Apollinaire] utilizes liturgical symbolism, it is to portray a popular doctrine: Unanimism").[63]

> La Moselle et le Rhin se joignent en silence
> C'est l'Europe qui prie nuit et jour à Coblence
> Et moi qui m'attardais sur le quai à Auteuil
> Quand les heures tombaient parfois comme les feuilles
> Du cep lorsqu'il est temps j'entendis la prière
> Qui joignait la limpidité de ces rivières
>
> O Paris le vin de ton pays est meilleur que celui
> Qui pousse sur nos bords mais aux pampres du nord
> Tous les grains ont mûri pour cette soif terrible
> Mes grappes d'hommes forts saignent dans le pressoir
> Tu boira à longs traits tout le sang de l'Europe
> Parce que tu es beau et que seul tu es noble
> Parce que c'est dans toi que Dieu peut devenir
> Et tous mes vignerons dans ces belles maisons
> Qui réflètent le soir leurs feux dans nos deux eaux
> Dans ces belles maisons nettement blanches et noires
> Sans savoir que tu es la réalité chantent ta gloire
> Mais nous liquides mains jointes pour la prière
> Nous menons vers le sel les eaux aventurières
> Et la ville entre nous comme entre des ciseaux
> Ne réflète en dormant nul feu dans ses deux eaux
> Dont quelque sifflement lointain parfois s'élance
> Troublant dans leur sommeil les filles de Coblence.
>
> (The Moselle and the Rhine join in silence
> Europe prays night and day for Coblence
> And I who lingered on the quay at Auteuil

> While the hours were falling like leaves
> From the Autumn vines I heard the prayer
> That joined the limpidity of these rivers
>
> O Paris the wine of your area is better than
> What grows on our slopes yet on northern vines
> All the grapes have ripened for that terrible thirst
> My bunches of strong men bleed in the grape press
> You will drink all the blood of Europe avidly
> Because you are beautiful and you alone are noble
> Because it is in you that God can appear
> And all my wine growers in their fine houses
> Whose fires are reflected at night in our two waters
> It is in your fine black and white houses
> Ignorant that you are reality the growers sing your praise
> But with our liquid hands joined in prayer
> We lead the adventurous waters toward the sea
> And the city sleeping as between a pair of scissors
> Reflects no fires at all in its two waters
> Occasionally uttering distant murmurs
> And troubling the sleeping girls of Coblence.)

The poem's focus shifts next to the German city of Coblenz, situated, as Apollinaire says, where the Mosel and the Rhine rivers merge. The first verse was taken from an earlier poem entitled "Coblence," which evokes the "affreux monument" ("awful monument") to Kaiser Wilhelm I erected in the Deutsches Eck.[64] Although the poet visited the city at least twice during his *année allemande*, he does not appear to have had any particular affection for it.[65] Recalling one of his visits in "Zone," he merely says: "Tu es à Coblence à l'Hôtel du Géant." The reason Apollinaire devotes so many lines to this city, therefore, is because it is the center of the local wine trade. Why Europe would want to pray all day and night in Coblenz, which is not a pilgrimage site, is not immediately clear. Although it contains some lovely old churches, there is nothing about them that would normally elicit this response. In contrast to the first stanza, which is spoken by Apollinaire, the second is uttered by Coblenz itself. While apologizing for the inferior quality of its wine, the city invites Paris to sample it nonetheless. Once again, Apollinaire equates wine and blood in an image worthy of Hieronymous Bosch: "Mes grappes d'hommes forts saignent dans le pressoir" ("My bunches of strong men bleed in the grape press"). This probably refers to the many wars in which the city has been involved over the years. Although Coblenz's wine has not been consecrated by the Church, like that offered by Rome, it is sacrificial wine just the same.

The next line invokes the poem's original premise, that Paris intends to drink all the wine in Europe, but in keeping with the preceding verse, the wine has been changed into blood. A eulogy for the French capital occupies the following six lines. In addition to being beautiful and noble, Paris represents humanity's highest point of evolution—one that has even given birth to God. This statement is followed by two geographical metaphors that exploit Coblenz's position as a riverain city. Unexpectedly, the first metaphor explains why Europe prays all day and night at Coblenz. Because the Rhine and the Mosel form two sides of an isosceles triangle with the Deutsches Eck at its apex, Apollinaire compares them to a pair of hands joined in prayer. And since the rivers border the city on both sides, viewed from above they resemble an open pair of scissors. Like the first verse of the preceding stanza, the last four lines of this stanza are borrowed from "Coblence." At some point in the city's speech, night has descended, the lights have been extinguished, and Coblenz has fallen asleep. The only sound that can be heard is that of a train whistle in the distance.

> Les villes répondaient maintenant par centaines
> Je ne distinguais plus leurs paroles lointaines
> Et Trèves la ville ancienne
> A leur voix mêlait la sienne
> L'univers tout entier concentré dans ce vin
> Qui contenait les mers les animaux les plantes
> Les cités les destins et les astres qui chantent
> Les hommes à genoux sur la rive du ciel
> Et le docile fer notre bon compagnon
> Le feu qu'il faut aimer comme on s'aime soi-même
> Tous les fiers trépassés qui sont un sous mon front
> L'éclair qui luit ainsi qu'une pensée naissante
> Tous les noms six par six les nombres un à un
> Des kilos de papier tordus comme des flammes
> Et ceux-là qui sauront blanchir nos ossements
> Les bons vers immortels qui s'ennuient patiemment
> Des armées rangées en bataille
> Des forêts de crucifix et mes demeures lacustres
> Au bord des yeux de celle que j'aime tant
> Les fleurs qui s'écrient hors de bouches
> Et tout ce que je ne sais pas dire
> Et tout ce que je ne connaîtrai jamais

Tout cela tout cela changé en vin pur
Dont Paris avait soif
Me fut alors présenté.

(The cities replied now by the hundreds
I could no longer make out their distant words
And the ancient city of Treves
Mingled its voice with theirs
The whole universe concentrated in this wine
Containing seas animals plants
Cities destinies and singing stars
Men kneeling on heaven's shore
And docile iron our great companion
Fire that we love like we love ourselves
All the proud dead united under my forehead
Lightning that shines like the birth of a thought
All the names six by six the numbers one by one
Kilos of paper twisted like flames
And those who will bleach our bones
The immortal verses that patiently grow tired
Armies drawn up for battle
Forests of crucifixes and my lakeside houses
Bordering the eyes of the woman I dearly love
Flowers crying out from mouths
And everything I am unable to describe
Everything that I will never know
All that all that changed into this pure wine
For which Paris thirsted
Was then presented to me.)

At this point, the scene suddenly erupts in a chorus of contending voices. Located further down the Mosel River, Triers adds its voice to hundreds of other cities that hasten to pay tribute to Paris. So many contribute to the wine destined for the French capital that Apollinaire boasts that the wine contains the entire universe. And indeed the catalogue of the cities' contributions is impressive. As Greet observes, the poet describes the universal wine in Unanimist terms.[66] Besides such human pursuits as love, war, religion, and poetry, it includes every person living or dead, all the animals, minerals, and plants on the planet, fire, lightning, astronomical bodies, and every conceivable name and number. In addition, tons of paper are reserved for "les bons vers immortels," which are simultaneously immortal lines of poetry and immortal worms. Apollinaire employed this line previously in "Adieux" and "Le Ciel se couvre un matin de mai."[67] The list of contributions is so exhaustive it even includes everything Apollinaire cannot put into words and everything he will never know. All this and more goes into the marvelous wine destined to quench Paris's thirst. For some reason, however, it is presented to Apollinaire rather than to the French capital.

> Actions belles journées sommeils terribles
> Végétation Accouplements musiques éternelles
> Mouvements Adorations douleur divine
> Mondes qui vous rassemblez et qui nous ressemblez
> Je vous ai bus et ne fus pas désaltéré
>
> Mais je connus dès lors quelle saveur a l'univers
>
> Je suis ivre d'avoir bu tout l'univers
> Sur le quai d'où je voyais l'onde couler et dormir les bélandres
>
> Ecoutez-moi je suis le gosier de Paris
> Et je boirai encore s'il me plaît l'univers
>
> Ecoutez mes chants d'universelle ivrognerie
>
> Et la nuit de septembre s'achevait lentement
> Les feux rouges des ponts s'éteignaient dans la Seine
> Les étoiles mouraient le jour naissait à peine.
>
> (Actions lovely days terrible sleeps
> Vegetation Couplings eternal tunes
> Movements Adorations divine sorrow
> Worlds resembling you and resembling us
> I drank you down without quenching my thirst
>
> But I learned what flavor the universe has
>
> I am drunk from having consumed the whole universe
> On the quay where I watched the water flow and the barges sleep
>
> Listen to me I am the throat of Paris
> And I will drink the whole universe if I wish to
>
> Listen to my songs of universal intoxication
>
> As the September night gradually concluded
> The bridges' warning lights flickered out in the Seine
> The stars died away and the day began to dawn.)

The first stanza summarizes all of the things the different cities have contributed in the course of the poem. As we have seen previously, the wine is truly universal, encompassing every aspect of human endeavor plus the entire physical world. By the time the reader reaches the end of the stanza, Apollinaire has swallowed all the wine and is ready for more. Standing on the quay at Auteuil, he watches the river pass by and the skiffs bob peacefully up and down. Not only does he still savor his recent experience, but he also glories in his marvelous intoxication. Drunk both with wine and success, the poet boasts that he could do it all over again. As Morhange-Bégué and Pierre Lartigue remark, one of Apollinaire's fundamental character traits was "la volonté de faire reculer les frontières de l'univers poétique jusqu' à l'illimité" ("the desire to roll back the frontiers of the poetic universe as far as infinity").[68] Returning to his original point of departure, he addresses the "Hommes de l'avenir" "(Men of the future") once again. "Ecoutez-moi," he exclaims, "je suis le gosier de Paris" ("Listen to me, I am the throat of Paris"). Just as everything in the world funnels through Paris, so everything in Paris funnels through Apollinaire. "Vendémiaire" celebrates not only the French capital as the center of the world but also Apollinaire as its poetic mouthpiece. His "chants d'universelle ivrognerie" ("songs of universal intoxication") contain everything the world has to offer distilled into wine. As Morhange-Bégué and Lartigue note, the wine is both the source and the symbol of his inspiration.[69] "Vendémiaire" concludes with a flourish and a pair of rhyming alexandrines. As day dawns and the stars disappear, the bridge lights are extinguished like candles in the water.

Notes

1. Michel Décaudin, *Le Dossier d'"Alcools,"* rev. ed. (Paris: Minard, 1965), 126–27.

2. Philippe Renaud, *Lecture d'Apollinaire* (Lausanne: L'Age d'Homme, 1969), 153.

3. Richard Stamelman, *The Drama of Self in Guillaume Apollinaire's "Alcools"* (Chapel Hill: North Carolina Studies in the Romance Languages and Literatures, 1976), 40.

4. Décaudin, *Le Dossier d'"Alcools,"* 127. By contrast, Jean-Claude Chevalier believes Apollinaire took the idea from *L'Enchanteur pourrissant* (Chevalier, *"Alcools," analyse des formes poétiques* [Paris: Lettres Modernes, 1970], 202–3).

5. Stamelman situates the bird below the earth instead of above it (*The Drama of Self*, 41–42).

6. Claude Morhange-Bégué and Pierre Lartigue, *"'Alcools.'" Apollinaire* (Paris: Hatier, 1991), 31; Robert Champigny, "Le Temps chez Apollinaire," *PMLA*, Vol. 67, No. 2 (March 1952), 8; and Marie-Jeanne Durry, *Guillaume Apollinaire,* Vol. 3 (Paris: SEDES, 1964), 178.

7. Stamelman, *The Drama of Self*, 42.

8. Ibid., 44; Anne Hyde Greet, tr., *Alcools* (Berkeley: University of California Press, 1965), 229; and A. E. Pilkington, ed., *Alcools* (Oxford: Blackwell, 1970), 125.

9. Scott Bates, *Guillaume Apollinaire*, rev. ed. (Boston: Twayne, 1989), 78.

10. Madeleine Boisson, "Paysages célestes," *Du paysage apollinarien*, ed. Michel Décaudin (Paris: Minard, 1991), 96.

11. See Guillaume Apollinaire, *Oeuvres poétiques*, ed. Marcel Adéma and Michel Décaudin (Paris: Gallimard, 1965), 98.

12. Durry, *Guillaume Apollinaire*, 3:207.

13. Renaud, *Lecture d'Apollinaire*, 160–61.

14. Stamelman, *The Drama of Self*, 46.

15. Décaudin, *Le Dossier d'"Alcools,"* 128.

16. Greet, tr., *"Alcools,"* 227–28.

17. Géralde Nakam, "'O Corneille Agrippa, l'odeur d'un petit chien . . .' Alcools Cortège," *Revue des Lettres Modernes*, Nos. 249–53 (1970), 156–58.

18. Renaud, *Lecture d'Apollinaire*, 154.

19. Décaudin, *Le Dossier d'"Alcools,"* 128.

20. Durry, *Guillaume Apollinaire*, 3:180.

21. Champigny, "Le Temps chez Apollinaire," 5.

22. Renaud, *Lecture d'Apollinaire*, 155.

23. Durry, *Guillaume Apollinaire*, 3:183–84.

24. Morhange-Bégué and Lartigue, *"'Alcools.'" Apollinaire*, 32.

25. Jeanine Moulin, *Guillaume Apollinaire: Textes inédits* (Lille: Giard, 1952), 42.

26. Décaudin, *Le Dossier*, 226.

27. Guillaime Apollinare to Madeleine Pagès, July 30, 1915, Guillaume Apollinaire, *Tendre comme le souvenir* (Paris: Gallimard, 1952), 70.

28. See Décaudin, *Le Dossier*, 220–26.

29. Georges Schmits, "'Vendémiaire,'" *Les Etudes Classiques*, July 1964, 248.

30. Décaudin, *Le Dossier*, 224; LeRoy C. Breunig, "The Chronology of Apollinaire's *Alcools*," *PMLA*, Vol. 67, No. 7 (December 1952), 919.

31. Henri Meschonnic, "Signifiance de 'Vendémiaire," *Revue des Lettres Modernes*, Nos. 327–30 (1972), 41–63.

32. Schmits, "'Vendémiaire,'" 260–62.

33. Guillaume Apollinaire, "Simultanisme-Librettisme," *Les Soirées de Paris*, June 15, 1914. Reprinted in Apollinaire, *Oeuvres en prose complètes*, Vol. 2, ed. Pierre Caizergues and Michel Décaudin (Paris: Gallimard, 1991), 976.

34. Stamelman, *The Drama of Self*, 153.

35. Philippe Renaud, *Lecture d'Apollinaire* (Lausanne: L'Age d'Homme, 1969), 137.

36. Ibid., 156, and Robert Couffignal, *L'Inspiration biblique dans l'oeuvre de Guillaume Apollinaire* (Paris: Minard, 1966), 140.

37. Antoine Fongaro, *Apollinaire poète: Exégèses et discussions 1957–1987* (Toulouse: Presses Universitaires du Mirail-Toulouse, 1988), 13–14 and 148.

38. Roger Lefèvre, ed., "*Alcools*": *choix de poèmes* (Paris: Nouveaux Classiques Larousse, 1965), 88.

39. S. I. Lockerbie, "*Alcools* et le symbolisme," *Revue des Lettres Modernes*, Nos. 85–89 (Fall 1963), 29.

40. Didier Alexandre, *Guillaume Apollinaire*: "*Alcools*" (Paris: Presses Universitaires Françaises, 1994), 17.

41. Marc Poupon, "Notes sur quelques énigmes de 'Vendémiaire,'" *Apollinaire: Revue d'Etudes Apollinariennes*, No. 4 (November 2008), 50.

42. Greet, tr., "*Alcools*," 283.

43. Poupon, "Notes sur quelques énigmes," 51.

44. A. E. Pilkington, ed., *Apollinaire*: "*Alcools*" (Oxford: Blackwell, 1970), 161.

45. Couffignal, *L'Inspiration biblique*, 161.

46. Lefèvre, ed. "*Alcools*," 91.

47. J. Patrick Truhn, "The Wave of Wine: Revolution and Revelation in Apollinaire's 'Vendémiaire,'" *Romanic Review*, Vol. 72, No. 1 (January 1981), 43.

48. Guillaume Apollinaire, *Oeuvres poétiques*, ed. Marcel Adéma and Michel Décaudin (Paris: Gallimard, 1965), 567.

49. See Antoine Fongaro, "Apollinaire, Gautier et les Sirènes," *Revue des Lettres Modernes*, Nos. 183–88 (1968), 64–71.

50. Truhn, "The Wave of Wine," 45.

51. Lefèvre, "*Alcools*," 91.

52. Truhn, "The Wave of Wine," 44.

53. Apollinaire, *Oeuvres poétiques*, 718.

54. Renaud, *Lecture d' Apollinaire*, 170.

55. Lefèvre, ed., "*Alcools*," 92.

56. Greet, tr., "*Alcools*," 284.

57. Pilkington, ed., *Apollinaire*, 161.

58. Greet, tr., "*Alcools*," 284–85.

59. Truhn, "The Wave of Wine," 46.

60. Renaud, *Lecture d'Apollinaire*, 170.

61. Poupon, "Notes," 51–52.

62. Lefèvre, "*Alcools*," 92.

63. Couffignal, *L'Inspiration biblique*, 141

64. Guillaume Apollinaire, *Le Guetteur mélancolique*, ed. Michel Décaudin (Paris: Gallimard, 1980), 158. For some reason, "Coblence" does not seem to have been included in his *Oeuvres poétiques*.

65. See Louis Brunet, "Le Voyage d'Apollinaire à travers l'Allemagne au printemps 1902," *Apollinaire: Revue d'Etudes Apollinariennes*, No. 6 (November 2009), 35–36.

66. Greet, tr., "*Alcools*," 285.

67. Apollinaire, *Oeuvres poétiques*, 332–34 and 521.

68. Morhange-Bégué and Lartigue, "*Alcools.*" *Apollinaire*, 33.

69. Ibid., 32.

~

CHAPTER EIGHT

A Modern Muse

"Zone" is probably the most influential poem that Apollinaire ever wrote. Its impact both on modern French poetry and on modern poetry in general has been incalculable. Although it was the last work in *Alcools* to be composed, Apollinaire placed it first for a very good reason: it represents a major breakthrough, one that many poets today are still exploiting. Whether it truly deserves to be called "cubist" has been debated by critics for years. What matters, however, is not the label one attaches to the poem but the radical new aesthetic that it introduced. While Apollinaire had been creating patchwork poetry for many years, as we have seen, his efforts were neither extensive nor systematic. All that changed with the publication of a revolutionary new composition that depicted the world more than just prismatically.

"Zone"

One of Apollinaire's best-known poems, "Zone" was composed only a few months before it appeared in *Les Soirées de Paris* in December 1912.[1] A slightly different version was published in *Der Sturm* in April 1913. Besides these two documents, a rough draft exists of nearly the entire poem. Until it was replaced on the second proofs of the *Soirées de Paris* version, the work's original title was "Cri." In October, while Apollinaire, Francis Picabia, and Marcel Duchamp were visiting Picabia's wife, Gabrielle Buffet, in Switzerland, near Etival, the poet read a first draft aloud. When asked about the title, he hesitated at first and then confided it would be called "Zone." For this reason, it has been suggested that the title refers to the *zone franche* near Etival, where goods could pass back and forth without being taxed. Perhaps with equal justification, it has also been suggested that the title alludes to a dilapidated area surrounding Paris, outside the former fortifications, where Apollinaire and his friends used to go occasionally to eat: "Sur cette zone," Pascal Pia declares, "campait une société bigarée, composée de chiffonniers, de vanniers, de raccommodeurs de porcelaine, de tondeurs de chiens, de bagotiers et de rôdeuses peu appétissantes" ("This zone was inhabited by a whole motley society of rag pickers, basket makers, porcelain menders, dog clippers, porters, and vagabonds").[2] Since *zone* derives from the Greek word for "belt," as LeRoy Breunig points out, the title could also describe the circular course of Apollinaire's walk, which proceeds from one morning to the next.[3]

Interestingly, the prosody in "Zone" is unlike any we have encountered before. At first glance, most critics would probably agree with Anna Boschetti that "l'alexandrin, régulier ou faux à dessein, alterne dans 'Zone' avec des vers libres" ("the alexandrine, regular or deliberately false, alternates with free verse").[4] This is certainly a pattern that occurs in other poems by Apollinaire. However, leaving aside the question of what constitutes a proper alexandrine for the moment, the poem contains surprisingly few *vers libres*. Although there seems to be some disagreement about how to describe the latter, *Le Petit Robert* provides the following definition: "vers non rimés et irréguliers" ("verses that are unrhymed and irregular"). Following a detailed analysis, Jean-Pierre Bobillot concludes that fifty-eight verses in "Zone" contain more than twelve syllables, which fulfills one of the conditions for an alexandrine described above.[5] In addition, an appreciable number of verses contain fewer than twelve syllables. Nevertheless, even a cursory glance reveals that rhyme plays an important role in the poem. Despite their irregular lengths, many of the verses employ *rimes plates*. Following an equally meticulous analysis, Jeannine Kohn-Etiemble estimates that only eight or ten lines are unrhymed. The rest "comportent soit des rimes tout à fait classiques et canoniques, soit des assonances, soit au moins des échos sonores par consonnes accentuées ou par voyelles nasales de timbres voisins" ("include classical and canonic rhymes or assonances or at least sonorous echoes by accentuated consonants or nasal vowels of neighboring timber").[6] While some of these examples may not fit the Classical definition of rhyme, neither do they fit the definition of free verse. Apollinaire clearly took great pains to give his revolutionary new poem a solid aesthetic foundation.

Generally considered to be a modernist manifesto, Breunig notes, "Zone" is "perhaps the masterpiece of what one might call Apollinaire's peripatetic poetry."[7] Born in Italy and raised on the Côte d'Azur, the poet did not settle in Paris until he was nineteen. As such, he viewed the French capital through the eyes of a newcomer, one who was perpetually amazed at the treasures it contained. Fortunately, Paris was (and still is) an excellent city for walking. In order to save money but also to satisfy his boundless curiosity, the poet walked everywhere he could. Nothing made him happier than to introduce friends and colleagues to sights he discovered on his walks. Many of these adventures are recorded in a collection of essays entitled *Le Flâneur des deux rives*. Like François Villon and Dante Alighieri, who also paused to examine their lives in their early thirties, in "Zone," Apollinaire scrutinizes his past as he strolls through Paris. Beginning at sunrise, he walks all day and all night until dawn of the next day. As Marie-Jeanne Durry and Anne Hyde Greet have both noted, the poem's leisurely rhythm parallels the pace of a man walking.[8] In contrast to other poems we have examined, the plot of "Zone" is deceptively simple.

Although this is not the place to investigate the subject in detail, "Zone" is often cited as an example of cubist poetry. Since Apollinaire frequently visited Picasso's studio, often staying for dinner, he was able to follow the development of Cubist painting step-by-step. As we saw in Chapter 5, "Lul de Faltenin" may very well have been influenced by Picasso's *Les Demoiselles d'Avignon*. In the case of "Zone," there is little doubt that Apollinaire was attempting to accomplish in poetry what his friend had already achieved in art. Just as the Cubist painters sought to create an impression of simultaneity by superimposing multiple perspectives and overlapping planes, he switches back and forth from one personal pronoun to another and juxtaposes radically disparate experiences. Just as the Cubist painters abolished any trace of depth in their paintings, he employs the present tense almost exclusively and abolishes all traces of punctuation. While other similarities have also been detected between the works of Picasso and Apollinaire, the fact that they utilized different media has important repercussions. Despite Apollinaire's attempt to create a verbal collage, "Zone" remains a sequential rather than a simultaneous composition. It cannot be apprehended at a single glance like a work of art. Only after it has been deciphered can the various elements be reassembled to form a mental collage.

Since "Zone" consists of a series of scenes, Boschetti compares it to another sequential art form: film. "Rêve, méditation, dialogue, souvenir, hallucination, fantaisie, cauchemar, description d'une action réelle qui est en train de se dérouler" ("Dream, meditation, dialogue, memory, hallucination, fantasy, nightmare, description of an actual event that is happening")—the scenes fade in and out, she declares, like a series of dissolves.[9] In reality, however, each scene is clearly delineated and occupies its own discrete space. Each is deliberately juxtaposed with the others. Basically alternating between the present and the past, the poem itself is divided into six main sections. Three sections describe what the poet sees, thinks, and does, while two are devoted to various memories, and one contains an elaborate fantasy. Robert Couffignal divides "Zone" into two approximately equal halves, which he compares to Dante's *Paradiso* and his *Inferno*. Beginning with the Eiffel Tower, the first half (vv. 1–70) contains nine ascensional images. Following the airplane's ascent, the second half (vv. 71–155) contains a series of episodes "commencés dans la lumière et le bonheur [mais qui] s'achèvent dans les ténèbres et le malheur" ("beginning with light and happiness [but which] end with shadows and unhappiness").[10]

> A la fin tu es las de ce monde ancien
>
> Bergère ô tour Eiffel le troupeau des ponts bêle ce matin
>
> Tu en as assez de vivre dans l'antiquité grecque et romaine
>
> Ici même les automobiles ont l'air d'être anciennes
> La religion seule est restée toute neuve la religion
> Est restée simple comme les hangars de Port-Aviation.
>
> (You are weary at last of this ancient world
>
> Shepherdess O Eiffel Tower the flock of bridges is bleating this morning
>
> You have had enough of living in Greek and Roman antiquity
>
> Here even the automobiles appear to be ancient
> Only religion has managed to remain new religion
> Has remained as simple as hangars at the airport.)

As Bobillot remarks, the poem begins with "un incipit décidément bien ambigu" ("a decidedly ambiguous first line").[11] Why is the very first line concerned with the end of something? Who is "tu," and what has he done to make himself so tired? Where is "ce monde ancien," and how ancient is it? Does it encompass the year the poem was composed, for example, or is it prior to this experience? Unfortunately, the demonstrative adjective "ce" does not provide much help. Should it be translated as "this," one wonders, or as "that"? While five of the six available translations opt for the first choice, "this ancient world" is a contradiction in terms. How can something be contemporary and ancient at the same time? For the moment, these questions remain unanswered. Ironically, Apollinaire employs a quintessential Classical verse form to announce a break with the past. Citing the dieresis at the end of the line and the hiatus of "tu es," Bobillot claims that "Zone" would never have been accepted as an alexandrine historically. However, no less an authority than Marie-Jeanne Durry declares it is a perfectly fine example.[12] The fact that the line is composed of four carefully chosen anapests would seem to confirm her statement.

Little by little the reader begins to suspect that "tu," like the other pronouns in the poem, refers to Apollinaire himself. Indeed, as Boschetti observes, "Zone" functions very much like an interior monologue.[13] All of the voices from beginning to end emanate from the poet. This realization recasts the remarks in the first section in a whole new light. It seems to be Apollinaire now who is determined to break with the past—undoubtedly for aesthetic reasons. "From the opening line," David Berry remarks, "we are introduced to the device of *dédoublement*, ('doubling') in which the poet is revealed in his fundamental role of a spectator of himself."[14] Engaged in a reflexive dialogue, he maintains, Apollinaire struggles to achieve a sense of identity, stability, and self-awareness. This opinion is shared by several other critics as well. Whether it is actually true, however, remains to be seen. For one thing, there is remarkably little interaction between the "je" ("I") and the "tu" (or "vous") ("you") passages. On the surface, at least, they seem to have little in common. For another thing, second-person pronouns occur four or five times more frequently than first-person pronouns (fifty-nine vs. thirteen times), which undercuts the idea of an equitable exchange. Indeed, many of the first-person remarks are simply statements of fact: "J'ai vu" ("I saw"), "j'ai oublié" ("I forgot"), "je m'en souviens" ("I remember"), and so forth. According to all indications, switching from the first person to the second allows Apollinaire to distance himself from the past rather than to confront it. The conclusion is inescapable: this work is an aesthetic exercise rather than a therapeutic one. Alternating pronouns endow the poem with multiple perspectives like those cultivated by Picasso and his colleagues. Like Cubist paintings, "Zone" is composed of monolithic blocks that are juxtaposed with each other. Apollinaire's memories are simply that—memories and nothing more.

As Roger Lefèvre observes, the first line announces one of Apollinaire's favorite themes: the need to create something new.[15] Having stated his opinion, the poet hastens to give a stunning example: "Bergère ô tour Eiffel le troupeau des ponts bêle ce matin" ("Shepherdess O Eiffel Tower the flock of bridges is bleating this morning"). While the verse reminds Michel Décaudin of a line from Victor Hugo's "Pasteurs et troupeaux," any resemblance is purely imaginary.[16] However, Pierre Brunel is struck by an apparent paradox: that in order to evoke the modern world Apollinaire resorts to pastoral poetry.[17] The truth, I think, lies in the opposite direction. The poet utilizes a modern reference in order to breathe new life into the ancient genre. In other words, the line basically serves as an illustration. This is what we should be doing, Apollinaire seems to say, to bring poetry up to date. Although Brunel believes that he is parodying the ancient genre, scholars agree that the line exemplifies Apollinaire's aesthetics of surprise. Apollinaire has simply created a four-term homology: shepherdess / Eiffel Tower = sheep / bridges. François Rastier provides a detailed linguistic analysis.[18]In addition, as numerous critics have noticed, the line employs one of the poet's favorite rhetorical devices: paronomasia. The reason Apollinaire compares the Eiffel Tower to a shepherdess (bergère) is because it is located on the bank (berge) of the Seine. Since bridges cannot actually bleat, Lefèvre suggests the bleating sound is produced by tugboats on the river.[19] In contrast, Robert Faurisson believes it comes from automobiles honking their horns as they cross the bridges.[20] By way of confirmation, he points to the "troupeaux d'autobus mugissants" ("herd of mooing buses") in line 72.

The third and fourth lines make it clear that the "monde ancien"("ancient world") extends all the way up to 1912. Unfortunately, according to Apollinaire, the legacy of Rome and Ancient Greece is still very much alive. Paradoxically, even the automobiles—normally symbols of modernity—look as if they are ancient. At the beginning of the century, Décaudin explains, certain automobile bodies were modeled on those of horse-drawn carriages.[21] This first paradox is immediately followed by a second paradox. Despite its undeniable antiquity, Apollinaire insists that the Catholic religion is still brand new—as simple and as new as airplane hangars. Inaugurated in 1909, Port-Aviation was situated twelve miles south of Paris and the first organized airport in the world. The fact that Pope Pius X is the head of the Church, he continues, makes him thoroughly modern as well. Although Gilberte Jacaret believes these lines are strictly intended as satire, this is only partly true.[22] Apollinaire manages to be both sincere and insincere at the same time. On the one hand, Pius X was a conservative pope who repeatedly condemned the Catholic Modernist movement. On the other hand, since Christianity's message is ageless, in many ways he was ageless as well. More importantly, perhaps, the Pope was associated with modern aviation in Apollinaire's mind. In May 1911, he conferred his blessing on the aviator André Beaumont, who had just won a grueling four-day race from Paris to Rome. The following year, moreover, F. T. Marinetti sent the poet a copy of his recent novel *Le Monoplan du pape*.[23] The image of the Holy Father piloting an airplane in his pontifical robes was undoubtedly still in Apollinaire's mind when he sat down to write "Zone."

Having just insisted on Christianity's relevance for the modern world, Apollinaire represses an urge to enter a church and ask for confession. As Scott Saul observes, the constant remarks addressed to "tu" create "an air of big-city paranoia."[24] Even though nobody is looking out of the nearby windows, the windows themselves seem to be watching the poet. At the very least, they make him self-conscious. Suddenly ashamed to admit that religion still appeals to him, Apollinaire turns on his heel and walks away. Although the remaining lines are largely descriptive, they represent an important aesthetic statement. Seeking to distract himself, the poet stops to examine several advertisements posted on a wall. Because of their flashy typographical effects, he compares them to canaries singing in a cage. Taking his cue from Picasso and Braque, who had begun to incorporate letters and words into their paintings, Apollinaire announces that posters are a good source of poetry and newspapers a good source of prose. Combining verbal and visual elements, these were exciting projects. Some of the very first experiments with intermedia, they belonged to a larger project to integrate popular culture (including detective novels) into the artistic mainstream.

> J'ai vu ce matin une jolie rue dont j'ai oublié le nom
> Neuve et propre du soleil elle était le clairon
> Les directeurs les ouvriers et les belles sténo-dactylographes
> Du lundi matin au samedi soir quatre fois par jour y passent
> Le matin par trois fois la sirène gémit
> Une cloche rageuse y aboie vers midi
> Les inscriptions des enseignes et des murailles
> Les plaques les avis à la façon des perroquets criaillent
> J'aime la grâce de cette rue industrielle
> Située à Paris entre la rue Aumont-Thiéville et l'avenue
> des Ternes

> (This morning I saw a lovely street whose name I forget
> Clean and new it was the clarion of the sun
> The executives the workers and the pretty stenographers
> Pass by four times a day from Monday morning to Saturday evening
> The siren moans three times a day
> A rabid bell barks toward noon
> The inscriptions on the signs and the walls

The billboards the notices shriek like parrots
I love the grace of that industrial street
Situated in Paris between the rue Aumont-Thiéville and Avenue des Ternes)

Since much of "Zone" celebrates the modern age, Apollinaire's project to modernize poetry finds a counterpart in contemporary architecture (the airplane hangars) and in contemporary city planning. Stumbling across an industrial street in northeastern Paris, which Décaudin tentatively identifies as the rue Guersant, he employs a musical analogy to convey how clean and orderly everything appears.[25] Miraculously transformed into a golden bugle, the street resounds, to quote Berry, "with the music of sunlight and provid[es] a clarion call with which the sun announces the beauty of the modern industrial world."[26] As Saul observes, this is a professional world, where men and women are defined by their occupations.[27] As they come and go four times a day, the rhythm of their work is governed by the sound of rabid bells and moaning sirens. In 1912, people worked six days a week. Like the bells and sirens, the signs and notices are given animal identities. Because they are more colorful than some of the previous advertisements, Apollinaire compares them to shrieking parrots.

Voilà la jeune rue et tu n'es encore qu'un petit enfant
Ta mère ne t'habille que de bleu et de blanc
Tu es très pieux et avec le plus ancien de tes camarades
    René Dalize
Vous n'aimez rien tant que les pompes de l'Eglise
Il est neuf heures le gaz est baissé tout bleu vous sortez
    du dortoir en cachette
Vous priez toute la nuit dans la chapelle du collège
Tandis qu'éternelle et adorable profondeur améthyste
Tourne à jamais la flamboyante gloire du Christ
C'est le beau lys que tous nous cultivons
C'est la torche aux cheveux roux que n'éteint pas le vent
C'est le fils pâle et vermeil de la douloureuse mère
C'est l'arbre toujours touffu de toutes les prières
C'est la double potence de l'honneur et de l'éternité
C'est l'étoile à six branches
C'est Dieu qui meurt le vendredi et ressuscite le dimanche
C'est le Christ qui monte au ciel mieux que les aviateurs
Il détient le record du monde pour la hauteur.

(Behold the young street and you are still a baby
Your mother only dresses you in blue and white

You are very pious and with your oldest friend René Dalize
You love nothing so much as the pomp of the Church
It is nine o'clock the gas is turned down you sneak out of the dormitory
You pray all night in the school chapel
While eternal and adorable amethyst depth
The flaming glory of Christ revolves forever
He is the beautiful lily that we all cultivate
He is the torch with red hair that the wind cannot extinguish
He is the pale and scarlet son of the mournful mother
He is the tree perpetually bristling with prayers
He is the double gallows of honor and eternity
He is the six-pointed star
He is God who dies on Friday and is resurrected on Sunday
He is Christ who flies higher than the aviators
He holds the world record for height.)

Like most of the poem, this section is written in the simultaneous present. The fact that the street is young reminds Apollinaire of his own childhood on the Côte d'Azur. Using straightforward declarative sentences, he recalls in particular how pious he and his friends were. The reason he wore blue and white was because he was enrolled in the College Saint-Charles in Monaco, a Marianist establishment, and these were the colors of the Virgin Mary. The same memory occurs in an early poem entitled "Prière."[28] Apollinaire received his First Communion in the college chapel in 1892 and served as secretary of a student group called the Congrégation de l'Immaculée Conception. He was later reunited with his best friend René Dupuy (pen name René Dalize) in Paris. The critics agree that "flamboyante gloire" refers to Christ's halo, which seems to rotate in the flickering light of the sanctuary lamp. The line itself may allude to a painting, a sculpture, a stained glass window, or "un ostensoir en form de soleil" ("a monstrance in the shape of the sun"), which would explain the adjective "flamboyante."[29] Or in the case of a painting, the figure of Christ could be juxtaposed against a flaming sky. Couffignal cites two examples by Maurice Denis and Ignacio Zuloaga.[30] Although the amethyst has a role in Christian symbolism, as he notes, here it may simply describe a violet background. "On peut également penser," he concludes, "que les reflets rougeoyants de la veilleuse rouge . . . anim[ent] l'image divine" ("One can also imagine that the reddish reflections of the red sanctuary light . . . animate the divine image").

Prompted by the mention of Christ's name, Apollinaire begins to recite a litany like those he learned in his childhood. According to Couffignal, most of the metaphors in "Zone" come from the Bible or from the Catholic liturgy.[31] Sprinkled throughout both sources, the lily is a well-known symbol of purity. Similarly, the torch symbolizes Christ in his role as the Light of the World. The fact that it possesses red hair refers on the one hand to its flames and on the other to the popular belief that Christ was a redhead.[32] To be sure, the tree is a traditional image of the Cross and thus a symbol of resurrection. The "double potence" is much more puzzling until one realizes it has nothing to do with gallows. Shaped like a capital T, it is simply another type of cross—called a *croix potencée*. Finally, the six-pointed star or Star of David is commonly associated with Judaism. Since Christ was first and foremost a Jew, it is his emblem as well. Evoking his miraculous Ascension (described in Acts 1.9), the last two lines look forward to the following section. Although they strike the reader as a trifle irreverent, Apollinaire is technically correct. Since no one has ever been able to fly high enough to enter Heaven, Jesus holds the world's record. That he is able to outperform even the most experienced aviators emphasizes Christianity's eternal modernity.

> Pupille Christ de l'oeil
> Vingtième pupille des siècles il sait y faire
> Et changé en oiseau ce siècle comme Jésus monte dans l'air
> Les diables dans les abîmes lèvent la tête pour le regarder
> Ils disent qu'il imite Simon Mage en Judée
> Ils crient s'il sait voler qu'on l'appelle voleur
> Les anges voltigent autour du joli voltigeur
> Icare Enoch Elie Apollonius de Thyane
> Flottent autour du premier aéroplane
> Ils s'écartent parfois pour laisser passer ceux que transporte
> la Sainte-Eucharistie
> Ces prêtres qui montent éternellement élevant l'hostie

> (Christ pupil of the eye
> Twentieth pupil of the centuries he knows his business
> And changed into a bird this century like Jesus ascends in the air
> The devils in the abysses raise their heads to watch him
> They say he is imitating Simon Magus in Judea
> They cry if he knows how to soar he should be called a sorehead
> The angels flutter around the young performer
> Icarus Enoch Elijah Apollonius of Thyana
> Hover around the first airplane
> They occasionally give way to those whom the Eucharist elevates
> Priests who rise eternally elevating the Host)

Beginning with the last two verses of the preceding section, Giovanni Lista suggests that lines 40–70 actually date from 1910.[33] Continuing the previous discussion, the present section focuses initially on Christ. Not surprisingly, the first line has generated considerable debate:"Pupille Christ de l'oeil" ("Christ pupil of the eye"). Lefèvre suggests, for example, that it describes the Host in the center of the glass circle of a monstrance.[34] For Berry it recalls the idea of the pupillary soul, "where the pupil of the eye represents the seat of the soul, of life, and of the personality."[35]Claude Gandelman believes that the line evokes Christ surrounded by a mandorla in the tympanum of a medieval cathedral.[36] For Anca Mitroi, it suggests that Apollinaire is "a Christ-like visionary."[37] However, most critics think the verse is essentially a term of affection. Raymond Pouillart cites the Latin invocation "Custodi nos, Domine, ut pupillam oculi," which Apollinaire would have recited at Saint-Charles every evening during Compline.[38] The invocation derives from Psalm 17: "Garde-moi comme la prunelle de l'oeil" ("Keep me as the plum of the eye"; 17:8). The King James Version exchanges the plum for an apple: "Keep me as the apple of the eye." "Dans la tradition médiévale," Marc Poupon reports, "le rapport de la pupille à l'oeil correspond à celui du Christ à Dieu" ("In the Christian tradition, the relationship of the pupil to the eye corresponds to that of Christ to God").[39] He cites *The Seven Deadly Sins* by Hieronymous Bosch, in which the center of God's eye is occupied by an image of Christ. Finally, a number of critics detect wordplay in the first verse between "Christ" and *cristallin*—the crystalline lens of the eye. A similar *jeu de mots* exists between "pupille" in the first line and "pupille" in the second line. An excellent student of humanity, Christ has learned a lot about people during the two thousand years since his birth.

At this point, something absolutely amazing happens. The First Airplane revs up its single engine, taxis briefly, and climbs into the air piloted by Jesus. Symbolizing twentieth-century progress, it flies as effortlessly as a bird. As A. E. Pilkington remarks, the themes of religion and modernism are fused together through the image of Christ The Aviator.[40]Décaudin wonders if Apollinaire could have been inspired by two paintings he saw in Cologne during his *année allemande*. Two Stigmatizations of St. Francis show Christ on a cross flying through the air surrounded by fluttering angels.[41] Peter Read suggests that Apollinaire may have been inspired by Louis Blériot's cross-channel airplane, which was (and apparently still is) hanging in a deconsecrated church in Paris.[42] Personally, I wonder if the poet drew his initial inspiration from Marinetti's *Le Monoplan du Pape*. The title alone could have given him the idea of putting Christ in the cockpit. And although Gandelman believes Apollinaire drew on representations of Jesus in medieval cathedrals, he admits that the poet could have been inspired by Gazourmah "l'homme-avion" ("the airplane-man"), the hero of another one of Marinetti's books: *Mafarka le Futuriste* (1910).[43]

Not everyone is happy with the idea of Christ The Aviator. Saul accuses Apollinaire of replacing sacred metaphors with "visionary sarcasm."[44] But he completely misreads the poem in claiming that it spoofs the myth of scientific progress. The whole point of this section, most of which has not yet been examined, is that it celebrates the modern age and the invention of the airplane. As Berry declares, it is devoted to the apotheosis of the twentieth century.[45] According to Jacaret, the poet employs irony everywhere as a defense against his underlying anxiety. In "Zone," she continues, "il se moque des souvenirs de son enfance, de la religion, du Christ, de tous les êtres fabuleux ou réels qui ont été chantés" ("he mocks memories of his childhood, of religion, of Christ, of all the fabulous or real beings that were celebrated").[46] The problem with irony, which is a notoriously slippery trope, is that it exists largely in the eye of the beholder. In retrospect, nothing in Apollinaire's description of his childhood or his religious impulses seems inappropriate. There is no reason whatsoever to doubt his sincerity. The present section, in which Christ and the airplane are escorted to Heaven, falls into a different category. Since there is no attempt to be realistic, criteria such as sincerity and appropriateness are out of place. Whether one regards the episode as a fantasy or as a daydream, normal rules do not apply.

Although Apollinaire rejects the ancient world at the beginning of the poem, Hans-Robert Jauss points out, antiquity returns at this point "albeit in a mythical rather than historical form."[47] As The First Airplane ascends toward Heaven with Jesus at the controls, the devils down below shout all sorts of imprecations. They accuse the airplane of imitating Simon Magus, a sorcerer who lived in Samaria, not Judea, and whom according to legend was able to fly. The sin of "simony," or paying for a position and influence in the Church, is named after him. Confounding flying and stealing, the next verse is yet another example of Apollinaire's fondness for puns. Mariel O'Neil perceives the possible influence here of a text by Théophile Gautier.[48] Several critics also detect a potential reference to simony. As the airplane continues to rise, it is surrounded by numerous admirers—legendary and actual—who are also able to fly. In addition to a band of angels, these include a mythological character, two biblical personages, and an ancient philosopher. While Icarus' story is well known, Elijah and Enoch were transported to Heaven in a chariot of fire (see, for example, Second Kings 2.11). Apollonius of Thyana was a Greek Neo-Pythagorean philosopher who was reputed by his contemporaries to have worked many miracles. The tenth line of the stanza has been the subject of a certain amount of disagreement. Louis Allen argues persuasively that it is a misprint and that the second half should read: "ceux *qui* transportent la Sainte-Eucharistie" ("those *who* transport the holy Eucharist").[49] The latter are clearly the priests in the next line who are also accompanying the airplane. "Elevant l'hostie" refers to the ritual raising of the Host by a priest with his arms outstretched. Apollinaire jokes that the priests are literally elevating the Host, since the airplane is headed for Heaven.

> L'avion se pose enfin sans refermer les ailes
> Le ciel s'emplit alors de millions d'hirondelles
> A tire-d'aile viennent les corbeaux les faucons les hiboux
> D'Afrique arrivent les ibis les flamants les marabouts
> L'oiseau Roc célébré par les conteurs et les poètes
> Plane tenant dans les serres le crâne d'Adam la première tête
> L'aigle fond de l'horizon en poussant un grand cri
> Et d'Amérique vient le petit colibri
> De Chine sont venus les pihis longs et souples
> Qui n'ont qu'une seule aile et qui volent par couples
> Puis voici la colombe esprit immaculé
> Qu'escortent l'oiseau-lyre et le paon ocellé
> Le phénix ce bûcher qui soi-même s'engendre
> Un instant voile tout de son ardente cendre
> Les sirènes laissant les périlleux détroits
> Arrivent en chantant bellement toutes trois
> Et tous aigle phénix et pihis de la Chine
> Fraternisent avec la volante machine.

> (The airplane lands finally without folding its wings
> The sky fills with millions of swallows
> Crows falcons owls arrive at full speed
> From Africa ibises flamingos storks arrive
> Celebrated by story tellers and poets the Roc
> Glides by holding Adam's skull in its claws the first head
> And from America comes the little humming bird
> From China come long and supple pihis
> That have only one wing and fly in couples
> Next comes the dove the immaculate spirit
> Escorted by the lyre bird and the oscillated peacock
> The phoenix a pyre that engenders itself
> Veils everything in its ardent ashes for an instant
> Leaving the perilous straits the sirens
> Arrive all three of them singing
> And all of them eagle phoenix and pihis from China
> Fraternize with the flying machine.)

Just as human figures pay homage to the airplane in the first half, the sky is filled with millions of birds in the second half who also come to honor the aircraft. Apollinaire jokes that they come "à tire-d'aile"—swiftly but also by means of their wings. Since penguins don't fly, every continent is represented except Antarctica. Although many of the birds come from Europe, lyre birds arrive from Australia, hummingbirds from the Americas, and several avian species from Africa. Symbolizing the Holy Spirit, doves flock around the airplane as well. Large enough to carry an elephant in its claws, the legendary roc arrives from *The Thousand and One Nights*. Why it is carrying Adam's skull is never made clear. In addition, two more mythical birds appear: the Phoenix, which immediately bursts into flame, and the marvelous pihis from China. Apollinaire discovered the latter in an article published in the *Journal Asiatique* in 1896.[50] In a note, he specified that the male flies on the left and the female on the right. Since the Sirens are birds with the head and bust of a woman, as we saw in previous chapters, they fly all the way from Sicily. As in "Vendémiaire," Apollinaire mistakenly situates their territory in the Strait of Messina.

> Maintenant tu marches dans Paris tout seul parmi la foule
> Des troupeaux d'autobus mugissants près de toi roulent
> L'angoisse de l'amour te serre le gosier
> Comme si tu ne devais jamais plus être aimé
> Si tu vivais dans l'ancien temps tu entrerais dans un monastère
> Vous avez honte quand vous vous surprenez à dire une prière
> Tu te moques de toi et comme le feu de l'Enfer ton rire pétille
> Les étincelles de ton rire dorent le fond de ta vie
> C'est un tableau pendu dans un sombre musée
> Et quelquefois tu vas le regarder de près.

> (Now you are walking in Paris all alone in the crowd
> Herds of mooing buses pass near you
> The anguish of love clutches your throat
> As if you would never be loved again
> If you lived in olden times you would enter a monastery
> You are ashamed when you catch yourself saying a prayer
> You mock yourself and your laughter crackles like hellfire
> The sparks of your laughter gild the depths of your life
> It is a painting hung in a dark museum
> And from time to time you inspect it closely.)

All of a sudden Apollinaire's fantasy ends, and he returns to reality. Continuing on his walk through Paris, he encounters herds of lowing buses that recall the flocks of bleating bridges at the beginning of the poem. For a brief moment, we glimpse the pastoral setting once again. Lost in the anonymous crowd, the poet suddenly feels lonely and insignificant. His pain is exacerbated by the memory of Marie Laurencin, who broke off their relationship a few months earlier. In the olden days, he remembers, men who experienced such a painful loss would withdraw from the world and become monks. However, since he feels ashamed when he catches himself uttering a prayer, this route is obviously closed to him. Crackling like the flames of Hell, where he may yet end up, his self-mocking laughter conveys the recognition that his destiny lies elsewhere. Apollinaire concludes this stanza with a stunning metaphor for his life and the occasional self-examination it requires. Like an ornate portrait, it hangs in a dimly lit museum, where he goes to look at it from time to time. As we will see in a moment, the Doppelgänger is a recurring theme in his work.

> Aujourd'hui tu marches dans Paris les femmes sont
>   ensanglantées
> C'était et je voudrais ne pas m'en souvenir c'était au déclin de
>   la beauté
>
> Entourée de flammes ferventes Notre-Dame m'a regardé
>   à Chartres
> Le sang de votre Sacré-Coeur m'a inondé à Montmartre
> Je suis malade d'ouïr les paroles bienheureuses
> L'amour dont je souffre est une maladie honteuse
> Et l'image qui te possède te fait survivre dans l'insomnie et
>   dans l'angoisse
> C'est toujours près de toi cette image qui passe.
>
> (You are walking in Paris today the women are bloodstained
> As I can't forget it was during the decline of beauty
>
> Surrounded by fervent flames Our Lady regarded me at Chartres
> Your Sacred Heart's blood inundated me in Montmartre
> I am sick of hearing blessed words
> The love from which I suffer is a shameful illness
> And the image that possesses you causes you insomnia and anguish
> That image is always with you.)

Introducing a series of memories that help to define Apollinaire's identity, the next two lines are obscure. For some reason, he finds himself surrounded by bloodied women. Mitroi suggests the line refers to some kind of sacrifice.[51]

However, considering the implication of menstrual impurity, it could also be a misogynistic reaction to Marie's leaving him. Judging from the following line, impurity has been responsible for the decline of beauty in general. Seeking consolation, Apollinaire recalls two prior religious experiences: one before a statue of the Virgin Mary surrounded by burning candles in the Chartres Cathedral and the other at the Basilica of Sacré-Coeur in Montmartre, where he apparently received the body and blood of Christ. From one stanza to the next, Laurence M. Porter observes, "the blood of defilement becomes the blood of purification."[52] Unfortunately, since the last four lines are ambiguous, they could apply equally well to Jesus and to Marie Laurencin. The love that obsesses Apollinaire, that causes him such great anguish could be either divine or human. Fortunately, the preliminary manuscript reveals that Apollinaire was thinking of Marie.[53] The "maladie honteuse" ("shameful illness") from which he suffers is not love so much as pure, unadulterated lust.

> Maintenant tu es au bord de la Méditerranée
> Sous les citronniers qui sont en fleur toute l'année
> Avec tes amis tu te promènes en barque
> L'un est Nissard, il y a un Mentonasque et deux Turbiasques
> Nous regardons avec effroi les poulpes des profondeurs
> Et parmi les algues nagent les poissons images du Sauveur.
>
> Tu es dans le jardin d'une auberge aux envrons de Prague
> Tu te sens tout heureux une rose est sur la table
> Et tu observes au lieu d'écrire ton conte en prose
> La cétoine qui dort dans le coeur de la rose.
>
> Epouvanté tu te vois dessiné dans les agates de Saint-Vit
> Tu étais triste à mourir le jour où tu t'y vis
> Tu ressembles au Lazare affolé par le jour
> Les aiguilles de l'horloge du quartier juif vont à rebours
> Et tu recules aussi dans ta vie lentement
> En montant au Hradchin et le soir en écoutant
> Dans les tavernes chanter des chansons tchèques.
>
> (Now you are on the shore of the Mediterranean
> Beneath the lemon trees that flower all year long
> With your friends you go boating
> One is from Nice one from Menton two from La Turbie
> Frightened we watch octopi emerge from the depths
> And fish swim among the seaweed images of the Savior

You are in the garden of an inn near Prague
You feel very happy a rose is on the table
And instead of writing your story you watch
The rosebug sleeping in the rose's heart

Horrified you discover your portrait on Saint-Vit's agate wall
You felt extremely sad the day you saw it
You resemble Lazarus disoriented by the light
The hands on the clock in the Jewish quarter move counter clockwise
And your life slowly moves backward too
Climbing up to the Hradchin and listening
To Czech songs at night in the taverns.)

At this point, Apollinaire's recollections of the past begin to accumulate more rapidly, and we get more of an impression of simultaneity. The fact that the stanzas are shorter and change more quickly leads Durry to speak of "le kaléidoscope de la mémoire."[54] Décaudin calls attention to the possible influence here of a poem by Jean Moréas entitled "Fumées."[55] Recalling his boyhood on the Côte d'Azur, where the lemon trees are always in flower, Apollinaire remembers how he used to go boating with friends from neighboring towns like Nice, Menton, and La Turbie. Although they were frightened by the occasional octopus they discovered, they enjoyed seeing all the marine life. The memory of fish swimming around reminds the adult Apollinaire of the Greek acronym ICHTHUS (Jesus Christ Son of God the Savior). Still tempted to embrace religion, he sees images of Christ everywhere.

The next two stanzas recall Apollinaire's visit to Prague in March 1902, during the year he spent in Germany. Attempting to write a short story in the garden attached to his inn, he gazes distractedly at a beautiful rose only to discover that it harbors a voracious beetle in its center. Colored a metallic green, the rose chafer beetle (cetonia aurata) is a common European pest that feeds on pollen, nectar, and flowers. Borrowed from a poem Apollinaire sent Charles-Théophile Féret in 1911, the image symbolizes beauty eaten away from within.[56] In 1902, it would have evoked the poet's love affair with Annie Playden. In 1912, however, it clearly describes his affair with Marie Laurencin. Although Peter Por thinks the image may have been inspired by William Blake, "the canker in the heart of the rose" is a traditional topos, often symbolizing purity being consumed by sin.[57] It is found in no fewer than four of Shakespeare's sonnets: 35, 54, 70, and 95. Despite this ill omen, Apollinaire managed to finish writing Le Passant de Prague, which appeared in the Symbolist journal La Revue Blanche in June 1902.

The experience that affected the poet the most, however, occurred when he went to visit the Saint Vitus Cathedral. Admiring a large amethyst embedded in one of the cathedral's walls, he was suddenly astonished to recognize his own silhouette.[58] The experience was so unexpected, as he notes in "Zone," that it left him shaken. Like Lazarus raised from the dead and blinded by daylight, he was completely disoriented. Since the confrontation with one's Doppelgänger is a traditional omen of death, Berry explains, his reaction was perhaps understandable.[59] The other two tourist attractions Apollinaire visited were much less traumatic. Remembering that the clock's hands revolved counter-clockwise in the Jewish quarter, he remarks that he too is traveling back in time when he goes there. The other visit was to Hradcany Palace, the largest ancient castle in the world and situated on the same hilltop as the cathedral. Despite the poet's interest in sightseeing, one suspects that he looked forward to the evening even more, which he spent in the taverns drinking and listening to the local singers.

Te voici à Marseille au milieu des pastèques

Te voici à Coblence à l'hôtel du Géant

Te voici à Rome assis sous un néflier du Japon

Te voici à Amsterdam avec une jeune fille que tu trouves belle
et qui est laide
Elle doit se marier avec un étudiant de Leyde
On y loue des chambres en latin Cubicula locanda
Je m'en souviens j'y ai passé trois jours et autant à Gouda

Tu es à Paris chez le juge d'instruction
Comme un criminel on te met en état d'arrestation

Tu as fait de douloureux et de joyeux voyages
Avant de t'apercevoir du mensonge et de l'âge
Tu as souffert de l'amour à vingt et à trente ans
J'ai vécu comme un fou et j'ai perdu mon temps
Tu n'oses plus regarder tes mains et à tous moments
je voudrais sangloter
Sur toi sur celle que j'aime sur tout ce qui t'a épouvanté.

(Here you are in Marseilles surrounded by watermelons

Here you are in Coblence at the Hotel of the Giant

Here you are in Rome sitting under a Japanese medlar tree

Here you are in Amsterdam with a girl you find pretty but who is ugly
She is engaged to marry a student from Leyden
They rent rooms in Latin Cubicula locanda
I recall spending three days there and three more in Gouda

You are in Paris standing before the judge
Like a criminal who has been arrested

You have experienced sad and joyful voyages
Before learning about lies and old age
You suffered from love at twenty and at thirty
I have lived like a fool and I have wasted my time
You can no longer look at your hands and at every moment I feel like crying
Over you over the woman I love and over everything that has frightened you.)

As the pace accelerates, Apollinaire lists another half-dozen cities he visited, apparently in chronological order. Although no trace remains of a trip to Marseille, we know he visited Coblenz on August 28, 1901, on his way from Paris to Honnef, and again in May 1902—both times accompanied by the Viscountess Elinor de Milhau.[60] And while Apollinaire was born in Rome, this is the only indication we have that he ever returned to The Eternal City. By contrast, several traces remain of trips he took to Amsterdam. According to Pascal Pia, Apollinaire traveled to Holland several times between 1904 and 1908 on behalf of Jules Weil, his mother's partner, who was involved in the diamond trade.[61] Pia doubts that Latin was still spoken in Leyden and suspects the poet borrowed the anecdote about renting rooms from a book by Gustave Claudin. Correspondence between Apollinaire, his mother, and his brother reveals that he visited Holland in September 1905, from August to September 1906, and from mid-August to mid-September in 1908.[62] The story of his arrest and imprisonment in 1911, during the hysteria surrounding the theft of the Mona Lisa, has been told many times.[63] Illustrating the saying "no good deed goes unpunished," he spent five days in jail for trying to return two ancient Iberian sculptures stolen from the Louvre by somebody else. Attempting to summarize what he has learned so far about life, Apollinaire recalls his two great loves, Annie and Marie, but like François Villon before him, he concludes that he has wasted his youth. Overcome by grief, he can no longer bear to look at his hands. Pilkington speculates that this is because he has been branded a thief or because he feels unable to join his hands together in prayer.[64]

Tu regardes les yeux pleins de larmes ces pauvres émigrants
Ils croient en Dieu ils prient les femmes allaitent des enfants
Ils emplissent de leur odeur le hall de la gare Saint-Lazare
Ils ont foi dans leur étoile comme les rois-mages
Ils espèrent gagner de l'argent dans l'Argentine
Et revenir dans leur pays après avoir fait fortune
Une famille transporte un édredon rouge comme vous
     transportez votre coeur
Cet édredon et nos rêves sont aussi irréels
Quelques-uns de ces émigrants restent ici et se logent
Rue des Rosiers ou rue des Ecouffes dans des bouges
Je les ai vus souvent le soir ils prennent l'air dans la rue
Et se déplacent rarement comme les pièces aux echecs
Il y a surtout des Juifs leurs femmes portent perrruque
Elles restent assises exsangues au fond des boutiques.

(With eyes full of tears you regard these poor emigrants
They believe in God they pray their wives are nursing children
Their odor fills the waiting room at the Gare Saint-Lazare
They have faith in their star like the Three Wise Men
They hope to earn money in Argentina
And return home after making a fortune
A family carries a red quilt the way you carry your heart
That quilt and our dreams are both unreal
Some of the emigrants stay here in hovels on the
Rue des Rosiers or the rue des Ecouffes
I have seen them often at night they enjoy the fresh air in the street
And move only occasionally like chess pieces
They are mostly Jews their wives wear wigs
They slump exhausted in the back of their stores.)

Continuing on his way, Apollinaire comes across the Gare Saint-Lazare, which is filled with numerous emigrant families. Arriving at the Gare de l'Est from Eastern Europe, they have made their way across town and are waiting for a train to Le Havre or Brest, where they will board a ship for the Americas. Having been an emigrant himself most of his life, Apollinaire understands their situation and sympathizes with them. He knows what it is like to leave one's native land and settle in a country that speaks another language. In this case, however, the emigrants are sustained by their optimism and their religious faith. Since "Argentina" contains the French word for "money," they naturally hope to prosper. Unaccountably, this touching scene causes some critics to bristle. In the space of six lines, Saul declares, the poet moves from maudlin sympathy to acid irony. "Even their faith is a sham," he complains about the emigrants; "their spirituality is grounded in material prosperity."[65] The red comforter one family has carefully tucked around them occasionally elicits the same reaction. Given to Apollinaire by his mother when he left home, the comforter meant as much to him as it does to the emigrants. For some reason, however, Lefèvre finds it "vaguement ridicule et pathetique."[66]

> Tu es debout devant le zinc d'un bar crapuleux
> Tu prends un café à deux sous parmi les malheureux
>
> Tu es la nuit dans un grand restaurant
>
> Ces femmes ne sont pas méchantes elles ont des soucis
>   cependant
> Toutes même la plus laide a fait souffrir son amant
>
> Elle est la fille d'un sergent de ville de Jersey
>
> Ses mains que je n'avais pas vues sont dures et gercées
>
> J'ai une pitié immense pour les coutures de son ventre
>
> J'humilie maintenant à une pauvre fille au rire horrible ma
>   bouche.
>
> (You are standing at the bar in a crummy joint
> Drinking a cup of coffee surrounded by wretches
>
> At night you find yourself in a large restaurant
>
> These women are not evil they just have problems
> All of them even the ugliest has made a lover suffer
>
> She is the daughter of a policeman on Jersey
>
> Her hands which I hadn't noticed are rough and chapped
>
> I have tremendous pity for the scars on her stomach
> Now I humiliate my mouth to a poor girl with a horrible laugh.)

The next section is composed entirely of isolated snapshots. Entering a seedy part of town, Apollinaire stops for a moment to have a cup of coffee.

Later that night, he stops again to have dinner in a large restaurant. Having satisfied his appetite for food, he searches for a brothel where he can satisfy his sexual appetite. Judging from appearances, he seems to have moved on to a working-class neighborhood. After looking over the girls, he selects the daughter of a policeman on the island of Jersey, who probably moved to Paris because she was bored with small-town life. However, turning tricks is a hard way to make a living even—or especially—in a big city. When she touches Apollinaire, he feels her rough hands, and when she removes her clothes he sees several scars on her stomach. Her horrible laugh reveals even more about the life she has been living. Fully conscious of his momentary degradation, he kisses her passionately and throws himself on top of her. How nice it would have been, he thinks, to be making love to Marie instead.

> Tu es seul le matin va venir
> Les laitiers font tinter leurs bidons dans les rues
>
> La nuit s'éloigne ainsi qu'une belle Métive
> C'est Ferdine la fausse ou Léa l'attentive
>
> Et tu bois cet alcool brûlant comme ta vie
> Ta vie que tu bois comme une eau-de-vie
>
> Tu marches vers Auteuil tu veux aller chez toi à pied
> Dormir parmi tes fétiches d'Océanie et de Guinée
> Ils sont des Christ d'une autre forme et d'une autre croyance
> Ce sont les Christ inférieurs des obscures espérances
>
> Adieu Adieu
>
> Soleil cou coupé.
>
> (You are alone morning is about to dawn
> The milkmen clink their bottles in the streets
>
> Night withdraws like a beautiful mulatto
> Ferdine the False or Lea the Attentive
>
> And you drink this liquor burning like your life
> Your life that you drink like a burning liquor
>
> You walk toward Auteuil you want to go home on foot
> To sleep among your sculptures from Oceania and Guinea

They are Christs in other forms of other faiths
Lower Christs of obscure desires

Farewell Farewell
Sun slit throat.)

Following his brief experience in the brothel, Apollinaire finds himself back in the street. It is early morning, the milkmen are making their rounds, and once again he is alone. In keeping with the preceding episode, the dusky night slowly vanishes like two mulatto prostitutes on a Caribbean island. According to Pia, the poet borrowed "Ferdine la fausse" and "Léa l'attentive" from an erotic novel entitled *Une Nuit d'orgies à Saint Pierre-Martinique*.[67] To ward off the morning chill, Apollinaire stops at a bar and downs a quick brandy. This action is recorded in a striking couplet that expresses both his passion for life and his life of passion. Léon Somville provides a detailed semiotic analysis of these two lines, which, as he observes, represent a tautological construction.[68] Apollinaire compares alcohol to life and life to alcohol. No wonder he titled his first major book of poetry *Alcools*. Since he has not slept for twenty-four hours, Apollinaire heads back to his apartment in Auteuil. He looks forward to falling into bed surrounded by his collection of African and Oceanian sculptures (Figure 8.1). Crossing the Pont Mirabeau, as we know he always did, he spies "le troupeau des ponts" ("the flock of bridges") (Grenelle, Bir-Hakeim, and Iéna) on his right at the foot of the Eiffel Tower. In this manner, Marie-Louise Lentengre notes, "la fin du poème nous renvoie bien à son commencement, à ce retour chez soi et à soi, dans une même aube" ("the end of the poem sends us back to its beginning, returning home and to oneself again at dawn").[69]

From this point on, widespread disagreement exists not so much about how "Zone" ends but about how the ending should be interpreted. Since Apollinaire was fond of creating ambiguous situations, this is not terribly surprising. The first problem is to determine the relationship between Christ and the sculptures. Some critics prefer to contrast the two, and some prefer to compare them. In Couffignal's opinion, Apollinaire's tug of war with Christianity ends badly. Since Christ is vastly superior to the pagan deities, the fact that the poet seems to prefer the latter represents a tragedy in his eyes.[70] Although Mitroi basically concurs, she detects "a residual, albeit secularized, Christian desire for transcendence in a fragmented world."[71] In contrast to the first two critics, who take "inférieurs" at face value, Eric Sellin argues that the term simply means "nether."[72] It means the sculptures have come from southern regions of the globe. According to Apollinaire, in other words,

Figure 8.1. Senufo sculpture
Carl Einstein, *Negerplastik* (1915).

the native deities play the same role in their cultures as Christ plays in Christian societies. As Lefèvre declares, the conclusion is inescapable. Like the native religions, "le Christianisme est un mythe suscité par le besoin d'espérer et donc un rêve irréel" ("Christianity is a myth arising from the need to hope and thus an artificial dream").[73] There is essentially no difference between the two. This realization is not tragic, as Lefèvre unfortunately appears to imply, but is an important victory for Apollinaire. After vacillating the entire length of the poem, he finally decides to reject Christianity. He can no longer convince himself that the Christian myth is really true.

This decision prepares the reader for the last two lines, which confirm the preceding interpretation. Catching sight of the rising sun as he turns to enter his apartment, Apollinaire bids it—and us—farewell: "Adieu Adieu." However, these apparently innocuous words contain an additional message buried just below the surface. With very little effort, the original message can be modified to read: "Adieu à Dieu." This explains why Apollinaire says goodbye twice—the second "Adieu" allows him to create a play on words. Concise and to the point, the existential *jeu de mots* is worthy of Eugene Ionesco or Albert Camus. It also leaves no doubt as to the poet's sentiments concerning religion. With these final words, he breaks totally and completely with the Church. As Apollinaire disappears inside his apartment, we are left with the image of the sun and the enigmatic words: "Soleil cou coupé." Rastier provides a detailed linguistic analysis.[74] Although it is clear what these words refer to, it is not clear what they mean.

By 1913, to be sure, decapitation metaphors had been around for a long time. Apollinaire himself compared the sun to a decapitated head in "Les

Fiançailles" (see Chapter 6). While Décaudin mentions Victor Hugo and Lucie Delarue-Mardrus, the wounded sun had been a staple of Symbolist poetry for years. Mornings were a particular favorite, since the sun was often blood red and since dawn was the time reserved for guillotinings. The challenge was how to revive the metaphor and make it shine. Arguably the most brilliant conclusion in all of modern poetry, Apollinaire's verse took some time to solidify. He initially wrote "le soleil est là c'est un cou tranché" ("the sun is there it is a sliced neck"). By December 1912, the date of the poem's publication in *Les Soirées de Paris*, it had become more concise: "Soleil levant cou tranché" ("Rising sun sliced neck"). By the following April, when *Alcools* appeared, the conclusion had assumed its final lapidary form. While it is tempting to compare Apollinaire's sun to the dripping head of John the Baptist in "Salomé" (see Chapter 3), the image is actually quite different. The reference is not to a decapitated human head, as Saul suggests, but to a cleanly severed neck.[75] As Sellin notes, the image is that of a bloody stump seen in cross-section.[76] In other words, it is basically a round disc like the sun itself.

Discussing Apollinaire's creative use of echolalia, Décaudin cites "cou coupé" as a prominent example.[77] For some critics, the sound of the last two words presents a problem. Several writers are disturbed by the apparent presence of the word *coucou*, which can mean "yoo-hoo" as well as "cuckoo" in English. Didier Alexandre wonders how the word should be interpreted— "comme une dérision, un dégagement ou le prélude à un depart?" ("as derision, disengagement, or the prelude to departure?").[78] Although Brunel believes the line evokes the cuckoo's song, rather than the bird itself, both interpretations seem totally inappropriate.[79] And while Saul suggests the poet has gone mad, the English equation between "cuckoo" and "crazy" does not translate into French.[80] Inevitably, one is forced to conclude that this is a wild goose chase (or cuckoo chase). "Cou" is juxtaposed with "coupé" (rather than "tranché") purely for stylistic reasons. The repetition of the initial consonant [k] creates a chopping sound, the repetition of the initial vowel [u] creates an internal rhyme, and the final (oxytonic) accent evokes the crash of the guillotine blade.

Not surprisingly, perhaps, the last two lines appear to have a symbolic as well as a metaphorical function. In Jacaret's opinion, the death of the sun represents a clean break not only with everything that preceded it but also with any attempt by society to impose any form of constraint. "[Apollinaire] dit adieu au passé," she declares, "représenté par le soleil, archétype du Père, du chef, de la loi" ("[Apollinaire] says goodbye to the past represented by the sun, archetype of the Father, of the chief, of the law").[81] Speaking from a mythographical perspective, others claim the sun's execution symbolizes the

death of the solar hero. While the latter concept tends to be rather fluid, occasionally encompassing Apollinaire himself as we saw in "Lul de Faltenin"
(see Chapter 5), the figure that comes to mind in the present context is that
of Christ. Indeed, the poet evoked "le sang du Christ-soleil" ("the blood
of the Christ-sun") as early as 1902 in "Le Dôme de Cologne."[82] Thus the
Christian and the cosmic are fused together in the last two lines. Having previously said goodbye to God, Apollinaire then proceeds to execute his son.
"All that has remained of the poet's early religious faith," Berry translates,
"is finally killed off."[83]

Unlike Sellin, who claims that the last line gives the reader "a sense of soaring," most scholars find the conclusion a trifle depressing.[84] Garnet Rees believes it ends on "a note of unadulterated gloom," Lefèvre "dans le désespoir,"
and Pilkington "in despair and defeat."[85] Similarly, more than a few readers
feel that Apollinaire is prepared to kill himself by the end of the poem. Having
lost the love of his life and then his god, so the argument goes, he has nothing
left to live for. Faurisson thinks he is tempted to "finir avec l'existence," Porter
thinks he wants to retreat into "the symbolic suicide of a drunken sleep," and
Greet thinks he seeks to withdraw "into sleep or death."[86] Although we never
learn which solution the poet has decided to choose, it is almost certainly sleep
and not suicide. For one thing, his situation is not nearly as bleak as the preceding quotations would suggest. While he may have lost Marie, for example,
he has deliberately rejected Christianity and in doing so has gained a renewed
sense of reality. For another thing, the second half of "Zone" is actually not
all that gloomy. Apollinaire recalls numerous experiences in the past, some of
which were frightening or painful, as well as numerous places he has visited.
He encounters the emigrants in the train station, has a nice dinner, goes to a
brothel, and has a drink or two before heading home. Despite one or two negative experiences, he seems to have had a reasonably enjoyable day.

It is worth noting, moreover, that the death of the sun can be interpreted
in additional ways. For Mitroi, it constitutes "a symbolic sacrifice—a sacrifice
that produces light or knowledge."[87] By creating a new light source, Jacaret
adds, Apollinaire has become a god, a god who refuses to be bound by society's conventions: "Il refuse d'être esclave, il veut devenir le maître" ("He
refuses to be a slave, he wants to become the master").[88] From a symbolic
point of view, Lentengre believes the rising sun parallels the ascension of the
twentieth-century airplane piloted by Jesus. The blood Apollinaire spills on
the world is not just light but ascendant light: "image sublimée du poète lui-
meme, de sa vocation apollinienne" ("the sublimated image of the poet himself, of his Apollonian vocation").[89] The final word goes to Margaret Davies,
who notes that without the implication of day following night, "Zone" would

indeed be a tragic poem. As it is, she explains, "its end is no conclusion. All will start again and be reborn."[90] Following a good night's sleep, Apollinaire will awaken to a brand new day as powerful and as creative as before.

Notes

1. For the following details, see Michel Décaudin, *Le Dossier d'"Alcools,"* rev. ed. (Paris: Minard, 1965), 73–89.

2. Pascal Pia, "A propos de 'Zone,'" *Revue des Lettres Modernes*, Nos. 85–89 (1963), 154.

3. LeRoy C. Breunig, *Guillaume Apollinaire* (New York: Columbia University Press, 1969), 32.

4. Anna Boschetti, *La Poésie partout. Apollinaire, homme-époque (1898–1918)* (Paris: Seuil, 2001), 140.

5. Jean-Pierre Bobillot, "A la fin cou coupé: travail du vers et subjectivité dans Zone' d'Apollinaire," *Poétique*, No. 95 (September 1993), 304. For a study of the "vers libres longs" and the "vers libres courts," see 304–18 and 318–21 respectively.

6. Jeannine Kohn-Etiemble, "Sur 'Zone,'" *Revue des Lettres Modernes*, Nos. 576–81 (1980), 80.

7. Breunig, *Guillaume Apollinaire*, 31.

8. Marie-Jeanne Durry, *Guillaume Apollinaire: "Alcools,"* Vol 3 (Paris: SEDES, 1964), 215, and Anne Hyde Greet, tr.,*Alcools* (Berkeley: University of California Press, 1965), 211.

9. Boschetti, *La Poésie partout*, 138.

10. Robert Couffignal, "'Zone' d'Apollinaire: structure et confrontations* (Paris: Minard, 1970), 5–18.

11. Bobillot, "A la fin cou coupé," 308. For his discussion of alexandrines, see 8–10 and 301–3.

12. Durry, *Guillaume Apollinaire*, 3:187.

13. Boschetti, *La Poésie partout*, 138.

14. David Berry, *The Creative Vision of Guillaume Apollinaire: A Study of Imagination* (Saratoga, CA: Anma Libri, 1982), 52.

15. Roger Lefèvre, ed.,*"Alcools": choix de poèmes* (Paris: Nouveaux Classiques Larousse, 1965), 35.

16. Décaudin, *Le Dossier*, 86.

17. Pierre Brunel, *Apollinaire entre deux mondes: Mythocritique II* (Paris: Presses Universitaires de France, 1997), 3. His next comment appears on 17.

18. François Rastier, "Isotopies et expressions référentielles ou le soleil et la bergère," *Fabula*, No. 2 (October 1983), 109–10.

19. Lefèvre, ed.,*"Alcools,"*35.

20. Robert Faurisson, "Notes sur 'Alcools,'" *L'Information Littéraire*, No. 1 (January–February 1967), 35.

21. Décaudin, *Le Dossier*, 86.

22. Gilberte Jacaret, *La Dialectique de l'ironie et du lyrisme dans "Alcools" et "Calligrammes"* (Paris: Nizet, 1984), 93.

23. Gilbert Boudar and Michel Décaudin, *La Bibliothèque de GuillaumeApollinaire* (Paris: CNRS, 1983), 105.

24. Scott Saul, "A Zone Is a Zone Is a Zone: The Repeated Unsettlement of Guillaume Apollinaire," *Understanding French Poetry: Essays for a New Millennium*, ed. Stamos Metzidakis (New York: Garland, 1994), 161.

25. Décaudin, *Le Dossier*, 86.

26. Berry, *The Creative Vision*, 67.

27. Saul, "A Zone Is a Zone Is a Zone," 162.

28. Guillaume Apollinaire, *Oeuvres poétiques*, ed. Marcel Adéma and Michel Décaudin (Paris: Gallimard, 1965), 576.

29. Lefèvre, ed.,"*Alcools*,"37.

30. Couffignal, *L'Inspiration biblique*, 152.

31. Ibid., 151.

32. Faurisson, "Notes sur 'Alcools,'" 36.

33. Giovanni Lista, "Apollinaire et la conquête de l'air," *Revue des Lettres Modernes*, Nos. 380–84 (1973), 115–21.

34. Lefèvre, ed., "*Alcools*," 37.

35. Berry, *The Creative Vision*, 25.

36. Claude Gandelman, "Le Tympan futuriste du poème 'Zone' d'Apollinaire," *Zeitschrift für Vergleichende Literaturwissenschaft*, Vol. 18, No. 3 (1983), 297.

37. Anca Mitroi, "Apollinaire's 'Zone,' Catholicism, and the Paradox of French Modernity," *Religion and the Arts*, No. 13 (2009), 212.

38. Raymond Pouillart, "Lectures, souvenirs, et recréation chez Guillaume Apollinaire," *Revue des Lettres Modernes*, Nos. 123–26 (1965), 92.

39. Marc Poupon, *Apollinaire et Cendrars* (Paris: Minard, 1969), 15.

40. A. E. Pilkington, ed.,*Apollinaire: "Alcools"* (Oxford: Blackwells, 1970), 109.

41. Décaudin, *Le Dossier*, 87.

42. Peter Read, "Christ the Pilot in Apollinaire's 'Zone,'" *French Studies Bulletin*, No. 4 (Autumn 1982), 10.

43. Gandelman, "Le Tympan futuriste," 295, 297.

44. Saul, "A Zone Is a Zone Is a Zone," 165.

45. Berry, *The Creative Vision*, 54.

46. Jacaret, *La Dialectique de l'ironie*, 19.

47. Hans-Robert Jauss, "1912: Threshold to an Epoch. Apollinaire's 'Zone' and 'Lundi Rue Christine,'" *Yale French Studies*, No. 74 (1988), 41.

48. Mariel O'Neil, "Théophile Gautier et le modernisme de 'Zone,'" *Revue des Lettres Modernes*, Nos. 276–79 (1971), 109–10.

49. Louis Allen, "Apollinaire: 'Zone,' l. 51," *Modern Language Review*, January 1959, 74–75.

50. Décaudin, *Le Dossier*, 87.

51. Mitroi, "Apollinaire's 'Zone,'" 214.

52. Laurence M. Porter, "The Fragmented Self of Apollinaire's 'Zone,'" *L'Esprit Créateur*, Vol. 10, No. 4 (Winter 1970), 292.

53. Décaudin, *Le Dossier*, 78.

54. Durry, *Guillaume Apollinaire*, 3:169.

55. Décaudin, *Le Dossier*, 88.

56. Apollinaire, *Oeuvres poétiques*, 856.

57. Peter Por, "Notes en marge des textes d'Apollinaire," *Revue des Lettres Modernes*, Nos. 971–76 (1991), 134.

58. For a photograph of the amethyst, see *Europe: Revue Mensuelle*, Vol. 44, Nos. 451–52 (November–December 1966), between 192 and 193.

59. Berry, *The Creative Vision*, 55.

60. Louis Brunet, "Le Voyage d'Apollinaire à travers l'Allemagne au printemps 1902 (suite et fin)," *Apollinaire: Revue d'Etudes Apollinariennes*, No. 6 (November 2009), 35–36.

61. Pascal Pia, "Sur quatre vers de 'Zone,'" *Revue des Lettres Modernes*, Nos. 217–22 (1969), 208–9.

62. Guillaume Apollinaire, *Correspondance avec son frère et sa mère*, ed. Gilbert Boudar and Michel Décaudin (Paris: Corti, 1987).

63. See, for example, Laurence Campa, *Guillaume Apollinaire* (Paris: Gallimard, 2013), 352–64.

64. Pilkington, ed., *Apollinaire*, 112.

65. Saul, "A Zone Is a Zone Is a Zone," 170.

66. Lefèvre, ed., "*Alcools*," 42.

67. See Décaudin, *Le Dossier*, 89.

68. Léon Somville, "Deux Etudes," *Revue des Lettres Modernes*, Nos. 1303–9 (1996), 52–53.

69. Marie-Louise Lentengre, "Le Monologue du mal-aimé," *Littératures Contemporaines*, No. 2 (1996), 152.

70. Robert Couffignal, *"Zone" d'Apollinaire* (Paris: Minard, 1970), 18

71. Mitroi, "Apollinaire's 'Zone,'" 208.

72. Eric Sellin, "'Soleil cou coupé,'" *Romance Notes*, Vol. 14, No. 1 (Autumn 1972), 16.

73. Lefèvre, ed., "*Alcools*," 43.

74. Rastier, "Isotopies et expressions référentielles," 113–19.

75. Saul, "A Zone Is a Zone Is a Zone," 173.

76. Sellin, "'Soleil cou coupé,'" 14.

77. Michel Décaudin, "*Alcools*" *de Guillaume Apollinaire* (Paris: Gallimard, 1993), 59–60.

78. Didier Alexandre, *Guillaume Apollinaire. "Alcools"* (Paris: Presses Universitaires de France, 1994), 33.

79. Brunel, *Apollinaire entre deux mondes*, 8.

80. Saul, "A Zone Is a Zone Is a Zone," 173.

81. Jacaret, *La Dialectique*, 20.

82. Apollinaire, *Oeuvres Poétiques*, 538.

83. Berry, *The Creative Vision*, 76.

84. Sellin, "'Soleil cou coupé,'" 16.

85. Garnet Rees, ed.,*Alcools* (London: Athlone, 1975); Lefèvre, ed.,"*Alcools*," 43; and Pilkington, ed.,*Apollinaire: "Alcools*," 114.

86. Faurisson, "Notes sur 'Alcools,'" 37; Porter, "The Fragmented Self of Apollinaire's 'Zone,'" 288; and Greet, tr., *Alcools*, 213.

87. Mitroi, "Apollinaire's 'Zone,'" 215.

88. Jacaret, *La Dialectique*, 53

89. Lentengre, "Le Monologue du mal-aimé," 138.

90. Margaret Davies, *Apollinaire* (New York: St. Martins, 1964), 208.

~

Conclusion

With the publication of "Zone" in December 1912, Apollinaire's poetry entered a brand new phase, one that would result in the creation of simultaneous poems like "Les Fenêtres," conversation poems like "Lundi rue Christine," and visual poems like "Lettre-Océan." Although he had experimented with collage effects for many years, this was simply how he worked. Reflecting his eclectic imagination, the poems in *Alcools* were put together, metaphorically speaking, with scotch tape and glue. Except in the case of "La Chanson du mal-aimé,"which provides a setting for several smaller poems, Apollinaire was not conscious of doing anything out of the ordinary. He was not trying to make an aesthetic statement, he was simply trying to make a poem. As Cubism gained momentum, however, he gradually acquired a theoretical understanding of what he had been doing. The parallels between his poetry and Cubist painting must have seemed exciting. For the first time, Apollinaire was aware of belonging to the avant-garde, of being part of a larger group that was trying to create a specifically modern art. Following the publication of "Zone," his poetry became more self-conscious and his style more systematic. Although in some ways it became more daring, it also became more calculating and less spontaneous.

Therein lies the special attraction of *Alcools*, which in fact many people prefer to *Calligrammes*. The seventeen poems examined previously belong to a period in the poet's life when he was still trying to find his way. For this reason, they seem much more spontaneous and much more personal. Although Apollinaire wrote his share of Symbolist verses while he was growing up, he eventually realized he was not cut out to be someone's disciple. His impulse to stand on his own two feet was much too strong. He wanted to confront the muse face to face not through another other person. As Apollinaire struggled to free himself from his Symbolist masters, he experimented with a variety of styles in an attempt to develop his own poetic voice. Since he had no models to follow and since he refused to repeat himself, each poem had to be fresh and innovative. For this reason alone, it could be argued that *Alcools* is every bit as daring as *Calligrammes*. Apollinaire was basically working without a net. He had no way of knowing whether a poem would be successful or not because he had nothing to compare it to.

To be sure, this basically describes the poems that came after the "Rhénanes." Although the latter are lovingly crafted, the influence of the French Symbolists and the German Romantics is still discernible. Nevertheless, poems like "Nuit rhénane" and "La Tzigane" played an important role in Apollinaire's poetic evolution. By revealing the lyrical possibilities of the French language, they inspired him to develop his mature style. Filled with a new confidence, he returned to France determined to profit from what he had learned. Endowed with an epic breadth and an epic breath, "La Chanson du mal-aimé" helped him recover from his *déception amoureuse*. Although "L'Emigrant de Landor Road" was considerably shorter, it represented an important step in developing a new poetics. For the first time, Apollinaire created a fantasy world with its own logic and its own laws. Setting out to evoke the world of Greek mythology in "Lul de Faltenin," by contrast, he constructed a hermetic puzzle. Populated by enigmatic characters engaged in enigmatic tasks, the composition was totally obscure.

"Lul de Faltenin" was followed by two poems that in some ways were even more challenging. Adopting a visionary perspective bordering on the messianic, "Le Brasier" retraced the poet's attempts to reinvent himself. In order to accomplish this task, he consigned everything associated with the past to a fiery oblivion. Stung by accusations that his poetry was old fashioned, Apollinaire carried out a similar operation in "Les Fiançailles" aided by Jacques de Molay and the Knights Templar. Both poems employed a radical new language that proceeded by discontinuous leaps and bounds. Following this visionary period, Apollinaire adopted a style that was considerably more transparent. In "Cortège" and "Vendémiaire," language was reduced to a subordinate position. Its primary role was not to put stumbling blocks in the reader's way but to convey information. To a certain extent, both works were conceived as elaborate allegories. Both depicted Apollinaire engaged in the pursuit of enlightenment. While the first poem recounted his search for his authentic self, the second related his quest for universal knowledge. Evolving over a period of twenty years, all these poems culminated in "Zone" and the triumph of simultaneity. But that is a subject for another book . . .

Bibliography

Adam, Jean-Michel. *Pour lire le poème*. Brussels: De Boeck and Paris: Duculot, 1985.

Alexandre, Didier. *Guillaume Apollinaire. "Alcools.'"* Paris: Presses Universitaires de France, 1994.

Allen, Louis. "Apollinaire: 'Zone,' l. 51." *Modern Language Review*, January 1959, 74–75.

Apollinaire, Guillaume. *Correspondance avec son frère et sa mère*. Ed. Gilbert Boudar and Michel Décaudin. Paris: Corti, 1987.

———. *Le Guetteur mélancolique*. Ed. Michel Décaudin. Paris: Gallimard, 1980.

———. *Oeuvres complètes*. Ed. Michel Décaudin. Paris: Balland-Lecat, 1965–1966. 4 vols.

———. *Oeuvres en prose / Oeuvres en prose complètes*. Ed. Michel Décaudin and Pierre Caizergues. Paris: Gallimard, 1977–1993. 3 vols.

———. *Oeuvres poétiques*. Ed. Marcel Adéma and Michel Décaudin. Paris: Gallimard, 1965.

———. *Tendre comme le souvenir*. Paris: Gallimard, 1952.

Auffret, Serge, and Auffret, Hélène. *Le Commentaire composé*. Paris: Hâchette, 1968.

Bancquart, Marie-Claire. *Fin de siècle gourmande : 1888–1900*. Paris: Presses Universitaires de France, 2001.

Bates, Scott. *Dictionnaire des mots libres d'Apollinaire*. Sewannee, TN: privately printed, 1991.

———. *Guillaume Apollinaire*. Rev. ed. Boston: Twayne, 1989.

———. "Notes sur 'Simon Mage' et Isaac Laquedem." *Revue des Lettres Modernes*, Nos. 123–26 (1965), 68–77.

———. "Sur 'Lul de Faltenin.'" *Le Flâneur des Deux Rives*, No. 6 (June 1955), 7–9.

Baucomont, Jean et al., eds. *Les Comptines de la langue française*. Paris: Seghers, 1961.

Bellas, Jacqueline "L'Equivoque de Salomé dans la littérature et l'art 'fin de siècle.'" *Poésie et peinture du symbolisme au surréalisme en France et en Pologne*. Ed. Elzbieta Grabska. Warsaw: University of Warsaw, 1973.

Bernard, Oliver, trans. *Apollinaire: Selected Poems*. Harmondsworth: Penguin, 1965.

Berry, David. *The Creative Vision of Guillaume Apollinaire: A Study of Imagination*. Saratoga, NY: Anma Libri, 1982.

Bobillot, Jean-Pierre. "A la fin cou coupé: travail du vers et subjectivité dans 'Zone' d'Apollinaire." *Poétique*, No. 95 (September 1993), 301–23.

———. "L'élasticité métrico-prosodique chez Apollinaire: une lecture formelle des 'Colchiques.'" *Poétique*, No. 84 (November 1990), 411–33.

Bohn, Willard. *Apollinaire and the International Avant-Garde*. Albany: State University of New York Press, 1997.

———. *Apollinaire on the Edge: Modern Art, Popular Culture, and the Avant-Garde*. Amsterdam: Rodopi, 2010.

Boisson, Madeleine. *Apollinaire et les mythologies antiques*. Schena: Fasano and Paris: Nizet, 1989.

———. "Paysages célestes." *Du paysage apollinarien*. Ed. Michel Décaudin. Paris: Minard, 1991, 73–97.

Boschetti, Anna. *La Poésie partout: Apollinaire, homme-époque (1898–1918)*. Paris: Seuil, 2001.

Boudar, Gilbert, and Michel Décaudin. *La Bibliothèque de Guillaume Apollinaire*, 2 vols. Paris: CNRS, 1983 and 1987.

Bourdieu, Pierre. "Apollinaire, 'Automne malade.'" *Cahiers d'Histoire des Littératures Romanes / Romanistiche Zeitschrift für Literaturgeschichte*. Vol. 19, Nos. 3–4, 330–33.

Bowra, C. M. *The Creative Experiment*. London: Macmillan, 1949.

Breton, André. *Oeuvres complètes*. Vol. 3. Ed. Marguerite Bonnet, et al. Paris: Gallimard, 1999.

Breunig, LeRoy C. "Apollinaire et Annie Playden." *Mercure de France*, April 1, 1952, 638–52.

———. "Apollinaire's 'Les Fiançailles.'" *Essays in French Literature*, November 1966, 1–32.

———. "The Chronology of Apolllinaire's *Alcools*." *PMLA*, Vol. 67, No. 7 (December 1952), 907–23.

———. *Guillaume Apollinaire*. New York: Columbia University Press, 1969.

———. "Le Manuscrit de 'Lul de Faltenin." *Revue des Sciences Humaines*, new ser., Fasc. 84 (October–December 1956), 401–12.

———. "Les Phares d'Apollinaire. *Cahiers du Musée d'Art Moderne*, Vol. 81, No. 6 (1981), 63–69.

Brunel, Pierre. *Apollinaire entre deux mondes: Mythocritique II*. Paris: Presses Universitaires de France, 1997.

Brunet, Louis. "Le Voyage d'Apollinaire à travers l'Allemagne au printemps 1902." *Apollinaire: Revue d'Etudes Apollinariennes*, No. 5 (May 2009), 25–37, and No. 6 (November 2009), 25–37.

Burgos, Jean. "Sur les sentiers de la création." *Apollinaire, en somme*. Ed. Jean Burgos, Claude Debon, and Michel Décaudin. Paris: Champion, 1998, 181–276.

Cameron, John Wesley. *Apollinaire and the Painters: His Poetic Orphism*. Ph. D. diss. Indiana University.

Campa, Laurence. *Guillaume Apollinaire*. Paris: Gallimard, 2013.

Cansinos-Asséns, Rafael. *Salomé en la literatura (Flaubert, Wilde, Mallarmé, Eugenio de Castro, Apollinaire)*. Madrid: América, 1919.

Cellier, Léon. "Lecture de 'Lul de Faltenin.'" *Revue des Lettres Modernes*, Nos. 327–330 (1972), 67–86.

Champigny, Robert. "Analyse de 'Rhénane d'automne.'" *The French Review*, Vol. 33, No. 2 (December 1959), 123–30.

———. "Le Temps chez Apollinaire." *PMLA*, Vol. 67, No. 2 (March 1952), 3–14.

Chevalier, Jean-Claude. "Apollinaire et le calembour." *Europe*, Vol. 44, Nos. 451–52 (November–December 1966), 56–76.

———. *"Alcools": analyse des formes poétiques*. Paris: Minard, 1970.

"La Cinquième Vente de la Bibliothèque Jacques Guérin." *Que Vlo-Ve?: Bulletin International des Etudes sur Apollinaire*, 2nd series, No. 29 (January–March 1989), 24–26.

Clark, J. G. "De fil en aiguille: complément à une étude." *Revue des Lettres Modernes*, Nos. 576–81 (1980), 37–58.

Cooper, J. C. *An Illustrated Encyclopaedia of Traditional Symbols*. London: Thames and Hudson, 1978.

Coquet, Jean-Claude. "Sémantique du discours poétique. 'Les Colchiques' de Guillaume Apollinaire." *Littérature*, No. 6 (May 1972), 66–77.

Couffignal, Robert. *L'Inspiration biblique dans l'oeuvre de Guillaume Apollinaire*. Paris: Minard, 1966.

———. *"Zone' d'Apollinaire: structure et confrontations*. Paris: Minard, 1970.

Cranston, Mechtild. "Sortir d'Orkenise: Réflexions sur 'Onirocritique,''Le Brasier,' et 'Les Fiançailles.'" *Revue des Lettres Modernes*, Nos. 166–69 (1967), 53–73.

———. "Voyage en Rhénanie." *Du Monde européen à l'univers des mythes: Actes du Colloque de Stavelot*. Paris: Minard, 1968, 33–47.

Curnier, Pierre. *Pages commentées d'auteurs contemporains*. Vol. 2. Paris: Larousse, 1965.

Daubier, Louis. "'Les Colchiques' et les philtres d'Apollinaire." *Le Thyrse*, Vol. 70, No. 4 (July–August 1968), 19–21.

David, Jérôme. "On an Enigmatic Text by Piere Bourdieu." *Paragraph. A Journal of Modern Critical Theory*. Vol. 35, No. 1 (2012), 115–30.

Davies, Margaret. *Apollinaire*. New York: St. Martins, 1964.

———.Apollinaire, la peinture et l'image." *Que Vlo-Ve?: Bulletin de l'Association Internationale des Amis de Guillaume Apollinaire*. Nos. 21–22 (July–October 1979), 1–20. Paginated separately.

———. "'Le Brasier.'" *Etudes autour d''Alcools.'"* Ed. Anne de Fabry and Marie-France Hilgar. Birmingham: Summa, 1985, 1–13.

———. "'Lul de Faltenin.'" *Revue des Lettres Modernes*, Nos. 327–330 (1972), 89–93.

Debon, Claude. *Apollinaire: Glossaire des oeuvres complètes*. Paris: La Sorbonne Nouvelle, 1988.

———. "Image d'hier, image d'aujourd'hui." *Essays in French Literature*, No. 17 (November 1980), 81–91.

———. "L'Originalité des 'Rhénanes.'" *Histoire et critique littéraires en mouvement. Mélanges offert à Henryk Chudak*. Ed. Wieslaw Kroker. Warsaw: University of Warsaw, 2009, 73–92.

———. "Ouvrages et articles sur les poèmes d'*Alcools*." *"Alcools" en corps: Lectures et situation du recueil d'Apollinaire*. Ed. Jean-Yves Debreuille. Grenoble: Université Stendhal 3, 1999, 197–224.

Décaudin, Michel. *"Alcools" de Guillaume Apollinaire*. Paris: Gallimard, 1993.

———. "L'Année allemande." *Apollinaire: Revue d'Etudes Apollinariennes*, No. 6 (November 2009), 9–21.

———. *Apollinaire*. Paris: Livre de Poche, 2002.

———. "Compléments à un dossier." *Revue des Lettres Modernes*. Nos. 69–70 (Spring 1962), 57–61.

———. *Le Dossier d'"Alcools,"* rev. ed. Geneva: Droz and Paris Minard, 1965.

———. "L'Ecrivain et son temps." *Apollinaire en somme*. Ed. Jean Burgos, et al. Paris: Champion, 1998, 115–80.

———. "Un Mythe 'fin de siècle': Salomé." *Comparative Literature Studies*, Vol. 4, Nos. 1–2 (1967), 109–17.

———. "Obscurité et composition chez Apollinaire." *Cahiers de l'Association Internationale des Etudes Françaises*, Nos. 14–15 (March 1963), 119–25.

Deguy, Michel. "Encore une lecture des 'Colchiques' ou un poème de l'apophonie." *Poétique*, No. 20 (1974), 452–57.

Dickow, Alexander. "Sur 'Lul de Faltenin': Mallarmé selon Apollinaire." *Symposium*, Vol. 66, No. 4 (2012), 206–12.

Dininman, Françoise. "Toujours à propos des 'Colchiques.'" *Etudes autour d' "Alcools."* Ed. Anne de Fabry and Marie-France Hilgar. Birmingham: Summa, 1985, 25–40.

Durry, Marie-Jeanne. *Guillaume Apollinaire: "Alcools."* Paris: SEDES, 1956–1964. 3 vols.

———. "Sur 'La Tzigane.'" *Revue des Lettres Modernes*. Nos. 85–89 (Fall 1963), 76–89.

Edson, Laurie. "A New Aesthetic: Apollinaire's 'Les Fiançailles." *Symposium*, Vol. 36, No. 2 (Summer 1982), 115–28.

Empson, William. *Seven Types of Ambiguity*. London: Chatto and Windus, 1930.

Faurisson, Robert. "Notes sur *Alcools*." *L'Information Littéraire*, No. 1 (January–February 1967), 35–42.

Follet, Lionel. *"Encore Empédocle."* *Revue des Lettres Modernes*, Nos. 677–81 (1983), 136–39.

Fongaro, Antoine. "Apollinaire, Gautier et les Sirènes." *Revue des Lettres Modernes*, Nos. 183–88 (1968), 64–71.

———. *Apollinaire poète: Exégèses et discussions 1957–1987*. Toulouse: Presses Universitaires du Mirail-Toulouse, 1988.

————. "Des 'lys.'" *Que Vlo-Ve? Bulletin International des Etudes sur Guillaume Apollinaire*, 4th series, No. 14 (April–June 2001), 42–45.

Fonteyne, André. "Lul." *Revue des Lettres Modernes*, Nos. 380–84 (1973), 145–47.

Frazer, Sir James George. *The Golden Bough: A Study in Magic and Religion*. Abridged ed. New York: Macmillan, 1963.

Fröhlicher, Peter. *"Le Brasier" d'Apollinaire: lecture sémiotique*. Paris: Lettres Modernes, 1983.

Gandelman, Claude. "Le Tympan futuriste du poème 'Zone' d'Apollinaire." *Zeitschrift für Vergleichende Literaturwissenschaft*, Vol. 18, No. 3 (1983), 293–99.

Gateau, Jean-Charles. "'1909': entre la vamp, l'aéroplane et l'anarchie." *"Alcools" en corps, Lectures et situation du recueil d'Apollinaire*. Ed. Jean-Yves Debreuille. Grenoble: Université Stendhal-Grenoble 3, 1998, 129–37.

Gossiaux, Pol-P. "Clef de la 'Tzigane' de Guillaume Apollinaire." *Les Lettres Romanes*, Vol. 33, No. 3 (August 1979), 303–8.

Gothot-Mersch, Claudine. "'L'Emigrant de Landor Road' de Guillaume Apollinaire." *Cahiers d'Analyse Textuelle*, No. 8 (1966), 22–39.

Greet, Anne Hyde, trans. *"Alcools." Guillaume Apollinaire*. Berkeley: University of California Press, 1965.

Guilhembet, Jacques. "'Rhénanes.'" *L'Ecole des Lettres*, No. 12 (June 1992), 65–77.

Harrow, Susan. "'Les Fiançailles': cristallisation d'un amour." *Revue des Lettres Modernes*, Nos. 805–11 (1987), 119–34.

Hasselrot, Bengt. "Les Vertus devraient être soeurs, ainsi que les vices sont frères. Accord genre-sexe dans les figures généalogiques." *Revue Romane*, Special No. 1 (1967), 35–44.

Hubert, Etienne-Alain. "Autres Scolies sur *Alcools* d'Apollinaire." *Revue d'Histoire Littéraire de la France*, January–February 1998, 113–16.

————. "Erudition d'Apollinaire: quatre exemples." *Revue des Lettres Modernes*, Nos. 530–36 (1978), 83–91.

————. "Scolies sur *Alcools*." *Littératures Contemporaines*, No. 2 (1996), 245–54.

Iaria, Domenica, and Jean-Yves Tillmans. "Apollinaire et ses filles-fleurs." *Nuovi Annali della Facoltà di Magistero dell'Università di Messina*, No. 1 (1983), 302–13.

Jacaret, Gilberte. *La Dialectique de l'ironie et du lyrisme dans "Alcools" et "Calligrammes" de G. Apollinaire*. Paris: Nizet, 1984.

Jauss, Hans-Robert. "1912: Threshold to an Epoch. Apollinaire's 'Zone' and 'Lundi Rue Christine.'" *Yale French Studies*, No. 74 (1988), 39–66.

Johnson, Barbara. *The Critical Difference: Essays in the Contemporary Rhetoric of Reading*. Baltimore: Johns Hopkins University Press, 1985.

Kao, Shuhsi. "'Les Colchiques' d'Apollinaire et la modernité." *Essays in French Literature*, No. 17 (November 1980), 60–69.

Kohn-Etiemble, Jeanine. "De 'Bottom' à 'La Tzigane' par les chemins de traverse." *En hommage à Michel Décaudin*. Ed. Pierre Brunel, et al. Paris: Minard, 1988, 9–13.

————. "Sur 'Zone.'" *Revue des Lettres Modernes*, Nos. 576–81 (1980), 79–93.

Laforgue, Pierre. "'L'Emigrant de Landor Road': poète cou coupé." *Apollinaire: Revue d'Etudes Apollinariennes*, No. 11 (June 2012), 41–54.

Leclercq, P.-R. "Etude de texte: Guillaume Apollinaire: 'Mai.'" *L'Ecole des Lettres*, April 1976, 7–10.

Lefèvre, Roger. *"Alcools": choix de poèmes*. Paris: Nouvaux Classiques Larousse, 1965.

Legros, Georges. "'Sens' et 'Source'. A propos des vers 10–11 des 'Colchiques.'" *Cahiers d'analyse textuelle*, No. 16 (1974), 109–23.

Le Mollé, Roland. "'Les Colchiques' de Guillaume Apollinaire (architecture du poème et nature de la poésie)." *Annali della Scuola Normale Superiore di Pisa, Lettere, Storia e Filosofia*, Series 2, Vol. 37, fasc.1–2 (1968), 173–94.

Lentengre, Marie-Louise. "Le Monologue du mal-aimé." *Littératures contemporaines*, No. 2 (1996), 136–53.

Lévi-Strauss, Claude. *Le Regard éloigné*. Paris: Plon, 1983.

Lista, Giovanni. "Apollinaire et la conquête de l'air." *Revue des Lettres Modernes*, Nos. 380–84 (1973), 115–29.

Lockerbie, S. I. "*Alcools* et le symbolisme." Revue des Lettres Modernes, Nos. 85–89 (Fall 1963), 5–40.

Long, Harold C. *Plants Poisonous to Live Stock*. 2nd ed. Cambridge: Cambridge Agricultural Monographs, 1924.

Mathews, Timothy. *Reading Apollinaire: Theories of Poetic Language*. Manchester: Manchester University Press, 1987.

Meredith, William, trans. *Guillaume Apollinaire. "Alcools." Poems 1898–1913*. Garden City: Doubleday, 1965.

Merlin, I. "Poésie contemporaine. Guillaume Apollinaire: 'L'Emigrant de Landor Road.'" *L'Ecole des Lettres*, Vol. 60, No. 10 (February 15, 1969), 543–44.

Meschonnic, Henri. "Signifiance de 'Vendémiaire. *Revue des Lettres Modernes*, Nos. 327–30 (1972), 41–63.

Mitroi, Anca. "Apollinaire's 'Zone,' Catholicism, and the Paradox of French Modernity." *Religion and the Arts*, No. 13 (2009), 205–17.

Morhange-Bégué, Claude. "'Mai': Essai d'application d'une méthode stylistique." *Langue Française*, No. 7 (September 1970), 28–35.

Morhange-Bégué, Claude, and Pierre Lartigue. *"Alcools." Apollinaire*. Paris: Hatier, 1991.

Moulin, Jeanine. *Guillaume Apollinaire: Textes inédits*. Geneva: Droz and Lille: Giard, 1952.

Nakam, Géralde. "'O Corneille Agrippa, l'odeur d'un petit chien . . .' Alcools, Cortège." *Revue des Lettres Modernes*, Nos. 249–53 (1970), 156–58.

O'Neil, Mariel. "Théophile Gautier et le modernisme de 'Zone.'" *Revue des Lettres Modernes*, Nos. 276–79 (1971), 109–10.

Orecchioni, Pierre. *Le Thème du Rhin dans l'inspiration de Guillaume Apollinaire*. Paris: Lettres Modernes, 1956.

Perfézou, Laurence. *"Alcools." Apollinaire*. Paris: Bordas, 1988.

Pia, Pascal. "A propos de 'Zone.'" *Revue des Lettres Modernes*, Nos. 85–89 (1963), 153–55.

———. "Sur quatre vers de 'Zone.'" *Revue des Lettres Modernes*, Nos. 217–22 (1969), 208–9.

Pilkington, A. E. *Apollinaire: "Alcools."* Oxford: Blackwell, 1970.

Piron, Maurice. *Guillaume Apollinaire. "La Chanson du mal-aimé."* Paris: Nizet, 1987.

Potts, D. C. "The Interpretation of Apollinaire's 'Les Colchiques.'" *French Studies*, Vol. 26, No. 4 (October 1972), 430–33.

Pouillart, Raymond. "Lectures, souvenirs, et recréation chez Guillaume Apollinaire." *Revue des Lettres Modernes*, Nos. 123–26 (1965), 90–96.

Por, Peter. "Notes en marge des textes d'Apollinaire." *Revue des Lettres Modernes*, Nos. 971–76 (1991), 133–48.

Porter, Laurence M. "The Fragmented Self of Apollinaire's 'Zone.'" *L'Esprit Créateur*, Vol. 10, No. 4 (Winter 1970), 285–95.

Poupon, Marc. "L'Année allemande d'Apollinaire." *Revue des Lettres Modernes*, Nos. 183–88 (1968), 9–45.

———. *Apollinaire et Cendrars.* Paris: Minard, 1969.

———. "'Lul de Faltenin,' et l'etymologie." *Du Monde européen à l'univers des mythes.* Ed. Michel Décaudin. Paris: Minard, 1970, 132–51.

———. "Notes sur quelques énigmes de 'Vendémiaire.'" *Apollinaire: Revue d'Etudes Apollinariennes*, No. 4 (November 2008), 47–60.

———. "Sources allemandes d'Apollinaire." *Revue des Lettres Modernes*, Nos. 530–36 (1978), 7–36.

Rampant, Marie-Claude. "A propos de citrons." *Revue des Lettres Modernes*, Nos. 276–79 (1971), 110–12.

Ramsey, Warren. "Foreword." *Alcools. Guillaume Apollinaire.* Trans. Anne Hyde Greet. Berkeley: University of California Press, 1965, v–xxvi.

Rastier, François. "Isotopies et expressions référentielles ou le soleil et la bergère." *Fabula*, No. 2 (October 1983), 107–20.

Read, Peter. "Christ the Pilot in Apollinaire's 'Zone.'" *French Studies Bulletin*, No. 4 (Autumn 1982), 8–10.

———. "'Océan de terre' et la guerre des gaz dans *Calligrammes*" in *"Calligrammes" de Guillaume Apollinaire ou la poésie moderne.* Ed. Samir Mouzouki. Tunis: Université de Tunis: 2005, 31–40.

———. *Picasso and Apollinaire: The Persistence of Memory.* Berkeley: University of California Press, 2008.

Rees, Garnet, ed. *Guillaume Apollinaire: "Alcools."* London: Athlone, 1975.

Renaud, Philippe. "L'Effraie et le rossignol ou les énigmes du tremblement." *Revue des Lettres Modernes.* Nos. 249–53 (1970), 45–67.

———. "Herbiers et rituels ("Une Relecture de 'Colchiques')." *Apollinaire.* Ed. Pierre-Olivier Walzer. Fribourg: Editions Universitaires Fribourg, 1983, 57–70.

———. *Lecture d'Apollinaire.* Lausanne: L'Age d'Homme, 1969.

Revell, Donald, trans. *Poems by Guillaume Apollinaire. "Alcools."* Middletown: Wesleyan University Press, 1995.

Richer, Jean. "Le Destin comme matière poétique." *Revue des Lettres Modernes*, Nos. 166–69 (1967), 4–34.

———. "Une Prémonition d'Apollinaire: '1909.'" *French Review*, Vol. 39, No. 4 (February 1966), 491–95.

Riffaterre, Michael. *Semiotics of Poetry*. Bloomington: Indiana University Press, 1978.

Robichez, Guillaume. "Note sur quelques égarements d'Apollinaire dans *Alcools*." *Revue des Lettres Modernes*, Nos. 450–55 (1976), 125–36.

Roessler, Kurt. "Le Rire d'Apollinaire dans 'Nuit rhénane.'" *Apollinaire et les rires 1900*. Ed. Claude Debon. Paris: Calliopées, 2011, 149–55.

Saul, Scott. "A Zone Is a Zone Is a Zone: The Repeated Unsettlement of Guillaume Apollinaire." *Understanding French Poetry: Essays for a New Millennium*. Ed. Stamos Metzidakis. New York: Garland, 1994, 155–76.

Scepi, Henri. "'Un lyrisme neuf': Le Cas des 'Fiançailles' dans *Alcools* d'Apollinaire." *Apollinaire: Revue d'Etudes Apollinariennes*, No. 13 (September 2013), 13–28.

Schmits, Georges. "Apollinaire, le feu et le vol—'Le Brasier' et 'Pipe'" *Les Etudes Classiques*, April 1969, 110–48.

———. "'Le Brasier.'" Part I. *Les Etudes Classiques*, No. 35 (January 1967), 34–51. Part II. *Les Etudes Classiques*, April 1967, 145–74.

———. "'Vendémiaire,'" *Les Etudes Classiques*, July 1964, 247–62.

Scott, Clive. *Vers Libre: The Emergence of Free Verse in France 1886–1914*. Oxford: Clarendon Press, 1990.

Sellin, Eric. "'Soleil cou coupé.'" *Romance Notes*, Vol. 14, No. 1 (Autumn 1972), 13–16.

Shattuck, Roger. *The Banquet Years: The Origins of the Avant-Garde in France 1895 to World War I*. Garden City: Doubleday, 1961.

———, trans. *Selected Writings of Guillaume Apollinaire*. New York: New Directions, 1971.

Smith, Sir William. *Smaller Classical Dictionary*. New York: Dutton, 1958.

Somville, Léon. "Deux Etudes," *Revue des Lettres Modernes*. Nos. 1303–9 (1996), 33–62.

Stamelman, Richard Howard. *The Drama of Self in Guillaume Apollinaire's "Alcools."* Chapel Hill: North Carolina Studies in the Romance Languages and Literatures, 1976.

Steegmuller, Francis. Ed. *Alcools: Poems 1898–1913*. Trans. William Meredith. Garden City, NY: Doubleday Anchor, 1965.

———. *Apollinaire: Poet Among the Painters*. New York: Farrar, Straus: 1963.

Stepnowski, Adam. "'Les Colchiques' et le renouvellement du lyrisme." *Les Cahiers de Varsovie*, No. 11 (1984), 231–45.

Truhn, J. Patrick. "The Wave of Wine: Revolution and Revelation in Apollinaire's 'Vendémiaire.'" *Romanic Review*, Vol. 72, No. 1 (January 1981), 39–50.

Winspur, Steven. "The Uncertainties of Apollinaire's Language." *French Literature Series*, No. 18 (1991), 126–33.

Wolf, Ernst. *Guillaume Apollinaire und das Rheinland*. (1937) Frankfurt am Main: Peter Lang, 1988.

~

Index

~

About the Author

Willard Bohn is Distinguished Professor Emeritus of French and Comparative Literature at Illinois State University. While his interests encompass
modern literature and art in general, he has published extensively on
Guillaume Apollinaire, Dada and Surrealism, Italian Futurism, Giorgio de
Chirico, the Spanish and Catalan Avant-Garde, and modern visual poetry.
An active scholar with an international reputation, Professor Bohn is the
author of 171 articles and 14 books, including *Apollinaire on the Edge: Modern Art, Popular Culture, and the Avant-Garde* (2010), *Apollinaire and the
International Avant-Garde* (1997), *Apollinaire, Visual Poetry, and Art Criticism*
(1993), *Apollinaire and the Faceless Man* (1991), *The Avant-Garde Imperative:
The Visionary Quest for a New Language* (2013), *Reading Visual Poetry* (2011),
The Aesthetics of Visual Poetry (1986, 1993), *The Rise of Surrealism* (2001),
and *The Other Futurism* (2004).

Dr. Bohn has also lectured widely on a variety of topics in this country
and abroad at schools such as Yale University, the University of Oxford, the
University of Cambridge, the École Normale Supérieure, the University of
St. Andrews, UCLA, The University of Illinois, the Philadelphia Museum
of Art, Washington University, and the Sorbonne in Paris. He has been
the recipient of grants or fellowships from the National Endowment for the
Humanities, the American Council of Learned Societies, the American
Philosophical Society, the Fulbright-Hays Commission, the Camargo Foundation in France, the Gladys Krieble Delmas Foundation, and the Program
for Cultural Cooperation Between Spain's Ministry of Culture and United

States' Universities. In 1999, he was appointed Fowler Hamilton Visiting Research Fellow at Christ Church College, Oxford University, in 2005 the Oliver Smithies Lecturer at Balliol College, Oxford University, in 2006 Visiting Research Fellow at the Centre for Research in the Arts, Social Sciences, and Humanities, Cambridge University, and in 2008 Distinguished Research Fellow at the Institute of Advanced Study, Durham University. He is currently an associate editor for Purdue Studies in Romance Literatures and a member of the Consiglio Scientifico at the Fondazione Giorgio e Isa de Chirico in Rome.

Lightning Source UK Ltd.
Milton Keynes UK
UKOW02n0606151116
287644UK00001B/15/P